Brand Policy Determination

MARKETING SCIENCE INSTITUTE
SERIES OF BOOKS

PUBLISHED WITH ALLYN AND BACON, INC.

OTHER PUBLICATIONS

MARKETING SCIENCE INSTITUTE

3401 Market Street

Philadelphia, Pa.   19104

THE MARKETING SCIENCE INSTITUTE was established in 1962 in Philadelphia for the purpose of conducting the kinds of basic research that would serve to advance the productivity and efficiency of marketing. The Institute's research and educational activity is designed to (1) contribute to the emergence of a science of marketing, and (2) stimulate increased application of scientific techniques to the understanding and solving of marketing problems.

Financial support for MSI is provided by leading business firms. In addition, the personnel of these firms contribute generously of their time and ability as members of MSI committees, study groups, and as advisors and consultants on MSI research projects and reports.

All research reports and findings of the Marketing Science Institute are made generally available through publication. In compliance with MSI policy, publication of this report has been approved by a majority of the Board of Trustees.

MARKETING SCIENCE INSTITUTE

The Upjohn Company
Warner-Lambert Pharmaceutical
Company

Westinghouse Electric
Corporation
Wm. Wrigley Jr. Company

BRAND POLICY DETERMINATION

VICTOR J. COOK
Research Associate
Marketing Science Institute

and

THOMAS F. SCHUTTE
Assistant Professor of Marketing
University of Pennsylvania

Allyn and Bacon, Inc.
Boston

Foreword

BRAND POLICY IS one of the basic issues faced by managements in both small and large organizations at all levels of the market structure. Decisions by manufacturers or distributors to adopt private brand policies can affect their marketing programs and their overall corporate profitability.

The decision to follow a policy that does not encompass private labels can also have far-reaching effects. Brand policy has a unique dimension as well. Since a number of executives are either strong opponents or proponents of private brands for a variety of reasons, the issue has frequently been treated emotionally, rather than objectively; little research based on impartial analysis of the reasons for—and results of—adopting a given brand policy has been made publicly available.

That is why the Marketing Science Institute, convinced of the need for additional research in this important area, launched a major study of brand policy determination. It was begun under the direction of Thomas F. Schutte, MSI Research Associate. He was joined shortly after the study was started by Victor J. Cook, then Resident Fellow at MSI from the University of Michigan. On completion of the Resident Fellowship and the requirements for the doctorate, Mr. Cook remained with the Institute as Research Associate working as co-director of this study. Mr. Schutte left MSI at the end of August, 1966, to accept a teaching position at the University of Pennsylvania's Wharton School of Finance and Commerce; the completion of the study and development of this report were directed by Mr. Cook.

Following is a report to management on the results of MSI's study of brand policy determination.

WENDELL R. SMITH
President, Marketing Science Institute

Preface

THIS STUDY OF private branding was designed to identify and evaluate the factors taken into account by manufacturers and distributors in determining brand policy. The report provides information based on facts and analysis which can be helpful to many companies in evaluating their brand policies.

The first two chapters deal with an analysis of the problem and an examination of contemporary marketing structure.

Environmental forces affecting private branding are examined in Chapter 3, manufacturers' branding policies in Chapter 4, and the determination of branding policy by distributors in Chapter 5.

Nearly 200 corporate officers, most of them Vice Presidents, Presidents, or Board Chairmen, gave willingly of their time to provide a significant part of the information used in this study. We are deeply indebted to these men.

The business community was relied upon to provide estimates of trends in private brand sales in ten major industries. Information on the market share of private and national brands (at least as good as that available to management in each industry) was requested and obtained.

The full cooperation of two well-known research organizations and one major trade association also should be recognized. Through the efforts of James O. Peckham, Executive Vice President of A. C. Nielsen Company, the Marketing Science Institute was provided with specially prepared estimates of private and manufacturers' brand shares over a period of years for selected packaged food and household supply products. Howard A. Stone, President of Daniel Starch and Staff, developed estimates of private and manufacturers' brand share in several household appliance lines. Iver M. Olsen, Vice President of Market Research of the National Shoe Manufacturers Association, prepared estimates on market share by type of brand in his industry.

Approximately 50 other trade associations and organizations cooperated in this study. They provided detailed background on the industries with which they are affiliated, and suggested the names of companies and executives who might profitably be contacted in the study.

Several individuals deserve special mention for their support of this project:

Clarence G. Adamy
National Association of Food Chains

Guenther Baumgart
American Home Laundry Manufacturers' Association

Howard L. Binkley
Pharmaceutical Manufacturers' Association

Pauline Dunckel
Institute of Appliance Manufacturers

Dorothy Fey
The United States Trademark Association

Roy Harrison and Jack Simmons
The American Institute of Food Distribution, Inc.

W. W. Marsh
National Tire Dealers and Retreaders Association, Inc.

Albert H. Messer
Brand Names Foundation, Incorporated

A. J. Nesti
National Electrical Manufacturers Association

Theodore Nowak
Market Research Corporation of America

Paul Olsen
Drug Topics, Topics Publishing Co., Inc.

Donald Reath
N. W. Ayer & Son, Inc.

William A. Rossi and Frank Underhill
Boot and Shoe Recorder, Chilton Company

A. J. Rumoshosky
American Petroleum Institute

The assistance of 14 capable interviewers made it possible to bring the field work to a successful and rapid conclusion:

Seymour Baranoff
Pace College

F. William Beecher
Milwaukee Institute of Technology

Richard M. Clewett
Northwestern University

Jack R. Dauner
Saint Louis University

George S. Day
Columbia University

Carl T. Eakin
The University of Georgia

Frank H. Eby, Jr.
Villanova University

Henry Eilbirt
The City College of New York

Mervin D. Field
Field Research Corporation

Richard J. Lewis
Michigan State University

Ward J. McDowell
University of Cincinnati

Charles R. Spindler
Memphis State University

Stanley F. Stasch
Northwestern University

John W. Wingate
The City College of New York

Several members of the Marketing Science Institute staff made significant contributions: Wendell Smith, Jean Pumroy, Wilma Wilt, Donald Challis, Richard Hemsley, and George Potter.

We are particularly grateful for the careful review of the manuscript by William R. Davidson of The Ohio State University and Charles J. Fabso of the Philco-Ford Corporation.

While the contributions of many were necessary, we accept full responsibility for the findings, judgments, and treatment of the data.

VICTOR J. COOK
THOMAS F. SHUTTE

Contents

Highlights
of This Book

TO ASSIST THE business executive in determining whether his company's brand policy is of optimum efficiency, Victor J. Cook and Thomas F. Shutte undertook a study of brand policy determination among manufacturers and distributors across the country.

Their findings constitute a valuable guide for the great majority of businessmen who want to keep a step ahead of competition. There is information here that helps the marketing executive to determine whether or not his company is doing, or should be doing, what the competition is doing.

THE MIXED BRAND POLICY

Authors Cook and Schutte have examined the conditions favorable for the adoption of a mixed brand policy, which involves the sale of both national (manufacturers') and private (distributors') brands.

Manufacturers and distributors who are or might be contemplating such a policy (or who have not recognized the possibilities of a mixed brand policy) will find this book of particular interest.

The information in this book points up both the potentials and the limitations of a mixed brand policy, and reveals how the possibilities for its success will vary among different types of industries.

At the same time, questions are asked that every business executive should ask himself:

Which manufacturers adopt a mixed brand policy and why?

What can such a policy do that is not being done for a company under a straight manufacturers' or distributors' brand policy?

Once the decision to institute a mixed brand policy has been made, how should it be implemented?

Reaching Objectives Objectively

The question of implementation can be reduced to one of *objectives*. Does the company want profits in the short run, or is it wise to sacrifice immediate profits for long-term goals? Cook and Schutte provide a basis for an answer. And their findings are detailed enough so that they can be related to specific industries.

The authors present a variety of solutions. Much of their information is set forth as applying either to durable-goods or nondurable-goods industries. Generally, different sets of data must be applied to these two types of manufacturers.

Handling the Private Brand

From among the 65 mixed brand policy companies studied, two distinct company attitudes or orientations toward the private brand were discovered. And the authors found that the profit levels of these two groups were just as distinct as their attitudes toward their private labels.

The authors' tabulations will be a bit upsetting to the executive who assumes that his private brand policy is the most logical and profitable one possible. The great majority of the companies studied fall into the group whose private brand orientations are related to the substantially *lower* profit positions. Consequently, Cook and Schutte have enumerated the practices of the higher-profit group, consisting of those manufacturers who fully integrate private brand policy into every phase of corporate activity.

Drawbacks to Mixed Brand Policy

It was not the authors' intention simply to present a "prescription" for certain success with mixed brand policy. In fact, they indicate that such a policy, even when properly implemented, tends to fall a bit short of the profit level reached by the companies that can afford to rely exclusively on a national brand. Furthermore, they present a lengthy list of risks that firms face upon adopting mixed policies.

Environmental Factors

This book is not restricted to a consideration of conditions within companies.

It also relates the manufacturers' brand policies to general economic and industry conditions. The level of prosperity, extent of excess industry capacity, competitive structure of the industry, amount of national advertising for the product category, recency of the product, and percentage price differentials among competing brands—each of these variables is related to its effect on the private brand's share of market in a given product line.

FOOD FOR THOUGHT

The marketing executive will want to mull over these environmental variables and the private brand policy tendencies correlated with them.

He ought to acquaint himself with industry norms of brand policy determination either because his company may be (1) diverging from industry norms when it ought not to do so, or, on the other hand, (2) complying with industry norms, when it might be profiting by diverging from these norms.

Cook and Schutte found that the products with the greatest private brand share of market were in the *decline* stage of their life cycle. This finding presents the manufacturer with two diametrically-opposed possibilities.

Depending upon the nature of the product, a company continuing to manufacture a product in the decline stage could either heed the apparent warning of the findings and shift to extensive private branding, or it could "buck the trend " by marketing only a national brand, probably with little competition from other brands. If the product is not inherently outdated, but instead the "victim" of a new fad or of a general attitude that it is old-fashioned, then national brand emphasis could prove to have long-run profit potential. The product might even be lifted out of the decline stage and into a new period of growth.

Impossible of achievement? Perhaps. But the material in this book is certain to start one thinking about possibilities.

The relationship between the nature of the business environment and the market share of private brands is not as obvious as might be imagined.

Sets of variables may often be positively correlated up to a particular point, after which the correlation becomes negative. For instance, the authors report that national advertising in a given product category tends to grow with increases in private brand share only until this share reaches the 60 percent level, and then tends to decline.

THE RATIONALE OF THE DISTRIBUTOR

One other area explored in this book is that of the factors affecting attitudes of distributors toward adopting private brands. The information here is significant both for manufacturers and distributors.

If the manufacturer has a keen understanding of the distributor's profit possibilities, he may be able to place himself in a better bargaining position when he negotiates for an agreement to supply the distributor with private brand goods.

Decisions by Distributors

The authors warn that distributors' decisions are not affected only by motives of direct, immediate economic reward. They reveal how the nature of the product and the distributors' day-to-day merchandising needs may alter or even negate the efficacy of apparently obvious economic factors, in determining brand policy objectives.

In the case of durable goods, for example, short-run economic goals would be of less importance to the distributor than the aims to be achieved through long-run strategic policies. Knowledge of such variances in distributors' brand policy outlooks are invaluable to the manufacturer making decisions regarding his own company's brand policies.

Three Views

The Cook-Schutte findings, then, represent an attack on the problem of brand policy determination, on three fronts. The authors examine the policies of 119 manufacturers, and relate these policies to the companies' profit positions. They correlate environmental factors—economic and industry-wide conditions—with tendencies toward or opposed to private branding. Finally, they point up the considerations bearing upon distributors in their brand policy formulations.

BRAND POLICY AND THE NEW BRAND
OF EXPERTISE

With competitive business practices becoming increasingly sophisticated, and with brand policies providing a galaxy of sophisticated alternatives, a general knowledge of these alternatives and their consequences is essential for both the manufacturing and the marketing executive.

The book *Brand Policy Determination* was not intended to provide businessmen with neat or concise answers to questions about brand policy determination. But this book does provide the kind of information that helps the executive along the path leading to effective decision making.

STEUART HENDERSON BRITT
Editorial Director
Marketing Science Institute

Brand Policy Determination

I

The Problem

SOME OF THE world's largest corporations have set up special task forces to get the facts on private brands and their impact on policies and operations. There is good reason for this. Though private branding may look at first glance like a narrow marketing problem, it has much broader implications that command the attention of top management. Brand policy affects the entire stance of a company, from product development and production to finance and the price of corporate securities. A decision to produce, or not produce private brands can change the firm's market standing and affect its earnings for years to come. For distributors who develop their own brands, the effects can be just as far reaching.

Yet the interest in private branding has not generally been matched by in-depth analyses of the type which can become the basis of a well thought-out brand policy—one that looks to the future as well as considers the facts of the past.

PURPOSE OF THE STUDY

The overall purpose of the study is to identify and analyze the variables that manufacturers and distributors take into account in arriving at their brand policies.

In specific terms, the report attempts to develop answers to these fundamental questions:

Why are distributors' brands, or private labels, so strong in some product lines and not in others?

Why are trends in private brand sales different from one industry to another?

What are the factors taken into account by manufacturers and distributors in coming up with a brand policy?

1

What are the results of one brand policy compared with another?

BACKGROUND OF THE PROBLEM

Private branding is not new. It has, in fact, outlived many other marketing issues. In the two decades since World War II, there has been a resurgence of private branding. Distributors have captured large shares of volume with their own brands, and at the same time, there have been significant changes in retailing. The rise and fall of "fair trade" laws, the growth of discount houses, narrowing profit margins, and shortening product life cycles are some of the major changes. Giant retailers have gained a prominent position in the market. These and other events have given rise to a renewed interest in private branding.

The general importance of distributors' (private) brands in several major consumer product lines is shown in Exhibit 1. Private labels dominate some industries such as shoes, where they account for over 50 percent of sales volume. Industry differences are striking as well. While private brands account for an average of 33 percent of major appliance sales, their share of market falls to an average of 13 percent in selected packaged groceries, and about seven percent in portable appliances. One of the objectives of this study is to identify the factors that lead to these large differences in private brand sales among industries.

There are also wide differences in the trend of private brand sales among consumer products. The market share of private brands in some product lines grows dramatically over a period of a few years. In others, private brands have never become important, and in some cases distributors' brands gain a strong foothold, then begin to lose ground rapidly. Identifying the factors that lead to these changes is another objective of the study.

Finally, differences in the brand policies of manufacturers and distributors are important. Any company has three basic brand policy options. The first of these is a "manufacturers' brand policy." Here the company elects to produce, or a distributor to sell, only manufacturers' brands. The second is a "mixed brand policy," where a company produces, or sells, some combination of manufacturers' brands and private labels. The third option is a "distributors' brand policy." Here the company produces, or sells, only private brands.

It is sometimes found that companies of similar size and market share in the same industry have different brand policies. One firm will be heavily involved with private brand production, while another ignores this business. Some distributors, or retailers, do most of their volume in private brands, and others rely entirely on manufacturers' brands in one or more product lines. Thus, another task of this research is to explain why companies operate under given brand policies, and to determine the results associated with these policies.

EXHIBIT 1

DISTRIBUTORS' BRAND SHARE VARIES
(Average for Measured Products)

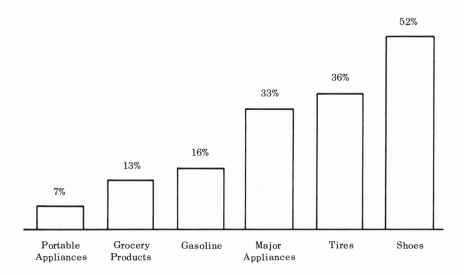

BASIC DEFINITIONS

The terms "manufacturers' (or national) brand" and "distributors' (or private) brand" are used throughout the study. These terms are defined on the basis of a single criterion—ownership of the brand name. A manufacturers' (or national) brand is one owned by a company whose primary or traditional business is production. A distributors' (or private) brand is one owned by a company whose primary or traditional business is distribution.

The major feature of these definitions is their workability. It is relatively easy to determine the owner of a brand name registered (or in application) at the United States Patent Office, Trademark Division. There are, of course, many unregistered brands used on a local basis, or for temporary purposes. These, however, account for such a small share of market as to be insignificant. Too, difficulties sometimes arise in identifying a company as primarily or traditionally a "manufacturer" or a "distributor," but usually the distinction is fairly clear-cut.

The use of brand ownership as the basis for definition is justified by more than workability. Ownership of a brand generally means a company has the authority to make the marketing decisions about the brand; decisions which determine whether the label is "low" or "high priced," "locally" or "nationally" distributed, and "advertised" or "unadvertised." And, the strategic position of the brand owner in a market—manufacturers compared with distributors—influences on the marketing actions taken by a company. Thus, it is both workable and sensible to distinguish between brands owned by distributors and manufacturers.

The terms "distributors" and "private" brand are used interchangeably in the report because they are widely accepted in the business community and usually taken to mean the same thing. Similarly, "manufacturers" and "national" brands are used interchangeably.

SOURCES OF INFORMATION

Since brand policy is basic to the overall marketing program of a company, information about the reasons for, and results of, a given policy are highly sensitive. By the same token, so is reliable share of market data for either private or manufacturers' brands. This sensitivity explains, in part, why only a limited understanding of the private brand issue exists.

Two broad-based sources of information were used in the study. The first was a series of intensive interviews, averaging some three hours in length, with top executives in nearly 200 manufacturing and distributing organizations. Of this total, 115 interviews were conducted with manufacturing executives and 77 with retailers, wholesalers, and officials of other distributing organizations. The companies included in the study represented adherence to all the important brand policy options. In this way, the information was collected from companies that operate under a manufacturers' brand policy, from those that follow a mixed brand policy, and from the viewpoint of those that rely entirely on private brands.

Second, data were needed to identify trends in private branding for various consumer products, so that impact of general economic forces on company brand policy could be evaluated. Many research organizations, syndicated marketing research services, trade associations, and business firms cooperated in developing these data. In grocery products and related lines, the A. C. Nielsen Company supplied the needed information. In major and portable appliances, and TV sets, figures were secured from the Starch Marketing Data Service. In other product lines, estimates were prepared by trade associations and business firms that had special information about a given industry. Complete details of the research design and methods used are presented in Appendix A.

ORGANIZATION OF THE REPORT

The next chapter presents a brief overview of the contemporary marketing structure. This material sets the stage for later analysis. It is followed by the three major chapters of the report. The first of these examines the economic forces which seem to affect brand policy determination (Chapter III). Next comes an analysis of the factors which tend to lead a manufacturer to adopt a given brand policy (Chapter IV). The final chapter (V) examines why private brands are adopted by different distributing organizations.

II

The Contemporary
Marketing Structure

IN ONE WAY or another, the private brand issue has some effect on marketing in practically every consumer product industry. It is important to thousands of manufacturing and distributing organizations—both small and large companies operating at nearly every level of distribution.

The overview developed in this chapter serves several purposes. First, it identifies the ten consumer product lines that are the focus of the analysis. Second, it shows how the similarities and differences among the ten lines serve as a basis for assigning all products to three general classes. This makes it possible to avoid needless concentration on minor product distinctions. Third, it provides a workable view of a complex distribution structure—a framework for looking at the various organizations in a simplified and meaningful way. Finally, it pinpoints the importance, or share, of private brand volume by type of distributor and major product line. This gives direction to later analysis, and allows the study to focus on the distributors most heavily involved in the sale of private brand merchandise.

SELECTING THE PRODUCT LINES

Thousands of products on which consumers spent a total of some $250 billions[1] in 1965 were possible selections. The products selected had to be representative on several counts:

The total dollar volume of selected products should account for an important part of consumer spending.

Brand choice by consumers should be involved in the shopping process.

6

Major product lines should be broad enough in scope to allow wide variation in the level of distributors' brand penetration from one product to another.

The selected product lines should represent a variety of shopping, consumption, and institutional characteristics.

RELATIONSHIP BETWEEN SELECTED PRODUCTS AND CONSUMER SPENDING PATTERNS

Five major nondurable product lines or industries were chosen for analysis. They accounted for about $56 billion out of a total of $177 billion in consumer spending on nondurables in 1964—approximately 32 percent. Expenditures on the selected durable goods ran about $10 billion, or some 17 percent of the $57 billion spent on consumer durables.

The fit between total spending on consumer products in 1964, and the ten major product lines selected for intensive analysis is

EXHIBIT 2

The Composition of Consumer Expenditures* − 1964
in the Aggregate and Within Product Lines Included in the Study

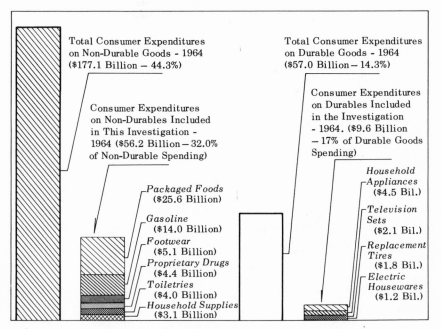

*Authors' estimates based on governmental and trade publications.

shown in Exhibit 2. This comparison is based on the definition of durable and nondurable goods used by the Department of Commerce. The major product lines or industries selected were:[2]

1. Packaged Foods	6. Footwear
2. Household Supplies	7. Replacement Tires
3. Proprietary Drugs	8. Electric Housewares
4. Toiletries	9. Major Household Appliances
5. Gasoline	10. Television Sets

The criteria used in defining the major product lines, and also a complete listing of the specific items included, can be found in Appendix B.

The selection of broadly representative products was undertaken with an eye toward isolating the more *general* determinants of brand policy and trends in private branding, so the findings are applicable in varying degree to consumer products other than those specifically included in the research.

CLASSIFYING THE PRODUCT LINES

Sixteen measures were selected, from among the many potentially useful ones, to identify the similarities and differences among consumer products. For example, one of these was average purchase price, another was durability of the product, and another the concentration ratio in manufacturing. These comparative measures are shown in Exhibit 3.

When the ten product lines were looked at against the comparative measures, strong differences began to appear. These differences add considerable depth to the notion of durable, and nondurable product classifications.

Generally speaking, markets for nondurable products may be viewed as ones with a high density of sellers and customers, coupled with a high frequency of transactions and products. In these product lines, changes take place rapidly and involve a large number of people.

On the other hand, markets for durables may be viewed generally as having a lower density of sellers, and customers, and a lower frequency of transactions and products.

Finally, a group of three product lines—footwear, portable appliances, and tires—though not related physically, fall between the extremes. They are identified as "semidurables." In this way, the sixteen comparative measures can be summarized in the durability scale and the result is a simplified grouping of similar product lines.

For example, the products grouped under the Nondurables heading are generally characterized by a low price per unit,

EXHIBIT 3

Classification of Product Lines Used in the Report

	NONDURABLES	SEMIDURABLES	DURABLES
	Foods	Portable	Major
	Drugs	Appliances	Appliances
	Household	Tires	TV Sets
	Supplies		
Comparative	Toiletries	Footwear	
Characteristic:	Gasoline		
● Average Price per Unit	Low*	Medium*	High*
● Change in Price Index (1947 to 1965)	Increase	Variable	Decrease
● Weight per Unit	Low	Medium	High
● Quantity Purchased/Year	High	Medium	Low
● Percent of Sales on Credit	Low	Medium	High
● Customer Search Time	Low	Medium	High
● Postponability	Low	Medium	High
● Durability of Product	Low	Medium	High
● After Purchase Service Need	Low	Medium	High
● Per Capita Consumption (Dollars)	High	Medium	Low
● Brand Awareness in Use	High	Medium	Low
● Intensity of Distribution	High	Medium	Low
● Industry Advertising/Sales	High	Medium	Low
● Concentration in Manufacturing	Low	Medium	High
● Sales per Man Hour Worked in Manufacturing	High	Medium	Low
● New Capital Investment/Plant in Manufacturing	High	Variable	Low

*The rankings for each group of products are *general tendencies*. Individual products may differ from the rankings shown here, but the fit was found to be close enough to justify the groupings.

small size, large number of purchases during a year, and limited use of consumer credit. Also, these products do not involve the consumer in much shopping around, and purchases are generally not postponable. Semidurables are more moderate on each of these counts, while durables tend toward the reverse of nondurable scores.

Looking at the other characteristics, nondurables fall into a group with little or no likelihood of after-purchase service, but with high per capita consumption and brand awareness during use. Again, semidurables register a moderate on each count and durables have a high likelihood of service with lower per capita consumption and brand awareness during use.

The relationship between durability and other product characteristics also tends to hold upstream in the market structure right to the original source of the product. For example, in nondurables, total advertising expenditures as a percent of sales, intensity of distribution, manufacturers' sales per man-hour worked, and new capital investment per plant are relatively high, with generally lower levels of concentration in manufacturing. This comparative analysis emphasizes two considerations that have a bearing on later analyses. First, the ten product lines selected for intensive study cover a wide range of the shopping, consumption, and institutional characteristics associated with brandable consumer products. Second, because the products classified in each of these groups tend to be quite similar, it is possible to use the general product groupings throughout the analysis which follows.

SUMMARY OF THE DISTRIBUTION STRUCTURE

Tracing the distribution systems of several major consumer products in today's scrambled product markets can be a complex task. While detailed description is not important here, some kind of organizing framework is necessary. The following exhibit represents one way to organize the thousands of different kinds of operations which have some relevance to the study.

EXHIBIT 4

Classification of Distributors

TYPE:	CRITERIA:		
	Merchandise Lines Offered	Number of Retail Outlets	Type of Ownership
General Merchandise Chain	General	Over 50	Central
Special Merchandise Chain	Special	Over 10	Central
Department Store	General	50 or less	Central
Affiliated Outlet	General/Special	10 or less per member	Affiliation
Unaffiliated Outlet	General/Special	10 or less	Independent
Supplier-Controlled Outlet	Special	Variable	Central/ Affiliation

Six general types of distributing organizations were identified. They were classified by the number of merchandise lines carried, the number of retail outlets involved, and degree of centralization of ownership.

Additional distributions may be made within each of the basic forms specified, but these are unnecessary in gaining a general perspective. For example, on the basis of customer service offering and price lines, one might divide the department store classification into (a) traditional, full-service department stores and (b) discount department stores.

Of the six types mentioned above, the first one is general merchandise chains. Chains in this category are identified by broad merchandise lines carried (both hard and soft goods), by the large number of retail outlets (over 50 units), and single corporate ownership with centralized management.

Next is the grouping of special merchandise chains. These chains are characterized by special or limited merchandise offerings (e.g., food chains); over 10 separate retail outlets, and corporate ownership with central management control.

Department stores are similar to general merchandise chains in terms of a broad merchandise line offering. Also, they often have single corporate ownership, with centralized management. But the department store is distinguished from the general merchandise chain on the basis of scale of operations. In this report, a departmentalized operation with less than 50 stores is called a department store organization. This dividing line tends to separate distributing organizations which are more or less intraregional in scope from those that cover large sections of the country.

The next two general classifications of distributors are affiliated outlets and unaffiliated outlets. The two operations share some basic characteristics; they tend to have limited or special merchandise offerings (though some small department stores fit the affiliated outlet category), and have fewer than 11 retail outlets under single ownership and central management. They differ in one important respect; the affiliated outlet is contractually integrated while the unaffiliated is not. Unaffiliated outlets may be thought of as independent retailers.

Membership in some form of affiliated operation, like cooperative buying groups, often provides the affiliated outlet with several advantages not available to the unaffiliated. Some examples might be: more favorable wholesale prices through pooled volume buying, exchange of market and operating information, and professional merchandise planning capabilities. Such gains in marketing capability can make the affiliated outlet an important force in private branding. Management control, however, tends to remain in the hands of cooperating retailers, and the affiliation itself typically exercises little control over individual operations, as compared with the degree of control maintained by management in corporate chain operations.

A final grouping of distributors is supplier-controlled outlets. These operations are simply special merchandise chains. But, they are an important departure from the special merchandise operation defined above. They represent forward integration by manufacturers, through corporate ownership, or by carefully controlled franchise agreements.

COMBINING PRODUCT LINES AND DISTRIBUTION

At this stage, the first three tasks of this chapter are complete. The product lines studied have been identified, compared with total consumer spending, and compared with each other. The result was a grouping of products on a "durability" scale. Next, a complex distribution structure was given some order. The result was a simplified classification of distributors established because of its relevance to this investigation.

These two results have a larger relationship, however. When the product line and distributor classifications are put together, a clear pattern of interrelationships emerge. This pattern, shown in Exhibit 5, identifies those distributors that are primarily responsible for private branding in each product line. For example, general merchandise chains were estimated to account for about 85 percent of total private brand sales in consumer durables—TV sets and major appliances. On the other hand, special merchandise chains dominate private branding in nondurables. They were estimated to account for over 70 percent of private brand volume in grocery products and household supplies, for example.

EXHIBIT 5

Estimated Percent* of Total Distributors' Brand Unit Volume in Ten Product Lines
Accounted for by Six Basic Types of Distributing Institutions—1965

Distributors	Major Product Lines									
	Nondurables					Semidurables			Durables	
	Packaged Foods	Household Supplies	Gasoline	Proprietary Drugs	Toiletries	Footwear	Replacement Tires	Electric Housewares	Television Sets	Household Appliances
General Merchandise Chains	**				20	25	60		50	85	85
Special Merchandise Chains	70	75	95	70	50	50	25			
Department Stores							20			
Affiliated Outlets	20									
Unaffiliated Outlets										
Manufacturer-owned Stores										

*Authors' estimates of the *general importance* of basic types of distributing institutions in accounting for distributors' brand volume in each product line. These estimates are *not* based upon a survey of firms.

**Estimates were developed only for those product lines where the given type of distributor accounted for at least 20 percent of private brand volume.

The relationships presented in Exhibit 5 lead to some points of focus for later analysis. In nondurable product lines, the principal emphasis is given to special merchandise chains, since these organizations dominate distributor branding. Though important in an absolute sense, affiliated outlets and their buying organizations receive secondary attention in the analysis. In durable product lines, the principal emphasis of later analysis is on general merchandise chains. These two distributing organizations also become a useful point of focus in semidurables, since their influence overlaps in these product lines.

Not only do certain types of distributors tend to dominate private branding in given product lines, but as might be expected, they share several operating characteristics. They are more or less integrated, by some form of either corporate or contractual backward integration.

They operate a large number of outlets, and each organization also tends to account for a relatively high unit volume in the given product lines.

SUMMARY COMMENTS

This overview of products, organizations, and private branding in different operations was designed to set the stage for the analyses which follow. The effect of results presented above on later analyses might be summed up in this way: more analytical attention is given to the types of organizations, marketing programs, and general product classes, while less attention is given to specific products.

III

Environmental Forces
Affecting Brand Policies

SINCE THE PRIVATE brand issue began to stimulate serious interest in the 1930's, many explanations of the growth in private brand sales have been advanced. Some of them relate to the operations of individual companies. From this viewpoint the "causes" of private branding are factors over which management has some control. These factors are examined in later parts of the report.

Another group of explanations relate to the economic climate and market conditions in which company policy is determined. The more general environmental forces may also have an effect on private branding. Even though management is not in a position to directly influence the outcome, companies can react to changes from the outside. Thus, it is sometimes claimed that industries, groups of firms, or consumers, react to changes in general economic conditions in a predictable fashion. This reaction contributes to certain changes in private branding. For example, one common idea is that excess productive capacity in an industry will lead to increased private brand production. The idea seems reasonable, but has not been subjected to serious evaluation over a broad range of consumer products.

TREND ANALYSIS

To evaluate the effect excess industry capacity, as well as other factors, might have on private branding, it is necessary to have reliable facts about what happens to private branding during periods of high and low excess capacity. In short, trends in private brand sales for different industries are needed. With this information, comparisons may be made between private branding and various general economic or marketing forces which might shape trends in private brand sales. (Trends in private brand sales for ten

14

major industries, covering generally the years from 1955 to 1965 are projected in Appendix D.)

Identification of the effect of environmental forces should contribute to a general understanding of the private brand issue. From the viewpoint of individual companies, if the effect of various economic conditions on private branding can be isolated, information about what is likely to occur under different circumstances can become a useful input in the process of brand policy determination. Even though a single firm cannot directly influence excess industry capacity, or levels of general prosperity, knowledge of their influence upon private branding will allow management to take advantage of expected changes.

NATURE AND PRESENTATION OF THE DATA

Estimates of distributors' and manufacturers' brand share in ten major industries were prepared by several commercial research companies and cooperating organizations. Among these were the A. C. Nielsen Company and the Starch Marketing Data Service. Restrictions placed on use of the market share data in this report differed considerably by source. For this reason, some specific product lines are fully identified while others are referred to only by number or letter. For example, A. C. Nielsen data on private brand share of market in packaged foods and household supplies were made available on the condition that market shares for specific products remain unidentified in this study. Hence, estimates of private brand share in each product line are masked in the following analyses by use of number and letter designations. The numbers assigned to products in one part of the chapter do not correspond to numbers assigned to products in another part of the report. In each section of the analysis, however, the products involved are listed in a footnote or an exhibit.

Finally, where conclusions presented in this chapter depend upon significant changes in the level of private or national brand share, significant levels of change were present according to the tests applied by the data sources. Further detail on the nature of the data appear in Appendix A.

ORGANIZATION OF THE ANALYSIS

Some explanations of how general economic and marketing forces affect private brand sales are widely accepted. Wide acceptance, however, does not establish validity. The purpose of this chapter is to analyze systematically the relationship between several environmental forces and private branding—to identify what happens to private brand sales under various conditions.

The factors to be evaluated can be divided into two classes. The first classification is general economic conditions and the second, general marketing forces. Within the two groupings, the following analyses evaluate each of these factors.

General Economic Conditions:

Excess Industry Capacity
The Level of General Prosperity
Degree of Economic Concentration

General Marketing Forces:

Amount of National Advertising
Stage in Product's Life Cycle
Price Differentials between Brands

The analyses deal with each factor, beginning with the group referred to as General Economic Conditions.

EXCESS INDUSTRY CAPACITY AND
PRIVATE BRAND SALES

If businessmen were asked what stimulates private brand production, one of the most common answers would probably be excess industry capacity. The implication is that if excess capacity persists in an industry, it will lead to an increase in private brand production. Proponents of this view argue that manufacturers sometimes build large production facilities for a product line, then as they begin to experience a drop in demand during intermediate term periods, look for ways to sell additional volume. One of these ways might be through private brand distributors.

Since manufacturers are supposed to view this added volume as plus business, their selling prices may be reduced enough to attract new or increased private brand sales.

At this point, the explanation generally ends without a discussion of what happens to private brand volume when industry capacity utilization returns to normal. A logical extension of the explanation would indicate that as excess capacity declines, sources of supply dwindle in number and private brand sales decrease. This is not very realistic for two reasons. First, in most industries there are several producers that make it their major business to supply products to private branders. Neither conditions of high nor low industry demand and output will alter the willingness of these manufacturers to produce private brands. Second, in both nondurable and consumer durable goods industries, few manufacturers are in a position to enter into or discontinue private brand production at will.

There is a difference between the motivation for an individual company to produce private brands, and the effect of excess capacity on an industry-wide basis. It is often true that capacity utilization in an industry does not reflect the degree of excess capacity in a specific company. For example, one company might have unused capacity available as a result of overbuilding facilities or due to the loss of a major customer. At the same time, the industry may be operating at a preferred level of capacity utilization. The single company might be prompted to seek private brand business at a time when there is little excess capacity in the industry.

It would be a mistake to confuse the motivations of management of a single firm with the effect of excess capacity on an industry-wide basis. Both conditions are examined in the report, but at this stage only the relationship between excess industry capacity and private brand sales is of concern.

Types of Comparisons Developed

There are at least three ways to look at the effect of excess industry capacity. The first is to take a number of product lines, and compare, on an overall basis, the amount of excess industry capacity with the level of private brand sales for various time periods. A second approach would be a comparison between groups of product lines, such as selected consumer durables and nondurables. Here the objective would be to find out if industries with the highest levels of excess capacity are also the ones with relatively higher private brand share of market. A third point of view would be to examine changes over time within a given product line or industry. Here, the approach is to relate changes in private brand sales to changes in excess industry capacity.

The analysis looks briefly at each of these three approaches. But first, it is important to establish a clear definition of excess industry capacity.

A Measure of Excess Industry Capacity

Capacity utilization for specific industries is an elusive concept and difficult to measure. "We are all familiar with...references to capacity, which seems to imply the existence of a body of statistics in which capacity is uniquely defined and measured with some precision at frequent intervals. Actually, no such body of statistics exists..."[1]

A measure of excess industry capacity was developed for use in this report. It is a modification of the technique used at the Wharton

School of Finance and Commerce of the University of Pennsylvania—the "Wharton Index of Capacity Utilization."

Excess industry capacity is viewed here as the difference between what an industry actually produced in one year, and what the industry would have been expected to produce as a result of output in the two or three preceding years (depending on industry conditions). A description of the methods used to estimate industry excess capacity in 26 lines, together with some illustrations appear in Appendix B.

General Comparison of Excess Industry Capacity and Private Branding

A series of comparisons were developed to identify the relationship between excess capacity and private brand share from an overall standpoint. These comparisons were based on 1) the index of excess industry capacity described above, and 2) an index of private brand share for 26 industries. Private brand share data generally covered the years from 1959 through 1965 for selected nondurables, and from 1954 through 1964 in semidurables and durables. All of the figures were converted to index numbers with a 1959-60 base period. These data were plotted on a scatter diagram so that comparisons could be made between excess industry capacity and private brand share for each industry and year for which data were available. In all there were 143 points on the scatter diagram. Each point matched capacity position with private branding at a given time.

This general comparison did not support the hypothesis that higher excess industry capacity is related to higher levels of private branding. Periods of relatively high excess capacity in the 26 measured industries were not associated with higher private brand share of market.

Another comparison was made following the same approach outlined above, except that the readings of excess capacity and private branding were not taken at the same point in time. Here, excess capacity was charted in one year and private brand share in the immediately following year. Inclusion of this lagged effect did not significantly change the relationship.

Private Branding and Excess Capacity in Industry Groups

Average excess industry capacity for all 26 industries over periods of both high and low capacity utilization was 104, with 100 equal to normal or projected output levels. The average private brand share of market for all industries studied was 14 percent. If industry groups where private branding is highest tend to be the ones which have been plagued by excess capacity, this should be revealed by comparing averages for industry groups with overall averages.

Since nondurables had persistently lower levels of private brand share, it might be expected that this industry grouping would show generally lower average excess capacity. And, since semidurables have had higher private brand sales, it might be expected that this group of industries would have higher levels of excess capacity. The pattern did not emerge.

Average excess capacity for nondurables and for semidurables was found to be about the same as for all industries combined. Yet the average private brand share for nondurables is nine percent, while in semidurables it is over 37 percent. The comparison can be seen more clearly in the following exhibit.

EXHIBIT 6

Excess Capacity and Private Brand Share for Industry Groupings

	Median Excess Capacity 100 = Actual Capacity Utilization (Index Number)	Median Distributors' Brand Market Share (Percent)
Nondurables (1959-65)	103.5	9.0
Semidurables (1954-1964)	104.0	37.5
Durables (1954-1964)	107.0	12.5
All Industries Studied	104.0	14.0

These figures suggest that industry groupings with the highest levels of private branding are not the ones that have experienced the highest and most persistent periods of excess industry capacity. In fact, over the years from 1954 to 1964, consumer durables, like refrigerators and washing machines, experienced the highest average excess capacity, while private brand share in durables averaged less than one-third the level found in semidurable goods industries during the same period.

Private Branding and Capacity in Specific Industries

Looking at what happens to excess capacity and private brand share of market within specific industries over a period of years might yield a clearer pattern, if some relationship does exist. In addition, it makes it easier to evaluate the effect of time lags, and should provide some indication of the chages that take place in private brand sales as capacity utilization returns to normal, if these aspects are important.

Two illustrations of the results in 26 industry comparisons are presented in Exhibits 7 and 8. The first is the gasoline industry; the second, replacement tires.

EXHIBIT 7

Excess Capacity and Private Branding in the Gasoline Industry*

*Authors' estimates of excess industry capacity; the method used is explained in Appendix B. Private brand share data for gasoline appear in Appendix D, page 305.

In these illustrations, as in most of the comparisons developed, it is possible to select a series of two or three years where excess capacity is related to private branding in a way which would tend to support the idea that excess industry capacity leads to increased private branding. Looking at the whole spectrum of years and specific industries, however, no meaningful or consistent pattern was identified.

EXHIBIT 8

Excess Capacity and Private Branding in Replacement Tires*

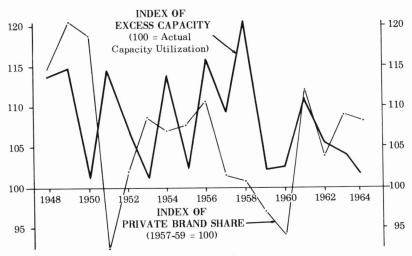

*Authors' estimates of excess industry capacity. The method used is explained in Appendix B. Private brand share data for replacement tires appear in Appendix D, pages 307 and 308.

The expected changes in private brand share were found in only one of the comparisons and then only if a two-year lag were allowed between the measurement of excess capacity and private brand share of market. This was a canned food product, and the results were not typical of the other 25 comparisons.

Summing Up

Excess industry capacity does not appear to be related to private brand share of market in nondurables, consumer durables, or semidurable goods. This conclusion seems to hold whether comparisons are based on an overall perspective, from the viewpoint of industry groupings, or in terms of specific industries, and with or without time lags. No consistent patterns seem to emerge.

It is possible that this is due to a lack of sensitivity in the data, or because of the difficulty of developing a precise measure of

excess industry capacity. But, it seems more likely that no relationship was identified because none exists. Perhaps excess
industry capacity was not intended as an explanation of what causes
private branding, but more as a rationalization for the existence
of private brand production. The effect of excess capacity on the
brand policies of individual manufacturers is, of course, still an
open question at this stage of the report.

THE EFFECT OF CHANGES IN GENERAL PROSPERITY

It is frequently suggested that changes in the level of general
prosperity will have a significant effect on the sale of private
brands. This is based on assumptions about the buying habits of
consumers and price differences between brands. The reasoning
is that during high prosperity consumers tend to buy national
brands, but during periods when the economy is depressed consumers are more likely to buy private brands because price
savings are then more important. Bad times, as seen by consumers,
can result from obvious signs such as spreading unemployment and
falling incomes, or from more subtle forces, like growing inflation and increased living costs as occurred in 1966.

In a report of research conducted in the mid 1950's, this comment
was made:

> It was generally agreed both by manufacturers and by distributors interviewed that
> high consumer incomes favor manufacturer brands. When consumer incomes are
> down and small savings seem more important there is greater opportunity for dis-
> tributor brands to gain on the basis of price differentials.[2]

A similar idea was suggested in a study conducted in the early
1940's:

> Distributors' brands have made their greatest gains in sales during periods of de-
> pression, when [price] differentials between manufacturers' and distributors' brands
> have tended to widen and such savings have had increased appeal to consumers be-
> cause consumers have become penny conscious at such times.[3]

Expected Differences Among Industries

These views of the relationship between levels of prosperity and
private brand sales tend to conceal differences among industries.
For example, on the basis of the characteristics of durable, semidurable, and nondurable goods industries developed earlier,[4] changes
in the level of general prosperity might be expected to have a
different effect on private brand sales in each group of product lines.

Since nondurables such as grocery products are relatively low-
priced, frequently-purchased items, consumers will buy them

regardless of the state of the economy. In addition, it is relatively easy to compare the price of items bought recently with the price of current purchases. This kind of direct comparison can also be made between private and manufacturers' brands in the same store. Finally, nondurable products, as a whole, are relatively non-postponable purchases. Some minimum level of consumption must be maintained in foods, household supplies, drugs, and gasoline, regardless of the level of economic activity. Nonetheless, there may be significant changes in the particular brands chosen.

The situation is different with consumer durables, and to some extent semidurables like portable appliances and replacement tires. Here, higher unit prices are involved, and products tend to be purchased infrequently. For example, the average interval between purchases is five to seven years for major appliances, so it is difficult for consumers to contrast the price of a current purchase with one made several years ago. Too, a high percentage of sales of private brand durable goods are made in stores which do not offer the choice of a manufacturers' brand. As a result, it is often difficult to make even current price comparisons among different brands of the same product at the point of sale. Finally, and of considerable importance in evaluating the effect of changes in general prosperity, durable goods purchases are relatively postponable. Unless a consumer durable is no longer serviceable, purchases tend to be postponed during a period of recession and perhaps during recovery as well.

This comparison of nondurables with durable goods industries suggests that different conclusions might be expected for each. Low prosperity might stimulate nondurable private brand sales, while high prosperity may favor manufacturers' brands. This appears not to be true with consumer durables and semidurables.

Types of Comparisons Developed

Since different results could be expected with nondurables as opposed to durables, comparisons were made which would allow for these differences. Nondurables were treated as one group, while durables and semidurables were treated as another. The analysis was directed toward determining the effect of the general level of prosperity on the sale of private brands.

Measuring the Level of Prosperity

Selecting periods of high and low prosperity, or tracing the course of a business cycle, is not difficult. A variety of measures are available; all generally consistent over time and taken at frequent intervals.

Levels of high and low prosperity in the United States economy are shown in Exhibit 9.

EXHIBIT 9

Periods of High and Low Prosperity
Compared With One of the Fourteen Indicators Used*

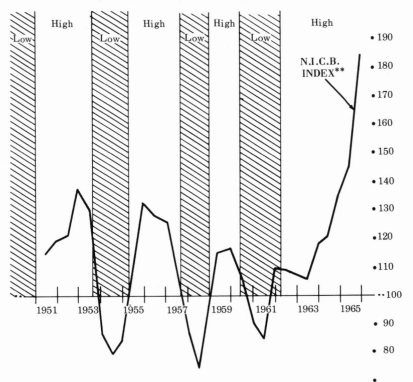

*The 14 measures used here to identify periods of high and low prosperity were developed by the National Bureau of Economic Research, and are published monthly by the Department of Commerce in *Business Cycle Developments.*

**Help Wanted Advertising as a Business Indicator, Technical Paper Number Nine, National Industrial Conference Board, Inc., New York. Data are seasonally adjusted and charted for mid-year (June) and end-of-year (December) points; 1957-59 = 100.

Since 1951 there have been four periods of relatively high prosperity and three of relatively low prosperity. These periods were measured by use of the 14 "roughly coincident indicators," or measures of business activity, developed by the National Bureau of Economic Research. Estimates are reported on a monthly basis in a Department of Commerce publication called *Business*

Cycle Indicators. Some of the items covered by the indicators are personal income, unemployment rate, amount of help–wanted advertising, and wholesale prices. An illustration of how one of the 14 measures compares with the high and low prosperity periods used is shown in Exhibit 9. Here, the National Industrial Conference Board's Index of Help–Wanted Advertising in Newspapers is plotted over each period of prosperity. This NICB Index is used in later illustrations because it has been found to be representative of changes in the other 13 measures of prosperity, and because it is more sensitive to change in economic activity than most of the other measures. Additional detail about selection of the periods and measures used is presented in Appendix B.

Prosperity and Private Branding in Nondurables

Comparisons were developed between changes in private brand share and changes in general prosperity in the 24 product categories of nondurable goods for which data were available. These products ranged from high to low private brand penetration. The share of market for each was traced from 1959 to 1965. The change in private brand sales during a period of low prosperity, running from early 1960 through 1961, was compared with the change in private brand sales for the same group of 24 product lines during the immediately following period of high prosperity, starting in early 1962 and continuing through 1966.

The result of this comparison between changes in prosperity and changes in private brand share in nondurables is shown in Exhibit 10. As a benchmark, each period of prosperity is shown in relation to the NICB Index. During the period of low prosperity, private branding increased significantly in about 90 percent of the 24 product lines examined (22 out of 24). For the same 24 product lines, private brand share of market decreased significantly during the following period of high prosperity in over 60 percent of the cases (15 out of 24).

Thus it appears that private brand share in selected nondurables tends to increase when the level of prosperity falls, and decrease when it rises. Exhibit 11 provides detailed information on this pattern.

In 15 of 24 nondurable product lines, private brand share changed in the way that would be expected if consumers switched from private to manufacturers' brands as prosperity rose. In many of these 15 product lines, there was a high correlation between changes in prosperity and changes in private brand share. To permit comparison between private brand sales and periods of high and low prosperity on a yearly basis, the NICB Index is used. For the examples presented in Exhibit 12, as well as for other comparisons shown in Appendix B, an upturn in the level of prosperity signals a downturn in private brand share. However,

EXHIBIT 10

Private Branding and the Level of Prosperity
in 24 Nondurable Product Lines*

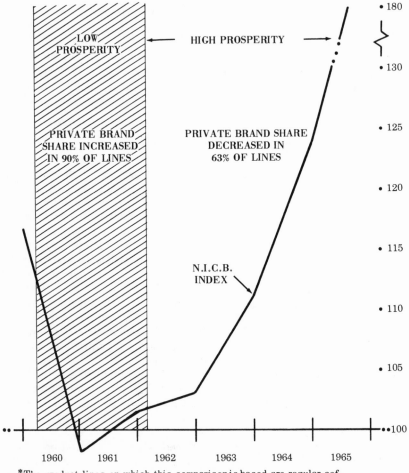

*The product lines on which this comparison is based are regular cof-
fee, salad dressing, mayonnaise, tomato juice, canned peaches, fruit
cocktail, canned pineapple, catsup, canned peas, canned corn, flour,
frozen meat pies, canned spaghetti, wax paper, gasoline, cleansing tissue, canned milk, powdered milk, packaged detergents, pineapple juice,
canned beans, toilet tissues, margarine, and soluble coffee.

the relationship seems to be fairly clearcut only for selected nondurable products.

As might be expected, it is generally true that decreases in
private brand share are accompanied by increases in manufacturers' brand share. However, this is not always true, as some

EXHIBIT 11

Patterns of Change in Prosperity and Private Brand Share
for Selected Nondurable Product Lines*

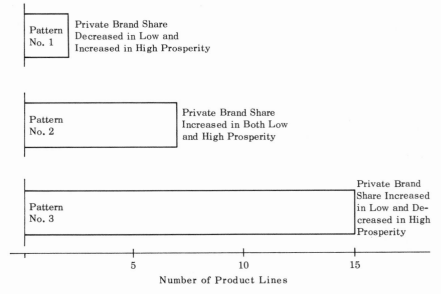

Number of Product Lines

*It is highly unlikely that these patterns could have resulted from chance causes, or
that private brand share and prosperity are unrelated.

sales are accounted for by local brands or unbranded merchandise
with shares too small to identify. Additional evidence is furnished
by tracing manufacturers' brand share of nondurable goods sales
as the level of prosperity increases. Data were available for manufacturers' brand share in 70 different grocery product lines, including some household supply items. In the period of generally
rising prosperity from 1962 to 1965, the share of manufacturers'
brands increased significantly in 45 out of 70 product lines—64
percent of the lines involved. In the drugs and toiletries industry
during the same period, manufacturers' brand share increased in
20 out of 24 product lines—in 83 percent of the lines. These data
add support to the contention that rising general prosperity is
favorable to manufacturers' brands and unfavorable to private
labels in nondurable product lines.

Background on the relationship

Even in these instances, however, the relationship between changes
in prosperity and private brand sales is not necessarily one of

28

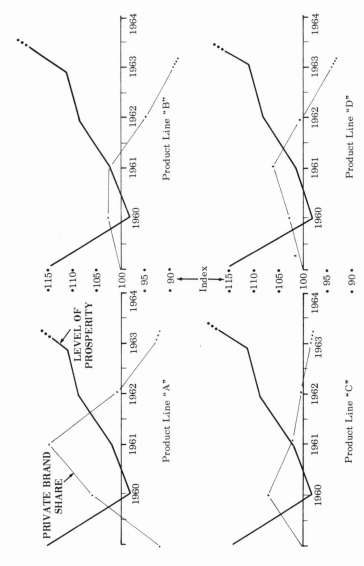

EXHIBIT 12

Changes in Prosperity and Private Brand Share
in Four Nondurable Product Lines*

*Similar comparisons for additional nondurable product lines are presented in Appendix B.

cause and effect. Many characteristics are associated with periods of high prosperity, which may tend to favor manufacturers' brand sales, and be unfavorable to private brands. A tendency for consumers to switch from private to national brands as prosperity increases is probably part of the explanation. It is probable that many consumers "upgrade" their purchases in this way with little knowledge of or interest in the branding policies involved. There are other factors too that may have a bearing. For example, producers of national brands may increase advertising during high levels of business activity. This would probably attract more customers to their brands. In addition, price differentials among brands may change during high prosperity. If they narrow, this might attract buyers to manufacturers' brands.

These and perhaps other factors are related to the tendency for high levels of prosperity to signal a downturn in private brand share of market for selected nondurables. The effect of some of these general marketing forces is examined later in this chapter.

Limitations on forecasting private brand share in nondurables

Whatever combination of events "causes" the relationship between prosperity and private branding, companies may want to use measures of economic activity to forecast changes in private brand share.

The usefulness of this approach would be limited by three factors. First, intermediate term projections are not too important to manufacturers of nondurable goods. In these industries, a year or two in the future may be too long a time span for consideration, since marketing plans and actions are often taken on a short term basis. Second, private brand share for all nondurables was not found to be closely related to changes in prosperity. There are exceptions. With some products, like regular coffee, there is a fairly close fit, and with others, like canned milk, the relationship does not hold.

Finally, historical relationships may not continue in the future.

Private branders; possible reaction to declining share

Private brand distributors can take merchandising and promotional steps to forestall the decline in market share. This is especially true in prolonged periods of high prosperity where there is time for such actions to take effect.

For example, private branders could shape their merchandising programs to magnify price differences during periods of low prosperity. Continuing to use this approach, when incomes are high and price savings not so important, will probably result in a loss of market share. Consumers can be given the idea, through advertising or in-store displays, that private brands are lower priced "substitutes" for manufacturers' brands. So, if price differences become less important during high prosperity, consumers are encouraged, by a distributor's own merchandising program, to turn away from private labels.

During periods of rising income and employment, distributors can move away from playing up price differences between brands. Private branders can adapt their merchandising programs to compete with manufacturers' brands on the basis of additional appeals (particularly nonprice ones) during high prosperity, and thus limit or prevent a downturn in market share. This would, of course, upset the historical relationship between prosperity and private branding in selected nondurables.

Prosperity and Private Branding in Semidurables
and Durables

Earlier in the analysis the characteristics of durable goods purchases were compared with those of nondurables. This suggested that changes in general prosperity may have a different effect on private branding in durables. Economic conditions of the last several years seem to bear this out.

Continuous increase in the level of prosperity has not signaled a decline in private brand share for either semidurables, like tires and shoes, or for consumer durables like washing machines and television sets. The share of distributors' brands in durable goods has actually increased significantly during the last five years. Generally, the gains in private brand share during this period of high prosperity have been greater than in the previous period from 1955 to 1960. Exhibit 13 traces changes in private brand share of semidurables over several periods of high and low prosperity. Private brand share of the replacement tire market does not follow the expected pattern; increasing when economic activity is low, coupled with a decrease when it is high. Almost the opposite occurs. Distributors' brand share tends to grow from 1951 through 1955, during generally rising prosperity. Then it falls off until 1958 as prosperity declines, and begins to increase with gains in economic activity during 1959. Over the entire decade, however, private brand share in replacement tires tends to hold at about the same long-term level; roughly 36 percent of unit volume. Private branding in footwear seems not to change predictably during fluctuations in prosperity. Distributors' brand share of the shoe market increased rather continuously from 1954 to 1959, and again from 1959 to 1964. While detailed data were developed only for these points in time, changes in private brand shoe sales between the measured years were estimated not to vary significantly from the trend shown in Exhibit 13.

EXHIBIT 13

Prosperity and Private Branding in Tire and Shoe Industries*

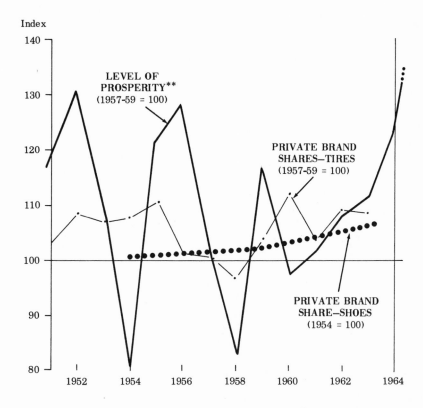

*Private brand share data for replacement tires and shoes on which these indices are based appear in Appendix D, pages 306, 307, and 308.
**National Industrial Conference Board Index. Annual Averages are charted.

A slightly different comparison was developed for consumer durables. For this part of the analysis, portable appliances, which were classified as a semidurable product, and put in with durable goods because private brand share data came from the same source. Changes in prosperity and private brand share were not compared on an annual basis. Instead, five-year periods were used because 1) the cost of private brand share of market data on an annual basis was prohibitive, and 2) changes are transmitted through the market for slow turning, higher priced consumer durables at a much slower rate than is true for nondurables, so annual data are not critical.

It was found that during the period of sharply rising intermediate term prosperity from 1959 to 1965, both the market share and the unit volume of private brand major appliances increased at an average annual rate almost double the rate of gain in the preceding period of generally falling intermediate term prosperity. Private brands of portable appliances increased at an almost constant rate, regardless of the state of economic activity. Only private brand TV sets had greater market share increases during low prosperity than in high, although their share did not decline with rising income and employment.

In consumer durables, rising general prosperity appears to favor private brands, rather than limit their growth in sales.

Background on the relationship

The factors affecting purchases of consumer durable goods examined earlier explain in large part the failure of private brand share to decline with improvement in the general economic climate. Buying is generally postponable, direct price comparisons at point of sale are difficult, and purchases need not be repeated during low and high points in prosperity. Still unexplained is why private brand share in durables tended to increase faster during high prosperity than low.

While the facts are not available, a partial explanation might be related to service. For example, higher prosperity does tend to accelerate the purchase of durable goods. Since after purchase service is an important part of the "product," increases in durable goods volume during high prosperity might tend increasingly toward outlets that provide the best service package. If a significant number of consumers believe these outlets to be the general merchandise chains, this would tend to favor distributors' brand purchases during high prosperity.

Summing Up

Earlier in the report, it was stated that excess industry capacity does not seem to affect private brand production. Changes in general prosperity, however, do have a predictable effect on private brand share of selected nondurable markets.

It may seem strange that an increase in excess industry capacity is not related to private branding, while a decline in economic activity is. It might be expected that declining economic activity would foster increasing excess industry capacity. Reasons for the differences in relation to private branding are several.

First, changes in excess capacity for specific industries may not correspond to changes in general economic activity. Capacity utilization in most of the industries examined in this report can change drastically without significantly affecting nationwide income and employment. Isolated changes in the "canned vegetable" or "washing machine" industry, for example, would probably have little effect on the economy as a whole.

Second, the conditions that give rise to excess industry capacity are quite different from those that mark periods of high and low general prosperity. One condition is the ability of a specific industry to produce additional volume in the short term. The other is based, in part, on the ability and willingness of consumers to increase their purchases of widely different products.

Finally, the assumption underlying the idea that either excess industry capacity or general prosperity can affect private branding is important. This assumption is that private brand distributors are more or less "passive." Take changes in capacity for example. When excess capacity becomes available, new private brand distributors suddenly appear to take up the slack. Or, existing ones rapidly increase their orders, just because capacity is available in the supplying industry and prices may be more favorable. This viewpoint, as illustrated in Exhibit 14, places private branders in a passive role; one which is hardly consistent with their market strength.

EXHIBIT 14

A Private Brander's Response to Economic Forces

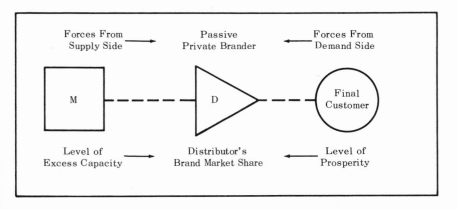

Distributors will probably respond to excess industry capacity only if they think it is in their best interest. Private branders can also react to forces from the demand side of the market but with less direct control.

In short, private brand distributors react to changing economic conditions just as readily as will suppliers or consumers. They may, it seems, be more restricted when it comes to influencing the buying patterns of consumers than they are in changing timing and volume of purchases from suppliers. As a result, changes in general prosperity have a stronger effect on private brand share than changes in industry capacity position.

ECONOMIC CONCENTRATION IN MANUFACTURING
DISTRIBUTION AND BRANDING

It has long been though that economic concentration is an important factor in shaping business developments. To some, evidence that a few manufacturers dominate an industry leads to the conclusion that monopolistic tendencies exist. This is often extended to mean that a few manufacturers decide on how things are done in the industry—from pricing to distribution.

The logical jump from control of output by a few manufacturers to monopolistic control of the industry is a big one; often not very realistic considering today's market structure. For one thing it overlooks the power distributors may have. The more general term economic concentration often has a special meaning, since it usually refers to concentration, or bigness in manufacturing.

Two other important facets of concentration should be considered. One is concentration in distribution. This refers to the degree of market control exercised by distributors through use of their own brands and in other ways. The other is concentration in branding, which considers the effect of concentration of market share in a few brands, and relates leading brands to either manufacturers or distributors.

Each of the three aspect of economic concentration—bigness in manufacturing, in distribution, and in branding—will be examined. The basic purpose is to determine the effect concentration may have on private branding.

The first part of the analysis deals with the response of private branders to concentration in manufacturing as measured by the percent of industry output accounted for by the four largest producers.[5]

Private Branders' Response to Concentration
in Manufacturing

Concentration in manufacturing seems to stimulate private branding rather than to restrict it. It was found that industries with lower concentration ratios tended to have lower private brand share of market than manufacturing industries with much higher levels of concentration. This relationship held for a number of different nondurable, semidurable, and consumer durable goods.

The conclusion is based on comparisons between concentration ratios in manufacturing and private brand share of industry volume. The relationship and a list of the industries involved are shown in the following exhibit.

EXHIBIT 15

Private Branding and Concentration in Manufacturing
for 22 Industries—1964*

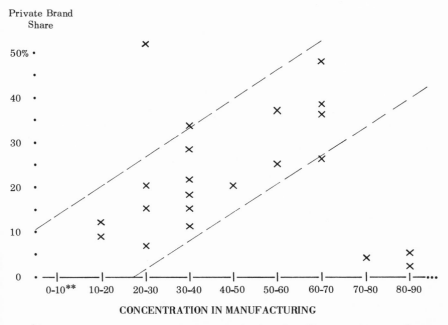

CONCENTRATION IN MANUFACTURING

*Authors' estimates of economic concentration based on *Economic Almanac*, Senate Hearings, NICB technical papers, and trade publications. The industries included are: packaged foods (nine product lines), health aids, toiletries, paper products, detergents, gasoline, shoes, TV sets, portable appliances, washing machines, refrigerators, dryers, and home freezers.

**Estimates rounded up in charting. Figures are percent of industry output accounted for by four largest producers.

In Exhibit 15 each point represents an existing level of concentration in production and the corresponding private brand share. The tendency for higher private brand share to be coupled with higher levels of production concentration is readily apparent.

Private Branding and Concentration in Distribution

In the context of private branding, the importance of concentration in distribution turns on the question of how distributors make use of the economic power they command. As a result, the notion of concentration in distribution is used here in a somewhat restricted sense. It refers to the percent of total retail sales in an industry captured by the top four distributors—or companies primarily involved with distribution activities. This approach excludes manufacturers who have integrated forward and are involved in retailing.

Suppose the top four distributors of a given product line, like replacement tires, account for 30 percent of retail sales. This control over volume at retail is one measure of economic power in the hands of a few distributors, and it might be reflected in the level of private brand share of market.

Overall, it was found that high concentration in distribution is not typically associated with high private brand share of market. Three specific conclusions are suggested by the comparisons developed in this analysis.

First, private branding in major appliances is dominated by four large chains that average nearly 100 percent of their appliance volume in private brands. Here, concentration in distribution is roughly 32 percent and the average private brand share for measured products is 33 percent. The large chains seem to equate their presumed economic power with their private brand merchandising, and smaller distributors account for very little private brand appliance volume.

Second, private branding in footwear is highly fragmented. Large distributors do a substantial portion of volume in their own brands, but concentration in distribution is estimated at 15 percent and private brand share of industry volume is over 50 percent, with many smaller distributors involved in private branding.

Third, relative to the other major industries examined, food distributors do not seem to be equating their presumed economic power with their private branding activity. While the top four chains account for about 20 percent of industry sales, they are estimated to do no more than 35 percent of this volume in their own brands.

There is one more way to look at how concentration of economic power might affect private branding. This is to consider concentration in branding.

Controlling Markets with Brands

In considering the private label issue, the importance of attempting to control markets by controlling brands hinges on three points: (1) the strength of leading brands already established as a restriction on new entries, (2) the frequency with which private labels are counted among the leaders in a product line, and (3) the importance of branded merchandise to consumers as guides to selection.

Measuring concentration in branding

The way in which control of markets through branding is measured is somewhat different from the way concentration in manufacturing is measured. The question is not how much volume do the top four manufacturers capture. Since concern is with control of markets, the question becomes how many brands control retail sales in a product line.

To provide a meaningful definition, market control was assumed to exist at an 85 to 95 percent level of brand penetration at retail. With this definition of market control, measurement of concentration in branding involves determination of the number of brands required to reach this level of sales in a product line, and then expressing this number as a percent of the total number available in the category.

For example, in a given product category, the market shares of the top five brands taken together might add up to 90 percent of retail sales. In another category, the shares of as many as 25 different brands might have to be included to account for 90 percent of sales. If 100 brands are marketed in each product category, then only five percent of the available brands account for 90 percent of sales in the first example, while in the second, it takes 25 percent of the brands to account for 90 percent of sales.

In this way a measure of concentration in branding becomes the percent of available brands which capture about 90 percent of retail sales. The different brand names included in a listing of those which together account for roughly 90 percent of sales may be thought of as market leaders, while the remaining brands available are nonleaders. As would be expected, application of this definition to the product lines included in the study meant that the many brands with low market penetration rarely appeared in the list of leading brands. In no case were more than 25 brands identified as market leaders in an industry, and usually only 10 to 12 brands fell into this classification.

Dominance by market leaders

It was found that, on the average, 20 percent of the brands available in a product line account for about 90 percent of total retail volume in that line. The remaining 80 percent of the brands share the other ten percent. In Exhibit 16 the percent of brands accounting for approximately 90 percent of sales in five major product lines is shown.

New brands, whether manufacturer of distributor owned, face a formidable array of market strength in trying to break into most consumer product lines. For some manufacturers, who turn to private brand production, and for most distributors, who stay exclusively with manufacturers' brands, the marketing resources needed to do otherwise and to compete with leading brands are not available. The stakes are too high.

EXHIBIT 16

Concentration in Branding in Five Industries 1963-64*

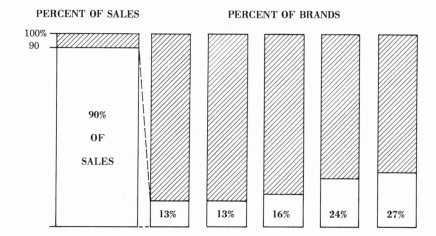

PERCENT OF SALES   PERCENT OF BRANDS

OF BRANDS CAPTURE 90% OF VOLUME IN:

Gasoline   Portable[1]   Tires   Groceries[2]   Major[3]
            Appliances   Appliances

*Based on the estimated minimum number of brands available in each industry; authors' estimates. [1]Average of 4 products. [2]Average for 71 products. [3]Average for 6 products.

Private brands as market leaders

In almost every product line examined, from major appliances to gasoline, from tires to groceries, private brands are typically represented among the group of brands identified as market leaders. It was estimated that, on the average, one out of every five leading brands is a private label, sponsored by a distributor. The market leading private brands also tend to capture a proportionate share of retail sales, or some 20 percent.

In Exhibit 17, averages for five major product lines show the estimated number of leading manufacturers' brands and private labels, together with their estimated share of retail volume. Private labels are among the leaders in each industry.

The effects might be different

While concentration in branding might tend generally to restrict the entry of new brands, the effects may be interpreted by manufacturers differently than by distributors. Manufacturers might produce private brands as one way to gain share of industry output without a large investment in marketing activities if only a few strong brands dominate the market.

EXHIBIT 17

Private Brands as Market Leaders—1963-64[*]

Industry	Manufacturers		Distributors		Total	
	Number	Share	Number	Share	Number	Share
Replacement Tires	15	53%	8	36%	23	89%
Major Appliances[**]	12	61	3	33	15	94
Grocery Products[**]	5	75	3	13	8	88
Portable Appliances[**]	6	78	2	7	8	85
Gasoline	16	79	2	6	18	85
Average	11	67%	3	22%	14	89%
	79% of market leaders are manufacturers'		21% of market leaders are private labels			

[*]Authors' estimates.
[**]Estimates for these three product lines are based on averages of the number of market leading brands in several specific product categories within each line. In major appliances, six product categories were averaged; in grocery products 71 categories were averaged; in portable appliances, three.

Distributors, however, may not view the situation in the same way. The success of market leading private brands could easily stimulate development of new brands by distributors who are only marginally capable of supporting these labels. If a few private brands meet with considerable success, other distributors might be tempted to follow the leaders. For example, in the major appliance industry, the ability of three private brands to achieve an average (in several product categories) of 33 percent of retail volume, might encourage other distributors to begin private branding in appliances.

The growing strength of major brands

Available evidence shows that the importance of branded merchandise has increased over the last several years. In durable goods, the average share of the top 15 brands was significantly smaller a decade ago than it is today. In the 1953-54 period, the 15 top selling brands accounted for an annual average of 87 percent of retail sales of consumer durables. In the 1963-64 period, the top 15 brands accounted for an average of 94 percent of sales. These top 15 brands include both manufacturers' and private brands.

In replacement tires, a semidurable good, the leading brands account for almost 90 percent of volume today as compared with just over 86 percent of volume in 1958-59. In nondurable goods, the share of leading brands in selected grocery products and household supplies has grown slightly over the last five years, with an average increase of about two percentage points, from 86 to 88 percent of volume.

The leading brands in durables have increased their strength largely because of increases in the share of a few private brands. In grocery products, the increased importance of brands has resulted largely from a growth in the share of manufacturers' brands.

It appears that consumers buy more major brand name merchandise today than they have in the past, whether it is a manufacturers' or a distributors' brand.

At this stage in the report, the effects of various general economic forces upon brand policy have been reviewed. Three broad areas were examined in some detail: industry capacity utilization, the level of general prosperity and concentration in manufacturing, distribution, and branding.

The major areas of concern in the remainder of this chapter have to do with general marketing forces: 1) patterns of national advertising, 2) stages in a product's life cycle, and 3) price differentials among brands.

NATIONAL ADVERTISING AND PRIVATE BRANDING

There are at least three viewpoints from which to look at the relationship between private branding and national advertising. One might be labeled "view with alarm," a second, "advertise a lot to keep out private brands." A third viewpoint is that the total national advertising in a given product line is not closely related to private brand share, since other factors may be more important.

The first attitude is illustrated by this comment:

> The mightiest common enemy of the national advertisers and their agencies is the growing level of competition from private brands.

> ... The challenge to advertisers and to their agencies is clear. Large manufacturers must have product quality and effective advertising to add value for their goods, or private brands will force many businesses to cutthroat price competition.[6]

Not unrelated to this view is a statement expressing the "advertise a lot to keep out private brands" viewpoint:

... those categories or product classes having the *greatest* losses [to private brands] had a *lower* advertising-to-sales ratio ... than the ... advertising-to-sales ratio characteristic of the major advertised brands in those product classes having the greatest gains.[7]

Comparisons Made

Comparisons were made between national advertising expenditures and private label share at specific points in time. Problems of data collection, as well as short-run fluctuations, led to the use of periodic data rather than an exhaustive examination of year-to-year changes. To insure reliability, advertising expenditures for two successive years were averaged and this mean became the estimate of national advertising for each point in time.

To determine what happens to national advertising expenditures under different conditions of private brand penetration, at least two approaches might be used: a cross-product analysis, where one product line is compared with another, and a time series approach, where advertising and private branding are compared over a period of years. The measure used might be either dollars spent on national advertising by market leaders, or advertising as a percent of industry sales.

Regardless of methodology, some data on national advertising are needed. Twelve industries, or product lines, were selected for close examination, ranging from low to high private brand share, (under 0.5 percent to over 80 percent), and representing consumer durables, semidurables, and nondurables. The product lines included in this analysis are: Shoes, Margarine, Gasoline, Electric Blankets, Tires, Washing Machines, Laxatives, Television Sets, Instant Coffee, Portable Appliances, Cereal (RTE), and Dentifrices.

Starting with this group of product lines, estimates were developed for national advertising expenditures. National advertising was defined as advertising in newspapers, television, and magazines placed and paid for by manufacturers directly or through their agencies to promote their own brands. Cooperative advertising and advertising allowances were not included. Full details of the sources and methods used are found in Appendix B.

Comparisons of Product Lines

One attempt to determine the merit of the three viewpoints concerning the relationship between national advertising and private brand share can be based on cross-product comparisons.

The advertising to sales ratio in 12 different consumer product lines is used in the first comparison. National advertising expenditures as a percent of total industry or product line sales are matched up with private brand share in Exhibit 18. Although the relationship is far from perfect, there is a tendency for a greater advertising to sales ratio (on the vertical scale) to be associated with a lower private brand share (on the horizontal scale).

EXHIBIT 18

Private Branding and National Advertising as a Percent
of Sales in 12 Industries, 1963-64

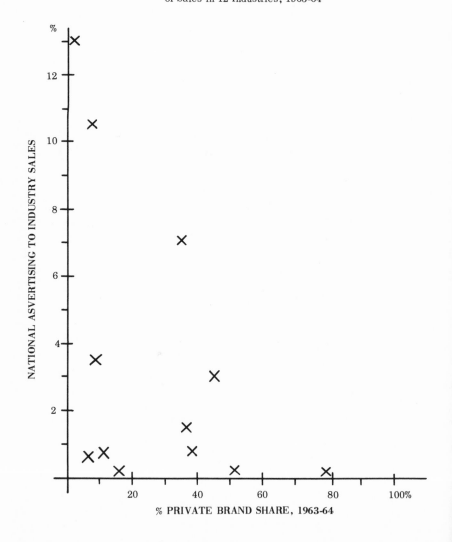

Using the same 12 product lines, another graph can be developed on the basis of dollars spent in advertising the leading manufacturers' brands. This is shown in Exhibit 19. Here private brand shares are plotted in increasing order from the low of 0.3 percent (product number one) up to 80 percent (product number 12). The estimated dollar expenditures on national advertising for each product are compared with private brand share. Without considering product differences which might be important, there is a slight tendency for higher dollar expenditures on advertising to be coupled with lower private brand share.

EXHIBIT 19

Private Branding and Dollars Spent on National Advertising 1963-64*

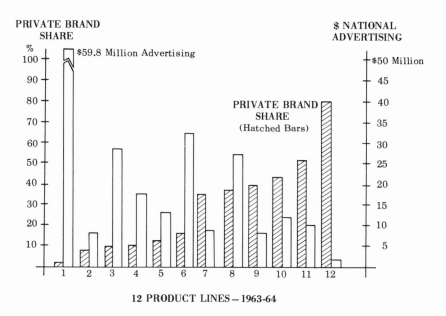

12 PRODUCT LINES – 1963-64

*Authors' estimates of national advertising expenditures. See Appendix B for description of methods used.

The conclusion drawn from these cross-product comparisons depends largely on the interpretative point of view. If the view with alarm position is taken, it might be concluded that private brands are responsible for eroding the position of national advertisers and their agencies. The larger the private brand share, the lower manufacturers' national advertising expenditures tend to be, both as a percent of sales and in terms of dollars spent. From this viewpoint, private branding becomes the independent variable.

Higher distributors' brand share "causes" lower natioanl advertising expenditures.

By simply reversing points of view—making national advertising
the independent variable—the same data lend support to the "advertise a lot to keep out private brands" position. Since distributors'
brand share of market tends to be lower in product lines with
higher national advertising, either as a percent of sales or in
dollars spent, advertising becomes the "cause" of limited private
brand penetration.

Finally, important product or market differences will exist in
any kind of cross-product comparisons. This lends support to the
third position that total advertising expenditures are not closely
related to private brand share.

There is probably some truth in each of these positions, but it
cannot be determined from comparisons of different product lines
alone. The information from cross-product comparisons added to
data on changes over time, however, might help to uncover the
situation that actually exists.

Changes in National Advertising Expenditures
and Private Branding

In order to help identify the relationship between changes in the expenditures of national advertisers and shifts in private brand share
of market, the following comparisons were developed.

First, a product line with extremely low private brand share is
shown in Exhibit 20. Here, national advertising was very high
(nearly 40 million annually or about 11 percent of industry sales
in 1958-59), and increased during the five-year period by almost
50 percent. In this industry, private brands have never been a
big factor and failed to gain share of market over the five-year
period. In this extreme case, national advertising was probably
one of the important factors limiting private brand sales. High and
increasing levels of national advertising can certainly be thought
of as partially responsible for restricted private branding.

At the other extreme, where private brands accounted for about
80 percent of retail sales in the 1963-64 period, the direction of
change in national advertising is reversed. Exhibit 21 shows the
relationship of advertising to private brand volume over the ten-
year period 1953-54 to 1963-64.

For this "high private brand share" product line, national advertising was comparatively low in 1953-54 (about one-half million
annually or 1.4 percent of sales), and declined over 60 percent during the decade. Private brand volume was relatively modest in
1953-54, but climbed to a dominant position in ten years. In this
extreme case, private brand share was probably one of the factors
leading to the decline in national advertising. The extreme cases

EXHIBIT 20

Changes in National Advertising and Private Branding for a Product Line*
where Private Brand Share Remains Under 1 Percent

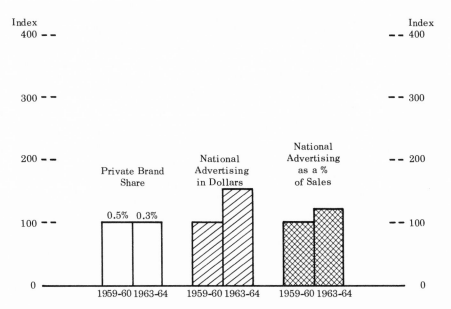

*Product line unidentified at request of data source

tend to support both the "advertise a lot to keep out private brands," and the "view with alarm" positions.

Changes in national advertising for product lines with successively larger private brand market shares (but between the extremes just examined) are shown in Exhibits 22 and 23. The remaining six comparisons developed for this analysis appear in Appendix B.

Most of the evidence suggests that national advertising continues to increase, even where private labels capture as much as 30 and 40 percent of sales volume. This raises questions about the notion that increased private branding will restrict growth in advertising expenditures.

It seems reasonable to suggest that increasing competition from private brands is partly responsible for increases in national advertising. However, the nature of the product itself may restrict private brand adoptions, while increases in the level of business activity tend to stimulate advertising, both in dollar terms and as a percent of sales.

Also, national advertising expenditures probably level off and decline with sharp increases and deeper penetration by private

EXHIBIT 21

Changes in National Advertising and Private Branding for a Product Line*
where Private Brand Share Reaches 80 Percent

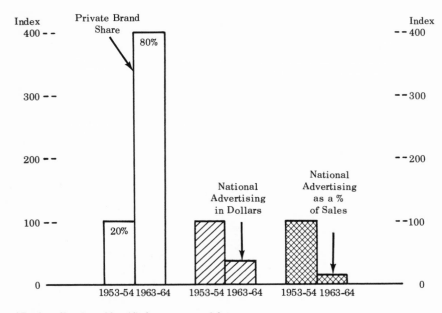

*Product line is unidentified at request of data source.

brands. Yet, a tendency for national advertising to be cut back would not be expected until private brands account for a majority of retail sales—probably over 60 or 70 percent.

Finally, the idea that advertising is responding to forces other than changes in private brand share has merit. Several other general marketing forces are likely to carry as much weight as does private branding in changing the patterns of national advertising. For example, the effect of changes in the product life cycle is examined later.

Are Advertising and Private Branding Related?

It would seem that neither the "view with alarm" nor the "advertise a lot to keep out private brands" position is supportable, except perhaps in the extreme cases. Between the extremes, national advertising does not decline because of increases in private branding. In fact, advertising expenditures seem to respond positively to increases in private branding. Conversely, rapid growth in national advertising does not seem to be matched by a decline in private brand sales.

EXHIBIT 22

Changes in National Advertising and Private Branding for a Product Line*
where Private Brand Share Reaches 7 Percent

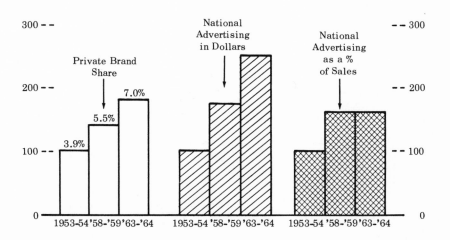

Changes in National Advertising and Private Branding for a Product Line*
where Private Brand Share Reaches 14 Percent

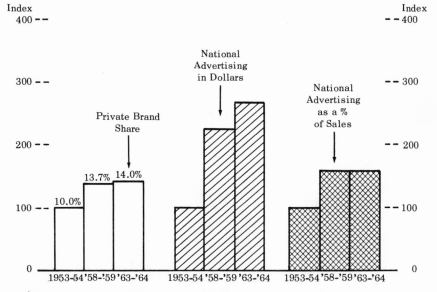

*Product lines unidentified at request of data source

EXHIBIT 23

Changes in National Advertising and Private Branding for a Product Line*
where Private Brand Share Reaches 35 Percent

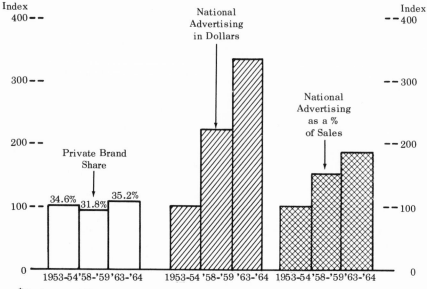

*Replacement tires

Changes in National Advertising and Private Branding for a Product line*
where Private Brand Share Reaches 51 Percent

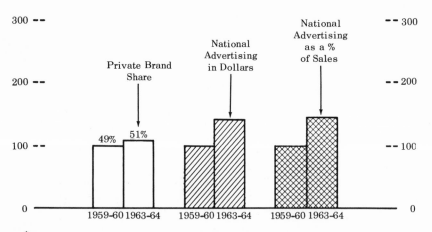

*Shoes

While national advertising might be expected to taper off as private brands reach 60 to 70 percent of retail sales, both this final decline, and the initial increases mentioned above, are influenced by changes in the market itself.

PRIVATE BRANDING OVER THE PRODUCT
LIFE CYCLE

The degree of market acceptance enjoyed by a product can directly affect many elements of marketing activity. It can influence advertising, pricing, distribution methods, and profits. It probably affects private branding as well. As a result, the product life cycle is a potentially useful concept for helping to explain why distributors' brands are successful in some product lines and not in others.

A Definition of the Product Life Cycle

The "product life cycle" is simply a way to trace the stages of market acceptance a product goes through from introduction to decline in use by consumers. Identification of the stages of market acceptance poses some problems.[8] The beginning point is easy to find for a product that is known to be new. The introductory stage starts with first sale of the new product. Following this, most expositions of the product life cycle simply label the next stages as growth, maturity, and decline in sales. This results in a large number of exceptions, since most products find their way into the pattern of consumption and seem never to drop entirely out of use. Salt, for example, would be thought of as being in the mature phase of the product life cycle. When will a sales decline take place? The decline stage is said to be a phase where many different sellers are involved, brand advertising is less important than it was, price competition is severe, physical product differences are slight, and industry-wide profits not as attractive as those of new products experiencing rapid growth in market acceptance. Most of these conditions apply, in some degree to the classic example provided by the salt industry, but sales volume continues to grow with population.

Other examples may easily be found where changes in market acceptance do not appear to fit the product life cycle concept. Among these are bread, shoes, branded packaged foods, aspirin tablets and chewing gum. If many product lines do not fit, the product life cycle would seem to be of relatively little value in explaining private branding or any other marketing action.

The idea of the product life cycle can be useful if it is strictly defined. To be meaningful, it must be measured in a way that makes its application to all products feasible, to permit identification of each stage in the life cycle, and show important changes in market acceptance which might affect a company's marketing program and profits. Since existing definitions do not do this, a somewhat different measure of the product life cycle is used here.

We will view the product life cycle quantitatively as the rate of change in product sales volume from one year to the next, measured in constant dollars (or in unit sales when these data are available). In short, the life cycle for a product line is defined as industry-wide marginal sales volume. The way this definition of the product life cycle fits into the picture of total sales, number of users, and population, is illustrated for a hypothetical product in Exhibit 24.

Measured in terms of rate of change, the product passes through these stages: introduction, increasing growth, declining growth, and finally saturation or decay depending on whether the product becomes an entrenched item in consumption patterns or begins to fade from existence. This measure of the product life cycle not only applies to all products and defines each stage in the cycle, it also pinpoints important changes in market acceptance. Marginal sales volume, over the long run, is a more sensitive indicator of changes in demand and profitability than total sales.

Applying the Measure

To trace the change in private branding over different stages in a product's life cycle, this measure was applied to 24 product lines:

Paper towels	Automatic washing machines
Electric refrigerators	Canned evaporated milk
Bathroom tissue	Aspirin tablets
Television sets (B & W)	Electric blankets
Synthetic detergents	Instant coffee
Preshave lotion	Adhesive bandages
Regular coffee	Personal deodorants
Baby powder	Liquid window cleaner
Portable mixers	Shortening
Margarine	Cleansing tissue
Footwear (excluding rubber)	Prepared puddings
Table salt	Replacement tires

The products represent nondurable, semidurable, and durable goods, and cover a wide range of private brand penetration. Backup data for product life cycle estimates in each of these 24 lines appear in Appendix B.

EXHIBIT 24

Tracing the Product Life Cycle for a Hypothetical Product

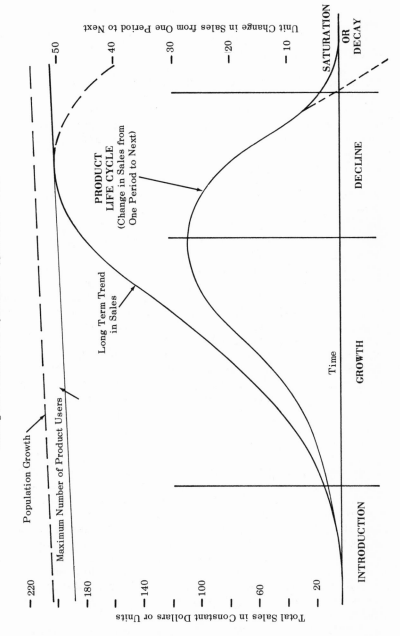

Private Branding in Different Stages of the Cycle

Product lines with a relatively high private brand share (over 30 percent in 1964) were all in the decline or decay stage of their life cycle. For example, Exhibit 25 shows the product life cycle for replacement tires from 1930 through 1964. This "high" private brand share product line is well into the decline stage of its life cycle. Six of the 24 product lines studied were in a similar stage of the life cycle. Private brands accounted for an average of over 44 percent of retail sales in these lines.

Products in the growth stage tend to have a relatively lower private brand share of market. Exhibit 26 shows a picture of one product line that falls into this group: "cleansing tissue." Three product lines out of 24 were plainly in the growth stage during 1964-65, and all had a relatively low private brand share averaging about 11 percent of retail sales.

These charts seem to support expectations. Some claim that private branders avoid new products until they are widely accepted. Or if not this, that during the early stages of a life cycle distributors do not have time to build up a large market share. Thus, some observers suggest it is natural for private brands to be relatively unimportant in the introductory or growth stages of the life cycle. In the decline and decay stages, however, products are well accepted, or passing out of use, and the time is ripe for distributors' brands to make sharp gains. As a result, it might be expected that private brands would become more important as a product enters the later stages of its life cycle.

This appears to be true. Products with a "high" private brand share were all in the decline or decay stage of their life cycle. But, many products in the same stage of market acceptance had a relatively low private brand share—less than ten percent.

Changes in Private Branding over the Life Cycle

In each of the 24 product lines examined, changes in private brand share were matched with movement through the life cycle. These comparisons furnished some rather consistent results: ones that add to an understanding of the patterns noted above.

First, the change in private brand share tends to stabilize as a product moves from the growth into the decline, saturation, and decay stages of the life cycle. The private brand share of market may be very high, say 80 percent, or very low, say two percent, in the final stages of the life cycle. The rate of change, however, tends to settle down at somewhere near the zero level, where gains and losses from year to year are very small.

Second, where private brand share is showing rapid increases, most product lines are in the growth stage of the life cycle. The rate of growth in private branding is often much greater than growth in market acceptance itself.

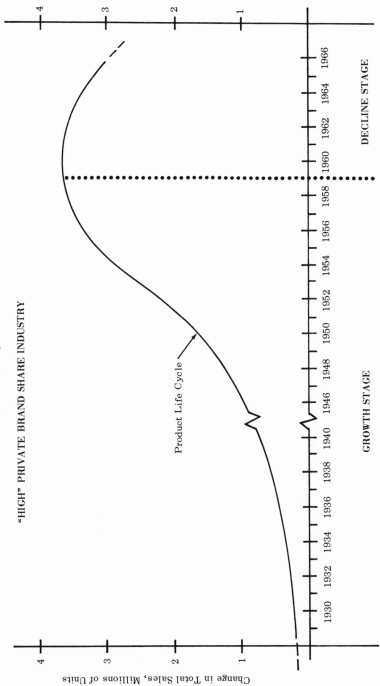

EXHIBIT 25

Stage in the Product Life Cycle and Level of Private Brand Share
in 1965 for Replacement Tires

"HIGH" PRIVATE BRAND SHARE INDUSTRY

Product Life Cycle

Change in Total Sales, Millions of Units

DECLINE STAGE

GROWTH STAGE

EXHIBIT 26

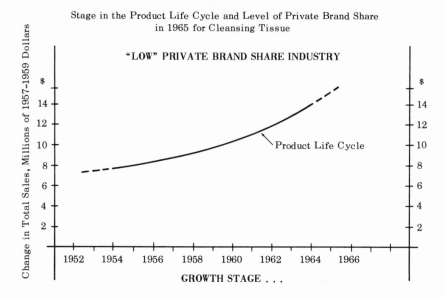

Stage in the Product Life Cycle and Level of Private Brand Share
in 1965 for Cleansing Tissue

The replacement tire line provides an excellent illustration of what appears to happen to private brand share over the life cycle. It shows a pattern repeated by the other product lines, and product life cycle and private brand share data are available on an annual basis from 1929 through 1964. Exhibit 27 shows how changes in private brand share for replacement tires compare with changes in market acceptance, or the product life cycle.

Since the long-term trend in replacement tires is representative of most product lines examined, closer consideration of Exhibit 27 is warranted.

Short and intermediate term effects, like changes in business activity and two war periods, were ironed out of all product life cycle estimates. As a result, it is clear that the growth stage for replacement tires began in the late 1920's and continued on through 1958. At about this time, replacement tires entered the decline phase of the life cycle. In the future, the rate of growth, or industry-wide marginal sales, will probably continue to slow down to the pace set by increases in population and new car purchases. Replacement tires will probably enter the saturation stage in the next few years.

Private brand share has not followed the same pattern. The greatest inroads were made by private brands during the growth stage. Before the life cycle peaked, the growth in private brand share began to slow down considerably. In fact, the change in private branding became negative at about the same time tires entered the decline stage. Since 1956, private brand share of

55

EXHIBIT 27

The Product Life Cycle and Private Branding in Replacement Tires 1930 to 1966

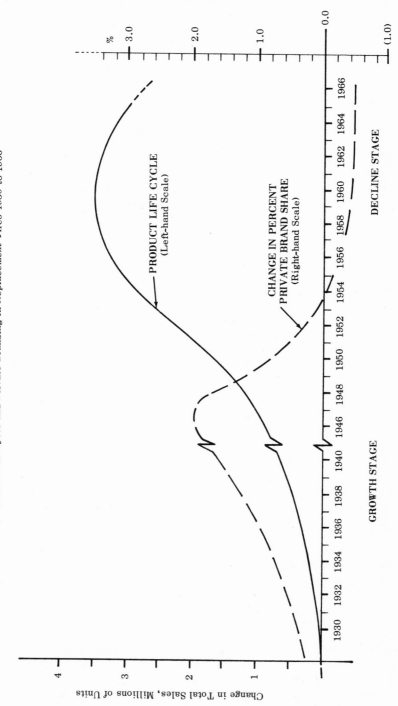

market has fluctuated slightly around a general penetration figure of about 36 percent. The long-term trend has been slightly negative, as compared with peak share of market in the late 1940's, but very near the no change level. In short, private brand share in replacement tires has tended to stabilize.

While private brand data were not available over such a long time span for other products, changes found during five-, six-, and ten-year periods in other lines seem to repeat the general pattern found in replacement tires. When the product is in its growth stage, private brands are making large gains in market share; gains which often exceed the growth in market acceptance. On the other hand, for products in the decline, saturation, or decay stages, the year-to-year change in private brand share tends to stabilize. Sometimes the rate of change settles down on the zero level. In other product lines private brands continue to grow at a constant, but slightly positive level. For some others the change in share stabilizes at a negative level, where private brands are losing market share.

For example, in two product lines studied (instant coffee and black and white television), private brands accounted for a relatively low share of market. Both of these products are in the saturation-decay stage of their life cycle, with constant but slight decreases in consumption. Growth in private brand share has leveled off, fluctuating around the no change level. This is a repeat of the result found in replacement tires.

At the other end of the private brand share spectrum, evaporated milk and margarine both have a "high" distributors brand share of market. Both are in the decay stage of their life cycles, and again, the change in private brand share has tended to stabilize near the zero level.

Since these comparisons deal with changes over the long term, or with secular trend, cyclical variation has been smoothed out of both the private brand share and product life cycle estimates. This becomes an important technical difference when compared with the analysis of changes in prosperity. Even so, in the case of coffee, for example, which declined in share during high prosperity, the downturn was strong enough to show up in a long-term trend.

A similar result was found in cleansing tissues, and combination refrigerator-freezers. Each of these products is going through the growth stage of its life cycle, and private brand share is increasing rapidly, faster than the growth in market acceptance itself. These results, as well as those found in the other 17 product lines tend to follow a pattern similar to the one followed by replacement tires.

The life cycle for electric refrigerators is especially striking. There are really two overlapping product life cycles involved, since "refrigerators" formerly were "single-door refrigerators," and today are primarily "combination refrigerator-freezers."

The end of one product life cycle and the beginning of the other can be measured simultaneously by change in unit sales volume (without having to adjust dollar consumption figures). This offers an unusual opportunity to trace the pattern of change in private brand share.

The results found in this product line are consistent with the general tendencies identified earlier. In the 1954-55 period, single-door refrigerators entered the decay phase of their life cycle, and have been in that stage ever since. But during the period of adjustment (decline of the old and introduction of the new product), the overall change in market acceptance took on the characteristics of the decline or at best saturation stage. During this five-year period, the change in private brand share remained stable near the zero level or about 0.1 of one percent growth per year. But, in the 1958-59 period when the new electric refrigerator, the combination model, really began to catch on, private brand share took off from its stable level and began to grow more rapidly than market acceptance itself, at an average annual rate of about 14 percent.

Another example is provided by black-and-white television sets. A graph of changes in private brand share compared with the product life cycle for this product is shown in Exhibit 28. Here, growth in private brand share began to decline rather sharply after black-and-white TV sets entered the decline phase. This may be the result of the extremely short period of time between introduction and decline stages for TV sets (only about five years

EXHIBIT 28

The Product Life Cycle and Private Branding in B & W Television Sets
Through 1964

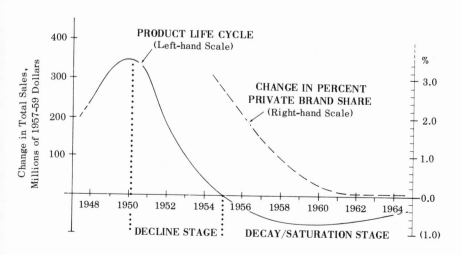

excluding the war period). Or, it may be because changes do not take place as quickly in consumer durables as in other product lines. In either event, for the years from 1958 through 1965, black-and-white television has been in the saturation or decay stage of its life cycle (it is difficult to say exactly which at this point in time) and the change in private brand share has stabilized very near the zero level.

Impact of the Product Life Cycle

Several conclusions based on the preceding examples can be drawn that probably apply to a wider range of consumer product lines than the 24 studied.

First, private branders seem to capitalize on favorable trends in market demand. When demand is growing at an increasing rate, so is private brand share, and often at a faster rate than demand itself.

Second, whatever inroads private brands are going to make will probably be made during the growth stage of the life cycle, rather than when the product becomes a fixed part of consumption patterns. Private brands seem to be stimulated by rapid growth in market acceptance, and they are likely to take a larger share of market during this period when sellers are not too concerned about the long-term future. By the same token, it is probably easier for manufacturers and distributors to maintain existing share of market after the product has entered the later half of its life cycle.

Third, private branders may not be considering just the most widely accepted products as the most attractive ones to put under their own brands. The development of suppliers and attainment of reasonable volume in products in the saturation or decay stages will be relatively easy. Yet, the payoff in terms of capturing a significant share of market, is probably considerably more limited.

Fourth, where private brand share is high, patronage built up for distributors' brands in dying product lines probably has some spill-over effect on lines still in the growth stage of their life cycle. For example, private brand patronage in wringer washing machines probably has a positive effect on the same distributor's sales of his own brand of combination refrigerator-freezers.

Finally, the response of national advertising to private branding can be traced in part to changes in the product life cycle. Both national advertising and private branding tend to respond to rapid growth in market acceptance. The fear that private brands will drive national advertising down should be discarded for the more logical idea that dying product lines will not be highly advertised. Also, the belief that large amounts of advertising will keep out private brands, should be tempered by a knowledge of the tendency for private brands to ride a rising tide of market acceptance.

TRACING THE EFFECT OF PRICE DIFFERENTIALS

One of the cornerstones of private branding has been the price differential. Price spreads usually exist between private and national brands, and some believe that these differentials are crucial to distributors' efforts to attract consumer purchases. It is a relatively common belief that the best way to limit or reduce private brand sales is to narrow price differentials between them and competing national brands.

Initial Consideration of Price Spreads

Price spreads among brands do exist in most product lines. But, the obvious price differentials between brands of margarine, for instance, may not be so apparent in consumer durables. Where price spreads do exist, are greater differentials between brands associated with higher private brand share? Directly related to the question of price strategy, is a narrowing of price differentials between brands in a given product line coupled with a decline in private brand share of market?

It was not possible to account for differences in quality among brands in the data available for this analysis. However, to provide answers to the questions above, data on percentage price differentials between private and manufacturers' brands in 21 nondurable, semidurable, and durable product lines were collected from several companies for use on a confidential basis.

Price differentials between private and manufacturers' brands were available for these nondurable product lines: salad dressing, margarine, canned evaporated milk, canned fruit, mayonnaise, pineapple, canned vegetables, frozen meat pies, soluble coffee, canned beans, toilet tissue, regular coffee, cleansing tissue, gasoline, and wax paper. In most cases, data covered the years from 1959 to 1964. In consumer durables, estimates of price differentials were available for TV sets, clothes dryers, refrigerators, air conditioners, automatic washing machines, and home freezers. In these product lines, estimates were for the 1963-64 period only.

Price Differentials and Private Branding

Comparisons made among product lines appear to support the idea that significant percentage price differentials between brands go with high private brand share. This applied only to nondurable goods, however, and even here the relationship was tenuous.

In simple "high-low" comparisons, selected nondurable product lines with a higher than average private brand share tended to have higher than average percentage price spreads between brands. At the other extreme, product lines with lower than average private brand share tended to have lower than average percentage price differentials.

A similar comparison of selected consumer durables failed to show a consistent pattern. Exhibit 29 reveals the relationship between the percent market share held by private brands in 1963-64, and the estimated percent price spread among brands in six durable lines.

EXHIBIT 29

Price Differential and Private Brand Share in Consumer Durables* 1963-64

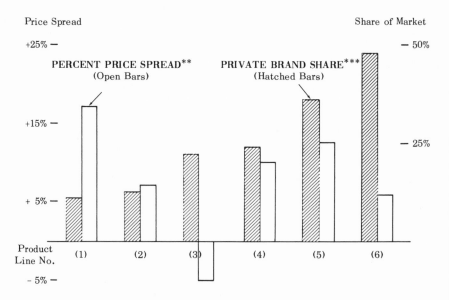

*These data are intended to identify general tendencies and caution should be taken in their interpretation since it was not possible to distinguish among differences in the quality/feature characteristics of product lines sold under distributors' as compared with manufacturers' brands.

**Percent by which the average price of private brands was estimated to be lower(+) or higher (-) than the average price of manufacturers' brands.

***Indices of private brand share for consumer durables appear in Appendix D.

If price differences were a prime factor shaping the degree of success enjoyed by private brands in consumer durables, there would be some tendency for wider differentials to be coupled with higher private brand share. This does not appear to exist. In fact, Exhibit 29 shows that the consumer durable line with lowest private brand share (about 11 percent) had the greatest estimated

price spread among brands, some 17 percent. At the other end of
the scale, the product line with the highest private brand share
market (nearly 50 percent of retail volume) had one of the smallest
price spreads, approximately six percent. In the consumer durable
product line where the distributors' brands captured about 21
percent of volume in the 1963-64 period, the price spread was
estimated to be in favor of manufacturers' brand (product line
number 3 in Exhibit 29).

A Closer Look at Price Differentials

Examination of the data presented in Exhibit 30 raised a question
as to the strength of the relationship between price spreads and
private branding for nondurables.

For example, product line number 13 shows a price differential in favor of private brands approaching 30 percent, and a
higher than average private brand share, or roughly 15 percent.
Product line number 3, near the bottom of the chart, has the
lowest price differential of all—less than five percent in favor
of private brands. This product line has a lower than average
private brand share of about nine percent of sales. Yet, its share
is only six percent less than private brand share for product
line number 13, while the price differential is almost 25 percent
lower.

Price differentials should make an important difference if
they are to provide a basis for pricing strategy. With this in
mind, the picture can be brought into sharper focus by tracing
the pattern of change in private brand share over time, as price
differentials change.

Private Brand Response to Changing Price Spreads

Exhibits 31 and 32 show the relationship between private brand
share of market and the percent price differential between brands
in 12 different nondurable product lines, on an annual basis.
Charting these data reveals an apparent lack of relationship
between changes in price differentials and private brand share.
Within reasonable limits, private brand share seems to be insensitive to changes in the percent price differential.

One or two product lines show a relatively high correlation
between changes in price spreads and distributors' brand share.
For each of these lines, however, there are several with similar
price patterns where private brand share appears to be unrelated.
Consider Exhibit 32, product line number 7, for example. Here the

EXHIBIT 30

Price Differentials and Private Brand Share
in 15 Nondurable Product Lines—1964

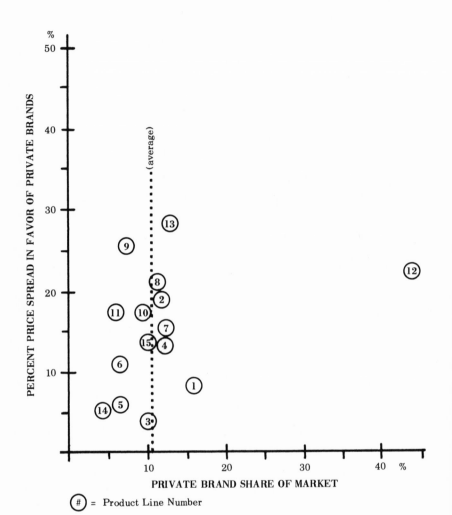

(#) = Product Line Number

percent price differential in favor of private brands dropped
consistently from a level of 22 percent in 1959, to about 15 percent by 1964. Over this period, private brand share increased and
then decreased, but by the end of the five-year interval, market
share had dropped from over 15 to about 13 percent of unit
volume. It might seem as if this were a reaction to narrowing
price spreads.

EXHIBIT 31

Changes in Price Differentials and Private Brand Share
for Selected Nondurable Product Lines*

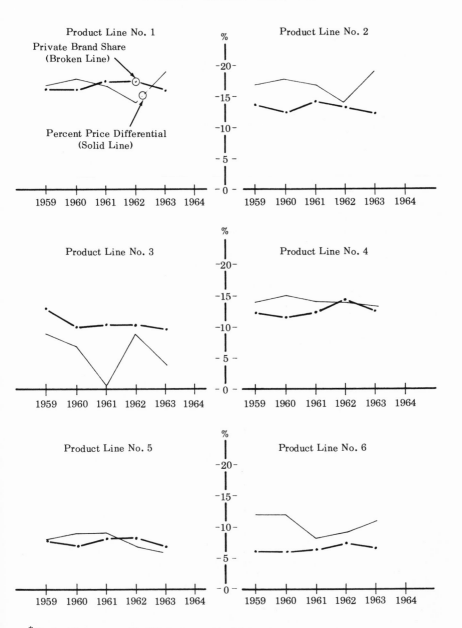

*Product lines are unidentified at request of data sources.

EXHIBIT 32

Changes in Price Differentials and Private Brand Share
for Selected Nondurable Product Lines*

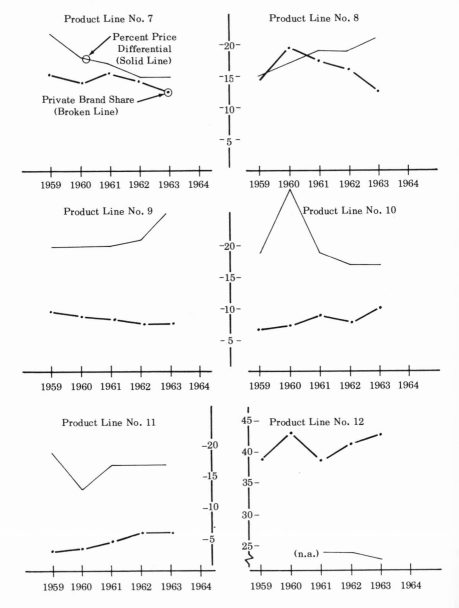

*Product lines are unidentified at request of data sources.

The opposite pattern can be seen, however, in product line number 10, Exhibit 32. Here the price spread in favor of private brands fell from about 30 percent to 18 percent in four years, while private brand share increased rather constantly from 6.5 to ten percent of retail volume.

The only basic conclusion to be drawn is that price differentials in many nondurable product lines can go up and down from one year to the next without any predictable relationship to private brand share of market.

Price Differentials in Focus

The success of private brands should not be pegged on the existence of large percentage price differentials. The sale of almost any brand will tend to be stimulated if its price is significantly lower than those of competing products. The ability to make direct comparisons would, of course, tend to make price differentials in nondurables more meaningful to consumers than in consumer durables where private and manufacturers' brands are less often sold on the same floor. This might be why grocery products with greater price differentials tend to have larger private brand shares. Within reasonable limits, increases or decreases in price differentials do not seem to have a direct effect on private brand share in intermediate-run periods of time.

CONCLUDING COMMENTS

The purpose of this chapter was to determine the effect of various economic and marketing forces on private branding.

Private branding was cast in the role of an activity that may—or may not—be influenced by industry structure, the business climate, national advertising, the product life cycle, and price differentials between brands. The reason for subjecting these factors to a process of systematic analysis was to gain an understanding of the environment in which manufacturers and distributors must go about the business of developing their brand policies.

Two major tasks remain. The first, and the one undertaken in the following chapter, is to identify and evaluate the factors taken into account by individual manufacturers in determining brand policy. The second, taken up in the final chapter, is to examine brand policy determination by distributors.

IV

Manufacturers' Branding Policies

THREE BRAND POLICY options are available to a manufacturer. A company can elect to produce only its own brands, and follow a "manufacturers' brand policy." Or, management may choose to produce both private and manufacturers' brands and follow a "mixed brand policy." Finally, a company may adopt a "distributors' brand policy," where it specializes in the production of private brands and does not produce a brand of its own.

There is little question why some market leaders committed entirely to their own brands refuse to go into private brand production. The company's size and market strength often leads management to believe it would give up more than it might gain by producing private brands—and such companies frequently have a history of success in the market and earnings to back up this belief. The characteristics of these companies are examined in the following pages. By the same token, there is little doubt why some companies specialize in the production of private labels. These operations are usually small, with limited capital backing and simply cannot afford to develop their own nationally advertised brands.

The unresolved issue in the area of manufacturers' branding policies, and the problem of central concern in this chapter, is why companies adopt a mixed brand policy, and what results—profits and sales—tend to be associated with such action. The importance of this issue can be brought into sharpest focus by examining briefly the marketing characteristics typical of companies following each of the three basic brand policy options.

MARKETING CAPABILITIES UNDER EACH BRAND POLICY

Companies with distributors' brand policy operate in every industry included in this study. Since these manufacturers do not market products under their own brands they are relatively unknown to consumers. With few exceptions, respondent firms committed to a distributors' brand policy were not established for the purpose of manufacturing private brands; they previously had produced only manufacturers' brands or both manufacturers' and private brands. Many date back to the earlier part of the century and some were among the first to establish leading manufacturers' brands in their industry. Most of these companies share a common characteristic. At a crucial point in their histories, usually prior to World War II, they lacked the management resources or the financial backing to strengthen a dwindling market position.

The current marketing capabilities of companies committed to a distributors' brand policy were created to serve the unique requirements of their principal customers—distributors who want a product manufactured under the private brand. As a result, the marketing programs of companies following a distributors' brand policy are typically considerably restricted in scope when compared with those of national brand manufacturers. While programs obviously differ from one company to another, companies with a distributors' brand policy may be characterized as follows:

Relatively low sales volume, often less than $50 million
Limited sales force
Restricted product research and development activities
Relatively limited capability in market planning and research
Limited warehousing and distribution facilities
Restricted consumer research staff and effort
Little organized promotion and advertising

In short, companies committed to a distributors' brand policy are essentially experts in the production of a given product line. The major marketing function is shifted to distributors. Only rarely does a company following a distributor's brand policy go into the production, distribution and promotion of its own brand—though management of some of these respondent firms expressed the hope to do so sometime. In essence, the distributors' brand policy is the best alternative open to these companies. Most of them do not have the strength necessary to compete effectively as producers of national brands.

At the other end of the scale of marketing capabilities is the company fully committed to the production and marketing of its own brands—to a manufacturers' brand policy. These companies are often giants in their industries. They have broad product lines, large brand shares and established distribution systems. Both day-to-day management and long-range planning involve a continuing search for ways to strengthen their market position. Again, characteristics differ among companies, but those fully committed to a manufacturers' brand policy are generally characterized by:

High annual sales volume, often over $500 million

Relatively large scale product research and development operations

Extensive warehousing and physical distribution facilities

Permanent staff personnel and large expenditures on continuing consumer and marketing research

Capability and experience in marketing planning and control

Established operations for customer market research and merchandise planning

Large sales force

Both "cooperative" and "national" consumer advertising and in-store promotion programs

Publicized guarantee or warranty programs, and where appropriate, the stocks, parts, and service operations to back them up

Successful operation under a manufacturers' brand policy obviously requires quite a different marketing capability than under a distributors' brand policy. Companies which follow a manufacturers' brand policy consider themselves to be specialists, not just in production, but in marketing and distribution as well, and often have the required management and capital resources to keep their complex operations going in a highly profitable fashion. Management of some of these firms does not view private brands as a serious threat, and in other companies management does not even view private brands as serious competition. There is little pressure on these companies to produce private brands, and management apparently sees no market opportunity in this course of action.

THE PROBLEM AND ITS SCOPE

The major concern of this chapter is with those companies, including many of the world's leading firms, with marketing capabilities and sales volumes similar to those listed above, which turn to private brand production under a mixed brand policy.

The company with a mixed brand policy often takes on some of the major characteristics of firms committed to manufacturers' brands, and some of those of distributors' brand producers. They are often large, well-established, experienced in marketing, and with sufficient financial resources to stay near the top of their industry with their own brands, but still produce private brands.

In all industries studied, it was found that an increasing number of manufacturers are turning to a mixed brand policy. It is probably the most common brand policy in existence today in most consumer product industries, both in terms of the number of companies involved and in the proportion of industry volume they account for. In addition, indications are that the mixed brand policy will become even more common in the future. This view is strengthened by the attitudes held by executives of companies still committed to a manufacturers' brand policy. Their management frequently expressed a softening attitude toward production of private brands, and considered it likely that their companies would switch to a mixed brand policy sometime in the future. This was true even among companies that have historically been strong proponents of the manufacturers' brand policy.

PURPOSE OF THE ANALYSIS

The basic purpose of this chapter is to explain the rationale underlying adoption of a mixed brand policy. After some brief comments about the nature of the data involved, the factors that were found to influence manufacturers to adopt a mixed brand policy are identified. Next, the profitability of respondent companies with each of the three brand policies is estimated and examined. Third, private branding as a marketing strategy is examined, and a case example furnished. Finally, the risks manufacturers associate with private brand production are commented upon in some detail.

NATURE OF THE DATA

The findings in this chapter are based on intensive interviews with top level executives in 112 different manufacturing organizations. The selection of respondent companies was purposely weighted in favor of those with a mixed brand policy, but a substantial number of manufacturers which followed the other two brand policies were also included. Manufacturers included in the study were divided among the three brand policies in this way: 33 companies had a manufacturers' brand policy; 65 were committed to a mixed brand policy; and 14 produced only private brands. The same ten industries, or product lines, examined in the previous chapter are the basis of this analysis, and the 112 manufacturing respondents are distributed about equally over the nondurable, semidurable, and durable goods industries.

The sample was purposive and the interviews themselves tended to be small case studies. The research was designed to obtain as much useful information as possible, from companies fairly representative of each brand policy in each industry. It is believed the results can be taken as typical of each industry and brand policy, even though they cannot be considered to be based on a representative cross section of the entire population of manufacturers. The limitations of a purposive sample are particularly important to keep in mind where comparisons are made of the profitability of companies following each of the three brand policies.

FACTORS LEADING TO A MIXED BRAND POLICY

Obviously the profit normally underlies the decision of a manufacturer to adopt a mixed brand policy. Here the specific factors important in influencing the choice of brand policy are identified and examined.

Some of the factors identified in this study as those influencing the adoption of a mixed brand policy have been recognized for decades, while some long thought to be crucial were found to be of only secondary importance. Other factors were identified which have come into prominence more recently.

Since brand policy has an impact on many areas of corporate activity, it is not surprising to find that the factors leading to a mixed brand policy involve not only marketing, but production, financial, and overall corporate considerations as well. The factors listed below were those named by executives of respondent manufacturers as instrumental in the adoption of a mixed brand policy by their firms. The factors are grouped roughly by principal area of activity into which they fall. They are not listed in order of importance.

Corporate:

1. An outcome of acquisition, merger, and diversification
2. Need for improvement in earnings per share
3. A necessary part of brand policy formulation

Financial:

4. An interest in a reduction in average collection period and improved working capital position
5. An attempt to get a higher return on investment

Production:

6. A stop-gap tactic to level our fluctuation in demand or output
7. An effort to improve stability in normal production scheduling operations
8. A basis for plant expansion and modernization (made possible by larger firm orders)
9. A way to reduce overall unit costs through economies of scale

Marketing:

10. A defensive measure to accommodate major customers
11. A way of achieving rapid market information feedback through distributors
12. A method of gaining access to knowledge of a major competitor's merchandising operations
13. An opportunity to influence indirectly merchandising programs of competitors
14. A means of lowering customer service costs through the opportunity to spread marketing overhead to private label accounts
15. A method of achieving more flexibility in pricing
16. An inability to maintain high levels of promotional competition in a product line or corporate division.

Overall Corporate Objectives Leading to a Mixed Brand Policy

A mixed brand policy frequently resulted from acquisition, merger and diversification activities.

For some companies, private brand production was started almost by accident, as when an acquisition or merger took place with firms doing substantial private label volume. More typically, companies in the study saw profit opportunities in the production of private brands. Management of some respondent companies checked the background of private brand manufacturers in the industry and found that these smaller companies often had unique private brand production capabilities and experience, and were also attractive investments in their own right. The result was the adaption of mixed brand policies by several large manufacturers through the acquisition of smaller firms specializing in the production of private brands.

Companies committed to a manufacturers' brand policy looked on this route to a mixed brand policy as providing immediate capability in private brand production, with minimum risk to the national brand franchise since the acquired firm could be operated as a separate subsidiary.

In addition, management in some of the companies in which interviews were held, considered acquisition of private brand manufacturers as a sound diversification strategy. In the search for broader consumer product offerings, diversification into unrelated lines could be accomplished with already established volume and product experience, and relatively low investment, through purchase of a smaller private brand manufacturer. Some companies did this with the thought of providing the management and capital required to produce and market new manufacturers' brands in the acquired facility after the private brand lines has been assimilated into the corporate family.

Acquisition or merger with a private brand manufacturer results in a mixed brand policy from the viewpoint of the corporation, even though consumers may be unaware of the relationship between the companies. Addition of a manufacturers' brand to the line of products already made by an acquired company can give a large manufacturer a three-sided, and in the opinion of the managements involved, an extremely forceful brand policy. The company taking such action has its leading national brand, plus a private brand subsidiary, and "controlled" or "associate" manufacturers' labels which, although not widely promoted or advertised, may be used as "fighting" brands to further increase corporate flexibility.

Some of the companies included in the study adopted a mixed brand policy with the express hope of bringing about an increase in earnings per share of corporate stock. Increasing earnings per share is closely related to increasing return on investment, at least in principal. Since respondents tended to separate the two, return on investment is taken up in the next section on financial considerations. Though the circumstances varied among the companies involved, the basic situation was the same—earnings per share had fallen for several years and the quickest way management could find to improve the picture was to compete for substantial private brand volume. One company's target earnings per share was reached in the year following its venture into the production of private labels. While plant capacity was available to cover the added business, it was not the simple availability of capacity that prompted the decision, although this was one of the factors involved.

Acquisitions, mergers, and diversification as well as an interest in increased earnings per share may be viewed as elements of overall corporate planning. The first is longer run in orientation, while a mixed brand policy stemming from a search for increased earnings is more a short-term tactic, and limited primarily to companies producing nondurable goods.

Between these extremes, another reason centered on overall corporate action emerged as a consideration in the adoption of a mixed brand policy. A number of companies looked on limited private brand production as a necessary part of brand policy formulation. The idea underlying this view was that the company could not arrive at the best policy with respect to private brands until it had had some experience. As a result, several companies had a mixed brand policy with less than one percent of output going to distributors under their own brands. Yet even this small volume gave the company what management believed to be valuable experience of use in long-term policy formulation.

Financial Advantages of a Mixed Brand Policy

Two factors stood out as gains in the capital strength of even large companies which resulted from a mixed brand policy that included substantial private brand volume. The first of these gains was a reduction in average collection period and the second improved return on stockholders' equity and retained earnings (or investment).

For some companies, adoption of a mixed brand policy marked an improvement in working capital position. The difference resulted from channeling more sales into a few large volume, quick-paying accounts (large private brand distributors), and proportionately less output into many small volume slower-paying accounts. The improvements in collection period had their greatest effect in industries where manufacturers rely on thousands of essentially independent wholesalers and retailers. For example, in the appliance and tire industries, several manufacturers found that average collection periods on large blocks of business were only a matter of days rather than months.

Improvements in return on investment appeared to cut across all industries. Private brand distributors as a group tend to be large-volume customers who pay quickly and require relatively limited service. In addition, there is a tie-in between increasing return on investment, and the ability to spread marketing overhead to private brand customers which is discussed later.

The effects of large customers on return on investment are easy to envision. They can be seen more clearly, however, in the case of some of the companies committed entirely to distributors' brands which were found to show regularly a return on investment two, three, and even four times as great as the averages for the particular industries in which the companies operate.

Gains in Production Efficiency Led Many Companies
Into Private Brand Production

From a short-term viewpoint, several companies found a mixed brand policy attractive as a stop-gap measure to level out swings in demand or output. Sudden declines in sales volume, temporary excess capacity, or overproduction were seen by some managements as problems that could be solved, at least partially, with private brand production.

For example, the petroleum industry has high capital investment costs with continuous production and high shutdown-startup costs. Refiners frequently sell excess output to independents for distribution under private brands. In the grocery industry, as another example, both quality and quantity of many food products are affected by factors beyond the control of the producer. Manufacturers buying under contract often receive a sizeable quantity of crop that does not meet their own brand's quality standards. Some food processors regularly sell this lower quality crop under private brands. Other food processors faced with the same problem chose to market their "substandard" quality under controlled labels owned by the company, but not widely advertised.

The production of private brands as a stop-gap maneuver seemed to appeal to a number of nondurable goods manufacturers, but was not as applicable to companies producing consumer durables. For product lines like washing machines or TV sets, manufacturers cannot enter into private brand production on the spur of the moment—too much long-term planning is needed. Withdrawal is equally difficult, since durable goods must be serviced over a number of years and this requires a manufacturer to maintain inventories of paints, trims, and parts for use by the private brand distributor.

All manufacturer respondents, however, expressed awareness of a longer term production efficiency related to private branding. This was the improved stability in normal production scheduling operations that resulted from contractual purchases by large volume distributors.

Though the stop-gap tactic and gains from improved production scheduling were cited by a number of manufacturers as part of the rationale underlying their mixed brand policies, these considerations were not crucial elements in any of the large, long-term private brand programs studied. Two other production advantages related to private branding, however, were extremely important to some manufacturers. These were the enhanced ability to undertake plant expansion resulting from large, firm private brand orders, and a general reduction in unit costs on both national and private brand volume through economies of scale.

One of the companies studied invested over $50 million in new production capacity on the basis of a long-term contract with one large private brand distributor. The contract not only made possible an immediate expansion and modernization of production capacity, but also allowed much of the manufacturers' own brand production to be diverted to new, more efficient plants. This was an important, twofold gain to the manufacturer. Without the firm private label contract, the large expansion would have been difficult to justify. Management found that the capital expansion and substantial increases in scale of operations through private brand volume, reduced unit costs on the national brand significantly— with a corresponding increase in gross profit per unit.

Other manufacturers, though not responding to new private brand volume with large building programs, experienced a significant reduction in unit costs on total volume as a direct result of private brand business. In one firm, the cost reduction was passed on to distributors in the form of increased margins. The company backed up the improved retailer profit potential with intensive trade promotion stressing the source of the increased margins. Retailers expressed little resentment of the supplier's new private brand program.

Gains in the Marketing Area were Important Factors
in Adopting a Mixed Brand Policy

It has long been thought that one of the principal factors underlying a producer's adoption of a mixed brand policy is his need to
accommodate an important customer. Under these circumstances
the mixed brand policy is adopted to prevent the loss of a significant amount of volume that would occur if an important customer
threatened to stop selling the producer's national brand unless he
produces a private label, and carried out the threat. This factor
was directly involved in the adoption of a mixed brand policy by
only a few of the manufacturers studied—but for these companies it was the most important motivation. Management believed
they could have lost sales of their own brands if they had not
produced the private label.

Three other closely related reasons for adopting a mixed brand
policy were given by a number of manufacturers. These reasons
were that the production of private brands provided:

1. rapid market information feedback
2. access to knowledge about a major competitor's merchandising operations, and
3. the opportunity to influence private brand programs.

Large private brand distributors with hundreds or even thousands of retail stores throughout the country generate large
quantities of marketing information in the normal process of
controlling their operations. The information available to chain
management can pinpoint changes in consumer demand as they
relate to such items as product features, price lines, and new
products.

Even if a private brand distributor keeps the details of his
market information secret, it will often be reflected in the price
lines, product features, and quality composition of his private
brand orders. Several manufacturers considered this a valuable
feedback that could not be gained cheaply or quickly in any other
way.

A more direct marketing advantage of their company's mixed
brand policy was pointed out by a number of respondent executives—
the detailed knowledge of the merchandising operations of major
competitors gained by supplying them with private brands. The
close working association between the manufacturer and his private
brand accounts allowed the supplier to exert some influence on
the product line and merchandising programs of a large competitor. One company included in the study found that its first
private brand account asked for (and got) the manufacturer's
help in merchandise planning. The producer and the distributor
agreed they would both be better off if the appeal of the private
brand were to be based on value rather than price, and that

traditional price levels would not be departed from significantly by the private label.

In addition, a few companies found that the knowledge gained through supplying private brands provided the basis for developing national brand marketing programs geared specifically to the large distributor's needs, that were attractive enough to persuade some accounts to discontinue long standing private brand policies in favor of a full commitment to national brands.

The opportunity to spread production overhead to added output under private brands has often been pointed out as an advantage to the manufacturer. A little recognized marketing advantage, however, was revealed by the study to be more important to many companies than the ability to spread manufacturing overhead—this advantage was the opportunity to spread marketing overhead.

For example, several companies found that even the largest distributors need the assistance of experienced manufacturers in developing private brand programs in some lines. This was particularly true when the distributor was taking on an entirely new line of merchandise under his own brand. Manufacturers' national brand marketing capabilities were important as well to smaller distributors going into private brands, even in product lines with which they have had considerable experience.

A company's national brand production and marketing capabilities were found to have a direct bearing on its ability to compete for and service private brand accounts. Product research and development is the most obvious capability attractive to private brand distributors. Often just as important were a company's experience and knowledge in such areas as merchandise line development and promotional program planning. Some companies found too that their ability to handle warehousing, inventory control, shipping, and billing to outlets was attractive to private brand distributors. Several respondent manufacturers believed the adaptability of national brand marketing experience and practice to private brand operations was basic to their mixed brand policy and partially responsible for winning large contracts from distributors.

Manufacturers indicated that one of the important reasons underlying adoption of a mixed brand policy was the high degree of pricing flexibility achieved.

Respondents seemed fully aware of the restrictions on pricing imposed by the Robinson-Patman Act. And they recognized the difficulties of justifying price differences, as noted in later discussion of the legal problems of a mixed brand policy. Yet, the production of private brands still offered an amount of flexibility in pricing to large distributors that would not be available under a manufacturers' brand policy.

For example, some executives believed that production of private brand merchandise for large distributors would minimize the probability of violating Section 2(a) of the Robinson-Patman Act.

With a mixed brand policy, companies can sell different products bearing private brands manufactured to the specifications of large distributors. As a result, some managements thought that products of "like grade and quality" were not being sold to buyers in competition with each other, and the chance of becoming involved in discriminatory practices was reduced.

Finally, it was clear that some manufacturers with broad product lines find it difficult to be leaders in both production and marketing over the full range of their product offerings. This was particularly true in industries characterized by high levels of promotional competition, involving large annual advertising and sales promotion expenditures, often as a necessary part of simple brand survival. Some of the manufacturers studied, though clearly market leaders in product categories accounting for most of their sales volume, were unable to maintain leadership in others, and in effect, chose to become specialists in manufacturing these product lines for private brand distributors. They adopted a mixed brand policy which allowed the flexibility of 1. continuing their national brand programs with substantially reduced promotional activities, and 2. recouping losses in volume under their own brands through private brand production, with the burden of promotional competition passed on to distributors.

APPROACHES TO PRIVATE BRANDING
UNDER A MIXED BRAND POLICY

One common thread was woven throughout the preceding discussion of factors leading to a mixed brand policy: there is a parallel between a company's approach to private branding and the durability of the product involved. Companies manufacturing consumer durables cannot approach private brand production with an in-again, out-again attitude.

Two basic approaches to private brand business were held by companies with a mixed brand policy. Several companies considered private brand volume "plus business" and priced on an incremental basis with no real long-term committment or planning. For these companies, their private branding operations were not in the mainstream of corporate activity. Another group of firms considered private brand volume to be an integral part of the business and treated private label sales much like sales under manufacturers' brands in terms of proportionate cost allocation and profit requirements.

The "Plus Business" Appproach to Private
Brand Pricing

Most of those companies included in the study whose executives looked upon private brand production as plus business, failed to allocate such costs as research and development, administration, factory burden, and marketing services. Under the plus business approach these costs were considered fixed and not fully applicable to the private brand segment of the business. Usually all indirect overhead costs were charged to the producer's own brands.

A sizeable portion of the manufacturers included in the study did not allocate research and development costs to private brands sales on a proportionate basis. A tabulation of the findings appears in Exhibit 33. Most of these firms had mixed brand policies and viewed private brand volume as plus business. To consider research and development costs as sunk cost chargeable only to the manufacturers' branded product sometimes resulted in an accounting understatement of private brand costs and an overstatement of private brand profitability.

EXHIBIT 33

How Companies with a Mixed Brand Policy Allocated Research and Development Costs in Pricing Private Brand Volume

Response	Manufacturer
Allocate all*	40%
Allocate some	20
Allocate none	34
Other	6
Percent of Companies	100
Number of Companies	50

How Companies with a Mixed Brand Policy Allocated Administrative Costs in Pricing Private Brand Volume

Response	Manufacturer
Allocate all*	44%
Allocate some	38
Allocate none	16
Other	2
Percent of Companies	100
Number of Companies	45

*On a basis proportionate to sales.

Nearly every durable goods manufacturer with a mixed brand policy used a proportionate allocation of research and development costs to the private brand segment of the business. By way of contrast, over half of the mixed brand policy grocery products and drugs and toiletries firms failed to allocate any research and development costs to the private brand segments of their business. This difference is an indication of the difficulty of approaching private brand production in consumer durables on a plus business basis, since it is most often a long-term proposition no matter what attitude prevails.

Approximately half of the manufacturers included in the study which followed a mixed brand policy did not allocate administrative costs to private brands. The difference in practices between durable and nondurable goods manufacturers noted in connection with the allocation of research and development costs were only slightly less evident with administrative cost allocation.

Among producers with a plus business approach to pricing private brands, the practice of ignoring administrative costs, even those directly related to marketing private brands, was not uncommon. For example, the vice president of one company studied flew from New York City to San Francisco periodically to service a large volume private brand customer, and charged the cost of these trips to general company overhead; not to the private brand account. Administrative cost allocation is perhaps more difficult for the mixed brand firm with a plus business approach since a distinct organizational structure does not exist for the private brand segment of the business. The marketing vice president for national brands often assumes the administrative role in managing the private brand accounts—sometimes unwillingly.

The Integrated Approach to Private Brand Marketing

In a significant number of respondent companies with a mixed brand policy management considered private brands to be an important part of the total sales picture. For these companies, private brand production was integrated with the main elements of corporate activity—from product research and development to distribution, from cutomer billing to capital investment programs. The company's management talent, production and marketing capabilities, as well as financial backing were put behind both manufacturers' brand and private label segments of the business as they were needed. And, of course, cost allocations and profit targets were shared proportionately by both types of brands.

The approach to private brand production of large companies with a mixed brand policy is sufficiently important to be examined further later in the chapter, in the discussion of private branding as a marketing strategy.

RELATIVE PROFITABILITY OF COMPANIES FOLLOWING DIFFERENT BRAND POLICIES

One of the purposes of this section is to develop some benchmarks on relative profitability among all manufacturers included in the study, according to their brand policies. Another is to compare profit performance among just those companies committed to a mixed brand policy and to determine which companies have, as a group, been most profitable with this policy. Identifying this group of companies provides a basis for attempting to determine why they have been more _profitable with a mixed brand policy than other companies.

The findings below provide some general information on the profit performance of manufacturers committed to each brand policy. It was found that industry differences were not significant in most instances. These data, however, were developed from the purposive sample described in Appendix A, and cannot, of course, be taken as representative of all manufacturers.

Measuring Relative Profitability

To accomplish the purposes mentioned above, the following financial ratios were developed for 87 of the 112 manufacturers included in the study:

1. $\dfrac{\text{Net profit after taxes}}{\text{Net sales}}$

2. $\dfrac{\text{Net profit before taxes}}{\text{Net sales}}$

3. $\dfrac{\text{Net profit after taxes}}{\text{Stockholders' equity}}$

4. $\dfrac{\text{Gross profit}}{\text{Net sales}}$

5. $\dfrac{\text{Selling, general, and administrative expenses}}{\text{Gross profit}}$

The information on many companies came from published reports, but for others, especially smaller private operations and some tightly held public concerns, estimates were developed from confidential material made available by the companies. All ratios used data for 1964. Respondent manufacturers were classified on the basis of brand policy and then compared with industry medians calculated for each of the five ratios used. Thus, the measure of relative profitability used here is the percent of companies above industry medians, and the percent below, classified by brand policy.

Profit Performance in Each Brand Policy

As a group, respondent companies with a manufacturers' brand policy were more profitable than producers with either a mixed brand or a distributors' brand policy. In addition, manufacturers with a mixed brand policy were more profitable than those committed entirely to private brand production. This pattern of profit performance among companies is illustrated for one of the five financial ratios—net profit after taxes as a percentage of sales—in Exhibit 34.

EXHIBIT 34

Net Profit after Taxes on Sales by Brand Policy of Manufacturers*

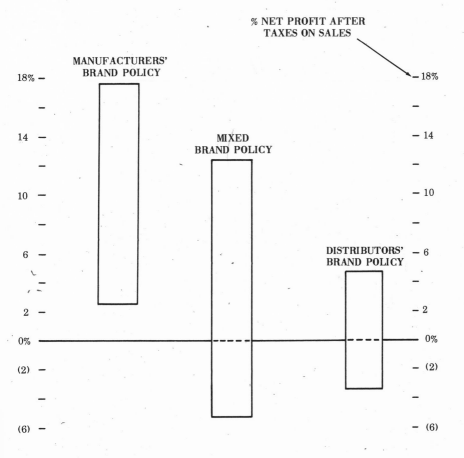

*Among manufacturers included in the study. These figures are not necessarily representative of all manufacturers in the industries studied.

More detail is shown in Exhibit 35 where the percent of firms included in the study which were above average performance and the percent below for each of the five financial ratios are classified

by brand policy. Manufacturer respondents committed to their own
brands outperformed both the mixed brand and distributors' brand
producers for each of the earnings ratios. Further, companies
with a manufacturers' brand policy had lower selling, general,
and administrative costs as a percent of gross profits than companies committed to either a mixed brand or a distributors'
brand policy.

EXHIBIT 35

Percent of Manufacturers Above and Below Average
in Profit Performance by Brand Policy

Financial Ratio	Manufacturers' Brand Policy (percent)	Mixed Brand Policy (percent)	Distributors' Brand Policy (percent)
Net Profit After Taxes			
Net Sales			
Above Industry Average*	77	43	39
Below Industry Average	23	57	61
Net Profit Before Taxes			
Net Sales			
Above Industry Average	81	45	32
Below Industry Average	19	55	68
Net Profit After Taxes			
Stockholders' Equity			
Above Industry Average	70	43	48
Below Industry Average	30	57	52
Gross Profit			
Net Sales			
Above Industry Average	71	52	25
Below Industry Average	29	48	75
Selling, general and administrative			
expenses			
Gross Profit			
Above Industry Average	34	54	48
Below Industry Average	66	46	52

*The average for each ratio was determined by obtaining the mean of four industry aver-
ages. The industry averages used in the study were: (1) median for manufacturers by brand
policy; (2) median of sample manufacturers by industry; (3) median for entire sample; (4) industry medians prepared by Robert Morris Associates, Inc.

For the earnings ratios, it is worth noting the descending pattern of the percent of above average firms going from companies
with a manufacturers' brand policy to those with a mixed brand
and then to the distributors' brand policy. On the net profit after
taxes to net sales ratio for example, the percent of companies
with above average performances in each brand policy declines
from:

77 percent with a Manufacturers' Brand Policy;
to 43 percent with a Mixed Brand Policy;
to 39 percent with a Distributors' Brand Policy.

This general tendency is true for three of the four earnings ratios used in the study, as can be seen in Exhibit 35. The exception, and a most important one to management, is the return on investment ratio (net profit after taxes to stockholders' equity) where 43 percent of the companies with a mixed brand policy are above average in performance as compared with 48 percent of the distributors' brand organizations.

For the expense ratio, the percent of companies with higher than average selling, general, and administrative expenses to gross profits was lowest for the manufacturers' brand producer and highest for the mixed brand firm.

These results are closely related to the observations made earlier in the chapter. The large companies leading their industries tend to rely solely on their own brands and have outstanding profit performances to back up this position. On the other hand, smaller companies that rely entirely on private brand production are not leading their industries either in sales or in profits, but most of them are probably following the best course available to them—specialization in the production of private brands. Management of some of these companies considers the results, especially return on investment, satisfactory in view of the alternatives. Others do not, and these private brand manufacturers often become subsidiaries of larger corporations that can supply the infusion of capital and market strength necessary to growth, while some, of course, become the victims of attrition.

Profit Performance of Companies with a Mixed
Brand Policy

Though performance of companies with a mixed brand policy was second to those with a manufacturers' brand, examples of highly profitable mixed brand organizations were found during the course of the study. It cannot be concluded that a manufacturers' brand firm is likely to suffer a loss in profits by adopting a mixed brand policy.

Approximately 40 percent of the companies with a mixed brand policy were above average in profit performance. This figure includes both the earnings and expense ratios. For example, Exhibit 36 shows the breakdown of the percent of firms with a mixed brand policy that scored above and below average in net profits on sales compared with the performances of the manufacturers' brand and distributors' brand producers.

Regardless of the profit measure used, it was found that among companies committed to a mixed brand policy the same ones scored above average on each measure. Those companies above average in net profit after taxes on sales were also above average in the other financial ratios. These same producers were the ones with the lowest percent of selling, general, and administrative expenses relative to gross profits.

EXHIBIT 36

The More Profitable, or Above Average, Manufacturers Committed to a
Mixed Brand Policy*

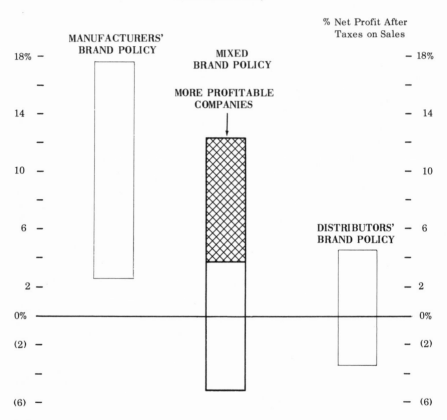

*Among manufacturers included in the study. These figures are not necessarily representative of all manufacturers in the industries studied.

CHARACTERISTICS OF THE MORE PROFITABLE
MIXED BRAND POLICY MANUFACTURERS

The manufacturers included in this study which were above average in profit performance are also the ones subscribing to an integrated approach to private brand marketing. The most significant characteristics of the private brand programs adopted by the more profitable companies are listed below:

1. A formal policy covering the production of private brands
2. A Private Brand Administrator
3. Careful selection of private label customers
4. Availability of corporate resources to the private brand program
5. The use of "known cost" contracts
6. Close management contact with private label customers

Formal Policy

Most of the more profitable mixed brand firms included in the study had formal policies covering the production and sale of private brands. These policies provided for private branding programs on a continuing basis as an integral part of each company's operation, rather than for the short term, in-and-out tactics that were used by some firms producing private brands.

In the more profitable companies with a mixed brand policy, the decision to produce private brands was made by top management and was supported at this level. In some of the less profitable firms, the private brand business appeared to have relatively little top level support even though top management obviously had approved their companies' entry into private branding.

The Private Brand Administrator

The more profitable mixed brand policy firms included in this study also had a full-time private brand administrator. All of these men were experienced in company management and in the production and marketing of private brands. Most of them reported directly to the vice president of marketing or his equivalent.

The private brand administrator was essentially the director of marketing of his firm's private brand operation. He coordinated and managed the selection, screening and servicing of private brand accounts. Above all, the private brand administrator was responsible for satisfying the private label customer and for making a profit.

Careful Selection of Private Label Customers

Most of the more profitable respondents with a mixed brand policy reported specific criteria used in selecting private label customers. While even the less profitable firms tended to have selection criteria these were generally informal and few in number. The more profitable producers usually had a larger number of formal criteria. While criteria for the selection of private brand customers of course varied from firm to firm, those listed below are reasonably representative of those used by the more profitable mixed brand producers:

1. Minimum volume requirements under the private label
2. Long term, annually renewable contracts
3. Financial stability of potential customers

Availability of Corporate Resources to the Private Brand Program

With an integrated approach corporate experience and resources were generally available to the private brand administrator in servicing private label customers. The availability of corporate resources—such as research and development staffs, marketing research data, and merchandising and promotional planning experience—for use in the private brand segment of the business was common among the more profitable companies following a mixed brand policy. The less profitable companies often did not make important corporate resources available to private brand customers, and in some companies, management seemed to ignore the act that private brands were being produced.

The Use of "Known Cost" Contracts and Close Management Contact with Private Brand Customers

To a limited extent, the use of known cost contracts—the type of contract which provides details on the manufacturers' cost structure—was one of the characteristics shared by the more profitable companies committed to a mixed brand policy. Too, the known cost contract often appeared responsible for a close management contact between supplier and customer; another distinguishing characteristic of the more profitable companies.

In contrast to the situation where the distributor releases specifications to several potential suppliers and often takes the best price—competitive bid contracts—the known cost contract tends to draw a supplier and private brand buyer into close, continuous management contact. The working relationship that can develop resembles closely the Value Analysis purchasing situation common among industrial suppliers and buyers. Development of a known cost contract often required such careful attention to the detailed elements of a manufacturer's cost-profit structure and the product requirements of the buyer, it served as a basis for long term commitment by both the manufacturer and distributor.

The detailed nature of the known cost agreement used in private brand production can perhaps best be understood from an example. The following exhibit summarizes an actual contract. This summary includes a list of the elements of known costs in the contract and an indication of the details involved in the particular situation. The example here was taken from the household appliance industry, where the known cost contract has been used by a number of companies for some time.

EXHIBIT 37

Summary of a Known Cost Contract

Elements of Known Costs

1. Direct Materials

2. Direct Labor

3. Factory Overhead

   Indirect Materials
   Indirect Labor
   Power, light, heat, water and rent
   Repairs and Maintenance
   Insurance
   Taxes
   Depreciation and Amortization
   Factory Employee Bonuses
   Warranty Expense
   Other Factory Expense

4. Administrative Expense

5. Product Engineering and Developing Expense

6. Pension and Profit Sharing Plans

7. Bonuses to Officers and Management

8. Other Income and Other Deductions

9. Selling Expense

10. Intercompany Transfers

11. No Profit Items
    (Profit Percentage not applied to these costs):

    Patent Royalties
    Prepaid Excise Taxes
    Prepaid Transportation
    Amortization of Special Power Tools

12. Profit Margins

Details of the Agreement

1. Minimum volume requirements based upon 80 percent of the customer's dollar requirements for a specified list of products.

Details of the Agreement (Continued)

2. Time requirements for fulfilling the contract:

    —length of contract (one year)
    —supplier's written statement of estimated manufacturing cost (November 1)
    —customer's revised estimates in manufacturing requirements for next succeeding quarter (estimate deadlines: January 1, April 1, July 1)
    —supplier-customer agree on estimated manufacturing costs for fixing billing charges (November 1)
    —customer places firm order at least 90 days prior to need.

3. Determination of billing prices—estimated manufacturing cost plus 6.3829 percent profit margin.

4. Supplier will not sell the same or similar product of like grade and quality to another customer at lower billed prices.

5. Customer has the right to notify supplier if he should receive offers from any competing supplier to produce any of the contracted products at lower prices. If the supplier-customer are unable to reach agreement on factory prices the customer may purchase from competing supplier after 30 days.

6. Within 120 days after the contract year, the supplier will determine actual manufacturing costs incurred by customer account—any variance between estimated billed amounts and incurred amounts will be promptly credited to or paid by customer.

7. Supplier promises to maintain adequate accounting and cost records based upon acceptable accounting procedures—all accounting records will be made available to customer at all reasonable times.

8. Supplier will inform the customer of need to purchase any special purpose tool and dies; upon customer approval in writing, the tools and dies will be purchased and marked "PROPERTY OF CUSTOMER".

9. Supplier tool and dies used for both the manufacturers' and private branded products will be amortized at rates mutually agreed upon by supplier and customer.

10. Supplier guarantees and warrants the product to be of good workmanship and materials, free of defects, and within conformity to accepted trade standards of quality, packaging, appearance and performance.

11. In the event of defectiveness or failure to conform to trade practices mentioned above, the supplier will permit return of products within specific time limits—within five years for major defects and one year for minor defects.

12. Supplier will store the product at its own risk and ship according to customer's specifications.

13. Supplier will produce the commodity at a time that fits reasonably well into production schedules. Any failure of the supplier to comply with customer's production instructions will permit the customer to buy said product from another manufacturing source.

14. Supplier will maintain for sale to customer an inventory of replacement parts—generally five years after each model season.

PRIVATE BRANDING AS A MARKETING STRATEGY
BY LARGE MANUFACTURERS

Many of the companies included in the study adopted a mixed brand policy for some combination of reasons that centered on correcting short-term problems or taking defensive actions. Several large companies, however, were identified that initiated private brand production as part of a basic marketing strategy aimed at strengthening an already enviable market position.

All of these companies have well-established, national brand names, and are either on top or near the top of their industries. They have annual sales of over $200 million and are multidivisional operations. These companies are recognized as leaders in product development and manufacturing. Their national distribution and marketing capabilities are fully established, with large, continuous advertising and sales promotion programs. Top management in each of them made the decision to produce private brands under a mixed brand policy as part of their overall marketing strategy of tapping new markets, and increasing their share of industry volume.

An Illustration

Several manufacturers included in the study fit each of these characteristics. For example, management of one household products company had undertaken a two-year study to evaluate the opportunities and the risks of adopting a mixed brand policy. The company had been committed to a manufacturers' brand policy in each of its consumer product divisions and had never produced private brands.

The results of the company's investigation indicated that its own brands would not suffer from a carefully planned program of private brand marketing. Management believed that private brand suppliers in the industry produced marginal quality compared with the company's own products. Their study findings led to the recommendation that the firm adopt a mixed brand policy and aim for that portion of the market supplied by companies specializing in the production of private brands for the large grocery chains. The Chairman of the Board and the President approved and fully supported this recommendation.

In summarizing the reasons why the company chose to use private branding as a marketing strategy, its Vice President for Marketing stated:

1. "Our best interests were in this area... We could no longer ignore private labeling because of the supermarket strength— and especially when private labeling was extensive in our product area."
2. "Most of our household products are easy to private brand...small producers can enter easily."
3. "We were advised that the percent of private label merchandise was growing—it's now between 11 and 23 percent of total chain store sales in most markets. We're losing millions in sales by refusing to produce chain brands."

4. "Most private labeling in the industry is on price basis and there's lots of competition...but we have special capabilities in these lines."
5. "In our product area there was little good quality private label."

Company executives saw a market opportunity in private brands, but they also believed they should develop a long-term commitment to a mixed brand policy in order to make private brand marketing a profitable part of overall operations. The program finally developed contained the following basic elements:

1. A two-year research program to evaluate the potential of private brand marketing,
2. Organized promotion to win accounts, including the preparation of a customer's handbook describing such things as the firm's private brand production capabilities, product quality control, and pricing and costing procedures,
3. High volume grocery chains as target accounts,
4. Assistance to private label accounts with promotional strategies and programs,
5. Similar products and containers (except for labels) as used for the manufacturers' brands; same formula and containers for each private brand account.

Exhibit 38 contains excerpts from a prospectus prepared by the company in an attempt to win a corporate chain's private brand business. This prospectus illustrates the planning underlying the company's promotional efforts in behalf of its new private brand marketing program.

Results of the Company's Private Brand Strategy

At retail, private brands produced for grocery chains by the company are doing well in sales. In fact, for one major grocery chain, the first quarter sales of the new private brand product resulted in a greater volume for the private label than the leading manufacturers' brand in the same chain (the leading brand was not the company's own label). After initial sales figures were known, the company's leading competitor stated that "it may be a bit premature to judge the success of their private brand program since so much promotional effort and money were used by the chains during the first quarter." However, the executive went on to comment on the manufacturer's private brand strategy by stating "...this is the first big producer to make a determined private brand effort in our industry."

EXHIBIT 38

Excerpts from a Private Label Prospectus

The National Brand Company, Inc.* proposes to manufacture a line of household product "X" for the Private Label Chain, Inc.*

A study of the current domestic market, as conducted at retail, indicates a real opportunity for sales and profit in retailing a line of private brand household product "X" provided:

1. The private label is of the best possible quality.

2. The private label offers the consumer a real savings over current retail prices of nationally advertised brands.

3. The private label offers the retailer the opportunity to make a better profit margin than that currently earned on nationally advertised brands.

4. The private label receives adequate shelf space and position; and adequate advertising promotional support by the retailer.

5. The private label is produced by a manufacturer with a high regard for strict quality control and a real sense of obligation to maintain a most satisfactory manufacturing and distributing process for the line.

*Fictitious Company Names.

The National Brand Company, Inc. submits that it is in a position to produce a private label line designed to fulfill the preceding requirements. A recent test of this proposal in a major regional chain operating stores in four different distribution areas proves the effectiveness of such a program and suggests that the rationale of the proposal is sound.

The National Brand Company, Inc. respectfully proposes, therefore, that we produce and sell to the Private Label Chain, Inc., a line of household product "X" carrying the distributor's brand with as wide a distribution as is possible.

The proposed line of household product "X" will be of exactly the same quality as products carrying the National Brand Company's labels.

The private brand will be in the same size containers, the industry standards, as now used for the National Brand Company's products.

The National Brand Company will agree to produce and label household product "X" against firm orders placed by the Private Brand Chain, Inc.

Sufficient lead time in the ordering process is essential in providing the best possible service to the Private Brand Chain, Inc.

The National Brand Company, Inc. has included label cost in its pricing of the proposed household product.

The following quoted prices include normal case markings provided costs are not greater than costs of case markings on manufacturer's own brands.

Proposed Private Label Chain Brand

Consumer's Price	$ xx.xx
Consumer's Savings	—
Retailer's Sales Income/Case	—
Retailer's Cost F.O.B. Plant	—
Assuming an average freight cost in	
000's pound shipments	—
Retailer's Delivered Cost	—
Retailer's Margin/Case	—
Retailer's Discount	—
Retailer's Total Markup	—
Percent Markup on Sales Income	%

The Company's National Brand

Consumer's Price	$ xx.xx
Retailer's Sales Income/Case	—

EXHIBIT 38 (Continued)

The Company's National Brand

Retailer's Delivered Cost	—
Retailer's Margin/Case	—
Retailer's Discount	—
Retailer's Total Markup	—
Percent Markup on Sales Income	%

Since all sales costs have been deleted from price quotations, in-store service on the private brand by the National Brand Company personnel is not to be considered.

In an effort to provide for adequate label and production runs, the minimum initial order is 000's cases.

Questions concerning this proposal should be directed to:

_____ , Senior Vice President

or

_____ , Senior Vice President

Each of the four grocery chains served by the company experienced increases in sales volume with the private label product. The increased sales volume and the higher dollar margin are contributing to the chains' profit expectations.

From the company's viewpoint, the Vice President of Marketing indicated that the decentralized product division showed a sales and profit improvement. Improvement in the company's operating results was shown by comparing returns from the year before with the year after private brand marketing began. Profits on net sales went from 3.0 to 3.2 percent. Net return on investment went from 7.4 to 8.2 percent. There was only limited improvement in the company's selling, general, and administrative expenses to gross profits, but management looked for more improvement here in the future.

Finally, the company improved its total share of the market since adoption of a mixed brand policy. The manufacturers' brand share of market remained stable during the first year of the new mixed brand program. The producer was successful, however, in reaching projected increases in total share of market for the year after private labeling began.

RISKS OF A MIXED BRAND POLICY

Several possible risks inherent in a mixed brand policy were identified by companies included in the study. As might be expected, the risks that appeared most critical to management were those which might have adverse effects on national brand marketing.

Adverse Effects on National Brands

The following risks of private brand production, some well recognized, were identified by companies as ones that could have adverse effects on sales of the manufacturer's own brands. The factors were not listed in order of importance.

Loss of trade support for the manufacturers' own brand
Recognition by consumers that products of the same manufacturer were available under both national and private labels
Loss of exclusive rights to new product developments
Disclosure of costs and operating data to a major competitor with "known cost contracts"
Competition from a major customer

Overall, executives seemed to believe the effects of these potential problems were far less severe than expectations had indicated they would be.

For example, manufacturers who relied on franchise outlets for distribution of their national brands were concerned, prior to adopting a mixed brand policy, that their wholesale and retail outlets would be severely critical of private brand production. Management in some companies feared this dealer criticism might result not only in a lessening of sales effort for the manufacturers' brands but in loss of franchises as well. For a few companies, these fears were justified. One manufacturer did in fact experience a loss of outlets and a decline in national brand sales. This loss, in a large part, was apparently a result of the mixed brand policy—though there appeared to be other factors that had a bearing.

Other companies were surprised to find that a survey of dealer organizations revealed that retailers were less critical of private brand production than management had feared they would be. Apparently retailers who compete with large private brand distributors were realistic about the brand policy problems faced by their suppliers and almost philosophical about a supplier's adoption of a mixed brand policy—"If they don't make private brands, someone else will." Some companies found ways to minimize adverse dealer reactions. One, mentioned earlier, found that wholesale price reductions made possible by production of private brands permitted wider retail margins which gained support for the policy change among dealers. Several manufacturers argued that adoption of a mixed brand policy through acquisition of a private brand manufacturer, because of the separation between the parent and subsidiary company, was especially helpful in allaying retailer criticism.

The problem of consumers recognizing products of the same manufacturer under both national and private brands cut across most industries. For product lines where personal selling and service at point of sale are a normal part of the marketing pattern, consumers can always be told by salesmen that the private brand is made by a certain manufacturer, even though that manufacturer's national brand is not available in the same outlet. This was frequently cited as a problem by manufacturers of appliances, television sets, shoes, and even gasoline. On the other hand, where products are sold on a self-service basis, as is true of most grocery store products, distributors commonly stock the private and national labels side-by-side on the shelf. Some manufacturers expressed concern because package design and container shapes were often the same under both brands. Of course, the problem of brand confusion by consumers arises even for companies that do not produce private labels, since a few distributors included in the study carried private label merchandise that intentionally duplicated the label, packages, and markings of established manufacturers' brands.

Many manufacturers seemed to be philosophical about the problem of consumers recognizing product similarities although they usually did all they could to minimize the risk. Some companies put provisions in contracts to prevent mention of the supplier's name in promotion. Others took steps to have product appearance as dissimilar as possible. Yet for some companies, the problems of consumer recognition of a manufacturer's product under both national and private brand was known well in advance and accepted as part of the private brand business.

Several of the mixed brand policy manufacturers studied worked with distributors on product research and development to the extent that distributors contributed significant amounts to R&D activities. Obviously, those private brand distributors wanted equal access to new product developments since they were contributing to the costs of this function. A few of the companies operating under this arrangement were on the verge of new product breakthroughs and felt certain the innovations would have to be made available simultaneously under their own and the private brands. Some manufacturers indicated they would "cross that bridge when we come to it." The president of one company saw simultaneous introduction of a major upcoming innovation under both his own and a widely distributed private brand, as carrying the advantage of fast, wide distribution and consumer acceptance, as well as the risk of consumer recognition that his company made the private label.

Many manufacturers included in the study saw disclosure of their factory and overhead costs to a major competitor through use of known cost contracts as an unavoidable problem of a mixed brand policy, though few executives believed this information would be used to their disadvantage. By the same token, competition from a major customer frequently cannot be avoided under a mixed brand policy. This was viewed as a special problem in nondurable goods where large chain distributors exercise substantial control over merchandising and pricing of both the national and private brands. A few companies in the grocery products industry cited examples of major buyers of manufacturers' brands using their control over national brand volume as a wedge to exact price concessions from the supplier on private labels. The vice president of marketing for one company noted that if his firm had refused to adopt a mixed brand policy it would not have eliminated private brand competition. But under a mixed brand policy these competitors became major customers as well, and thus added an additional dimension to the problem.

Other Risks of Private Brand Production

Certain risks have long been associated with private brand production. A number of these were also mentioned by executives interviewed in connection with this study. These are:

> Trading volume and dollars under the manufacturers' brand for volume and fewer dollars under the private label.
> Eventual dependence on a large private brand distributor through gradual increases in the proportion of output going to private brands.
> Governmental agency investigation of private. and manufacturers' brand pricing practices.

Among companies included in the study which followed a mixed brand policy, only a few associated a drop in sales of their own brands with private brand production. Most often, adoption of a mixed brand policy resulted in a substantial increase in total volume, and at least maintainence of previous sales levels under the manufacturers' brand.

While executives in most of the companies included in the study spoke of the potential danger of becoming dependent on giant private brand distributors, and of "the tail wagging the dog," many expressed a keen interest in increasing their private brand sales. Some looked hopefully to doubling and even tripling current levels of private brand volume, apparently without fear of being dependent on this business. Somewhat surprisingly, distributors sometimes put limits on the proportion of private brand volume from a single manufacturer. One large distributor limited purchases to about 40 percent of a single supplier's output in a given product line so it would not endanger the manufacturer's marketing and R&D capabilities, which could in turn reduce the company's value as a supplier.

Private brand production under a mixed brand policy can increase pricing flexibility and open up new market segments. But this policy can also complicate the problem of federal investigation of manufacturers' and private brand pricing practices. Violation of Section 2(a) of the Robinson–Patman Act which prohibits price discrimination among buyers of "like grade and quality" products is a problem faced by large companies under either a manufacturer's brand or a mixed brand policy.

Considerable confusion has existed in the past in the interpretation of the "like grade and quality" proviso as it affects companies with a mixed brand policy. This confusion was resolved by the Supreme Court in March of 1966. In its decision on the Borden Case, the Supreme Court held that differences in the market acceptance of private and national brands, no matter how commercially significant they may be, do not make the products of different grade or quality under Section 2(a) of the Robinson-Patman Act. Details on the legal history of the issue appear in Appendix C.

This decision highlights some special legal problems related to a mixed brand policy. For example, one large food products manufacturer, even before the Supreme Court decision of 1966, commented; "We can't afford to make private brands in product line X; the costs of manufacturing products physically different enough to make our own brand and a private label of 'unlike grade and quality' would wipe out the profits. And if we don't make the products physically different, the price differentials would certainly bring on an FTC complaint. We couldn't make private brands even if we wanted to."

Thus, some respondents believed it was necessary to maintain sufficient physical differences between products sold under private and national brands to remove the price differences to competing buyers from the "like grade and quality" proviso. Otherwise, these manufacturers felt they must fall back on the uncertainties of justifying price differences on the basis of cost. In the first instance, developing physical product differences between brands may make private label production uneconomic, and in the second, many companies are reluctant to face cost justification proceedings under an FTC complaint. The net result is to make a mixed brand policy unattractive on legal grounds for some manufacturers.

SUMMING UP

Many of the well established companies studied are coming to view private brand production under a mixed brand policy as a normal, profitable market opportunity. The rationale behind mixed brand policies of the companies included in this study was most often based on a combination of variables. Individually, some of the factors do not seem significant, but as a group, the advantages of a mixed brand policy were judged to outweigh the risks associated with private brand production even by some of the largest manufacturers. Managements in companies committed to a mixed brand policy appear to believe this is the most flexible of the three policy options; offering the opportunity to adapt quickly to basic changes in the market structure, and opening up large amounts of volume that would remain unavailable under a policy of producing only manufacturers' brands. Companies included in this study that integrated private brand production into the mainstream of corporate activity by developing well planned, long-term policies, apparently found this approach resulted in higher volume, greater overall market strength, and improved profits.

V

Distributors' Branding Policy

THE THREE LARGEST general merchandise chains in the United States do not regularly sell manufacturers' brands of major appliances, tires, TV sets, and electric housewares, or many other hard and soft good lines. Yet these chains have not always been committed to their own brands of durable goods.

One grocery chain does 77 percent of its frozen juice volume in private brands. Fifty-six percent of fruit cocktail sales, and 43 percent of margarine sales are in its own brand. Thirteen percent of the chain's detergent sales and nearly six percent of ready-to-eat cereal volume is in its private brand. At the other extreme, the chain does not even have its own labels in toilet soaps, canned soups, cigarettes, and cleaning compounds.

A majority of the pharmacies in America sell private brands of aspirin even though many of them do less than $100,000 total volume a year.

WHY PRIVATE BRANDS?

So far this report has examined some of the environmental conditions in the market and in the economy which affect private branding. It has given consideration to why manufacturers adopt one brand policy or another—and to the results associated with different policies. A key question remains unanswered: Why are many distributors interested in their own brands in the first place?

Looking closely at one industry, or one type of distributor, apart from all the rest, the answer may seem quite clear. Some maintain, for example, that the large general merchandise chains engage in private branding because they are so big and size brings buying power, which in turn can increase operating profits.

This may be true, but if size and buying power were the keys to private branding, many large chains which rely on manufacturers' brands in some lines would have their own labels instead.

At the other end of the scale thousands of small pharmacies, for example, sell distributors' brands. The explanation of size and buying power does not hold here. Perhaps if the corner pharmacist knew how to and did measure profitability more accurately he would sell only manufacturers' brands. Yet, accurate profit measurement in general merchandise chains is far more difficult than in a small retail store. This suggests that part of the reason for private brands in large retail operations is a lack of good profit comparisons. Perhaps these organizations would not offer as much private brand merchandise if they had more reliable measures of profitability.

There are a number of very large grocery chains; yet, in some lines, like toilet soap and soup, these chains sell manufacturers' brands in great volume. Thus "large size" and "lack of good profit measure" explanations are not adequate to fit all situations.

PURPOSE OF THE ANALYSIS

The purpose of this chapter is to provide answers to the question "why private brands?" by analyzing the influences that lead distributors to adopt private brand policies.

The analysis and findings developed here are based on intensive interviews with executives in over 70 distributing organizations—ranging from the largest chain operations to much smaller unaffiliated outlets. The organizations included represent commitments to each of the three alternative brand policies, but those with a "mixed brand" and a "distributors' brand" policy predominate.

This chapter is divided into three major parts. In the first, the minimum requirements for a private brand program are reviewed. This provides a basis for further analysis and helps to explain why practically all distributors engage in private branding in some lines, while in others only a few distributors offer their own brands.

The second part deals with the problem of determining relative profitability in different operations. It considers how private branders measure profits, the problems involved, and how comparative profitability relates to brand policy determination.

The chapter concludes with a partial explanation of why private brands occur in different situations and product lines and furnishes basic guidelines for a better understanding of the private brand policies of distributors.

THRESHOLD VOLUME AS THE MINIMUM
REQUIREMENT

Production economics and customer behavior are such that most distributors expect to sell at least some minimum annual dollar volume in a product line before adopting a private brand policy. This minimum annual dollar volume at retail is referred to as a private brand "threshold volume requirement."

The existence of a minimum requirement that varies widely from one product line to another is apparent in any evaluation of private brand programs. The president of a department store, heavily involved with the store's own brands in soft goods, commented, "We've started looking at private brands in appliances, but we aren't ready to go that route yet; we don't have enough volume." An appliance manufacturer, speaking of a distributors' fairly large private brand program in appliances, said, "They're large and look successful, but I think they're a borderline case. They barely have enough volume to keep the line full and justify production under the special brand." In grocery lines, suppliers often specify minimum order sizes for private brands that run into the tens of thousands of cases.

Before a distributor considers a private brand program, he should be reasonably certain of his ability to do a minimum amount of volume in the private brand and this minimum sometimes represents a substantial dollar commitment.

What Determines Threshold Volume

Three factors appear to be the major determinants of the threshold volume requirement in any product line: 1) the economics of production 2) consumer requirements and 3) the extent to which the distributor wants his private label product to differ from the supplier's other output. On the basis of these three criteria, threshold volume requirement can be satisfactorily estimated for any product line.

To illustrate the way these three determinants of threshold volume operate, to show how requirements differ from one product line to another, and to show how they affect private brand policy, several examples are provided, covering a wide range of products.

Threshold volume in aspirin tablets

Aspirin tablets are often manufactured to inventory for distribution under private brands. Firm orders in advance are usually not required. They can be purchased in bulk, packaged and labeled by any distributor, even those with the most meager financial resources and the most pessimistic volume expectations. For a total outlay of about $200, a small pharmacist can order aspirin tablets under his own brand, packaged in two or three different sizes. This amounts to perhaps a one-year supply or some 100,000 tablets.

Most consumers shopping for aspirin are not concerned about product age, hence shelf life is not a problem. Few customers will insist that they have a choice of buying the same private brand of other proprietary drugs.

From the distributor's point of view, the chemical characteristics of aspirin tablets are standard, with the label being the principal difference. Though all aspirin may not be the same, the differences do not usually concern the distributor. Promotion costs are negligible and inventory costs small, even with the purchase of several months supply.

Thus, the financial and management commitment required for a private brand policy in aspirin is extremely limited. A threshold volume requirement for aspirin tablets amounts to little more than $300 per year at retail prices.

Threshold volume in canned soups

Production, merchandising, and customer requirements for most packaged food products differ significantly from those associated with aspirin. The result is that threshold volume requirements for packaged food products are considerably higher.

In canned soups, for example, threshold volume for a chain operation is estimated to be about $160,000 annually at retail prices. The basis for this estimate is shown in Exhibit 39. Requirements in other grocery product lines (packaged foods and household supplies) would probably range between $50,000 and $400,000 annually. Initial estimates indicate that threshold volume tends to be lower in the grocery field for more standardized products, like paper napkins, and higher for more specialized items like soups, gelatin desserts, and scented toilet soaps.

On the production side, canned soups are a more specialized product than many other grocery items. Manufacturers require commitment for a comparatively large order before they will produce a private brand line.

Sufficient lead time against firm orders becomes important in the production process for soup. Packaging, pricing, inventory, delivery, and quality control are also critical elements. These factors are responsible for a considerably higher threshold volume than that found for aspirin.

The distributor is concerned with the taste and quality of canned soups, since taste differences are noticeable to consumers. In addition, distributors believe several varieties of soup must be made available; usually six to ten different kinds. This tends to

EXHIBIT 39

Estimated Threshold Volume Requirements* for a Private Brand Program
in a Packed Food Product—Canned Soups

Initial Merchandise Mix (Type of Soup)	Expected Sales Mix** (No. of Cases) (A)	Expected Revenue*** Per Case (B)	Components of Threshold Volume (A × B)
Tomato	14,800	$2.40	$35,520
Chicken	13,900	4.00	55,600
Vegetable	17,150	3.00	51,450
Beef	2,150	4.00	8,600
Mushroom	1,400	4.00	5,600
Split Pea	600	4.00	2,400
	50,000 Cases	Estimated Threshold Volume Requirement for Canned Soups	$159,170

*Authors' estimates based on information from interviews with private brand distributors and their suppliers.
**Based on two dozen cans per case.
***Authors' estimates of sales revenues per case at retail prices for a "typical" private brand program in canned soups.

increase the financial commitment required. A private brand policy can be adopted in soups, however, without consumers expecting to find the same private label available in many other lines. This tends to hold down threshold volume within the grocery product categories.

Threshold volume in appliances

Threshold volume requirements for merchandising a line of private brand appliances differ sharply from those of aspirin and canned soups.

It is estimated that the threshold volume in household appliances is roughly $10,000,000 annually at retail prices. The detailed basis for this estimate appears in Exhibit 40.

There are several factors which push threshold volume requirements in household appliances so high.

First, private branders believe consumers expect an outlet to carry a full line of household appliances. With this belief a distributor finds it difficult to build a private brand program in refrigerators, or in dishwashers, or in any single product within the household appliance category. The merchandise mix illustrated in Exhibit 40 represents a more or less standard offering of appliances and electric housewares under a private brand policy. This does not mean a distributor would be unable to buy individual products under his own brand, for production requirements alone would not stop him. But, distributors and their suppliers alike suggest building a private brand program in this fashion would not work out, unless several private brands were developed as elements of an overall merchandise plan.

EXHIBIT 40

Estimated Threshold Volume Requirements for a Private Brand Program
in Household Appliances*

Initial Merchandise Mix	Expected Sales Mix in Units (A)	Expected Retail Price per Unit** (B)	Components of Threshold Volume (A × B)
Electric Refrigerators	9,000	$260	$2,340,000
Ranges (Gas & Electric)	8,400	205	1,722,000
Automatic Washing Machines	7,000	220	1,540,000
Dryers (Gas & Electric)	3,600	160	576,000
Air Conditioners	5,400	200	1,080,000
Vacuum Cleaners	9,000	60	540,000
Disposers (Food)	2,600	60	156,000
Freezers	2,200	220	484,000
Dishwashers	2,000	190	380,000
Selected Electric Housewares***	31,000	15	465,000
		Estimated Threshold Volume in Appliances	$9,283,000

*Authors' estimates based on information from interviews with private brand distributors and suppliers.
**Authors' estimates of a normal merchandise mix and expected retail selling price under the distributors' brand during 1964.
***This group consists of the following products (estimated threshold volume in units): blenders (1,100); can openers (3,900); coffee makers (6,500); fry pans (2,400); irons (9,400); mixers (3,700); and toasters (4,000).

Merchandising and production tend to be closely related in the appliance line. For example, a mixed-brand producer making private brand appliances is legitimately concerned about consumers recognizing similarities between the manufacturers' and private brands. Both suppliers and distributors normally prefer products that differ materially under each type of brand—at least in appearance. This coupled with the common annual model change in appliances and continuing research and development costs does much to explain why a limited run of private brands can be unsound from both a production and a merchandising standpoint.

Additionally, every appliance sold creates a demand, or potential demand, for after-purchase service. This affects distributors and manufacturers alike. A stock of parts, trims, and paints for every line produced under the private brand must be readily available. For this reason, as well as high unit costs and substantial investment in inventory for both supplier and private branders, threshold volume requirements in household appliances are quite high.

Threshold volume in tires and shoes

Replacement tires and footwear are examples of the middle ground in product line threshold volume. Each of these two lines is estimated to have a private brand threshold requirement of about $1 million annually at retail.

The threshold requirement for replacement tires is based largely on the economics of production. Tooling up for the manufacture of private brand tires was found to be based on a minimum order of approximately 50,000 tires per year. This frequently involves an investment by the distributor, as he often owns the molds used by the manufacturer to produce the private label tire. At an average retail price of $20, 50,000 tires create a threshold volume of $1 million a year. This minimum allows for the production of several sizes and at least two styles, types and price levels.

In footwear, production commitment is a lesser factor in determining threshold volume. Here, the variety of consumer requirements is the paramount factor. A distributor could have almost any available type of shoe made up under his own brand with a minimum order of several thousand dollars (about two or three hundred pairs). One shoe style, however, does not provide a sound basis for a private brand program in shoes.

In a full-line shoe operation, it is mandatory for the distributor to offer several styles within each of the children's, men's and women's shoe classifications, at least two price lines in each, and a standard range of sizes. To provide a full line, distributors must often deal with several suppliers. Style changes, relatively rapid shifts in consumer preferences, inventory requirements, and display stocks push the threshold volume in shoes well above that required for aspirin and canned soups.

The Impact of Threshold Volume

Underlying the adoption of a private brand policy are, generally, reasons other than that of simply being able to sell more than estimated threshold requirements. Threshold volume requirements are a constraint, and a very effective one, particularly as they relate to household appliances or perhaps even replacement tires.

Threshold volume requirements explain why many distributors do not develop private brands in particular product lines. Smaller distributors simply cannot expect sufficient sales volume in their own brand to consider a private brand in some lines.

The Effect of Threshold Volume on Small Distributors

Threshold volume requirements have their greatest restraining force on unaffiliated outlets with limited financial strength. While practically every corner pharmacy could expect enough private brand volume to make such a program feasible in aspirin, few unaffiliated outlets could maintain a private brand program in such lines as appliances, tires, or packaged foods.

For example, based on the *Census of Business* it was estimated that in 1965 there were about 38,000 unaffiliated appliance, radio, and TV dealers in the country. Only about 300 of these had annual sales in excess of $1 million, and probably no more than five had total sales over $10 million. Considering the high threshold volume in appliances and that 90 percent of the private brand appliance sales are made by a very few general merchandise chains, it is not feasible for these outlets to adopt a private brand program.

In replacement tires, as another example, an estimate based on *Census of Business* data indicates there were about 19,000 unaffiliated tire dealers in the country in 1965. Only 200 of these were estimated to have tire sales in excess of $1 million annually. Threshold volume requirements alone keep most of these unaffiliated operations out of the private label tire business. Too, private branding in tires is dominated by special merchandise chains, like oil company outlets, and large general merchandise chains.

In grocery products, the comparatively smaller threshold volume requirements of between $50,000 and $400,000 in each product category still constitute a barrier for small, unaffiliated grocery operations.

The Effect of Affiliation

Membership in a cooperative or voluntary chain organization often makes it possible for smaller retailers to participate in private branding.

In addition to removing the volume restraint for the small retailer, cooperatives and voluntaries often provide another important ingredient of private brand programs—centralized product line development. Merchandising and promotional planning are also furnished by some organizations. Affiliation with a buying group makes it possible for smaller distributors (whether independent outlets, chains, or department stores) to buy in small quantities those private brand products from among a complete line, that best fit the outlets' particular merchandising needs.

Now that some benchmarks have been established which show when private brand policies become a realistic alternative for distributors in different product lines, analysis of the factors which lead to development of such a policy will be more meaningful.

ARE PRIVATE BRAND POLICIES UNDULY INFLUENCED BY GROSS MARGIN DIFFERENCES?

One of the charges most often leveled at private brand distributors is that they are overly influenced by high percentage gross margins or available markup on private labels. This comment summarizes the idea fairly well:

> [Distributors] eye the "lush" margin which their own brands seem to give them, but most of them really don't know the bottom line, because their accounting systems have not been set up to tell them the true net profit derived from each product.
> ... Even some of the most sophisticated, learned, intelligent, money-wise retailers have a blind spot when it comes to weighing the contributions to sales and profits of their own labels and manufacturers' labels on the scales.[1]

Measuring Private Brand Profitability in Durables

The nature of a distributors' brand policy makes direct long-term profit comparison with similar programs under manufacturers' brands virtually impossible. Since these chains do not carry national brands of durable goods they can easily be charged with lacking the information on which to judge relative profitability.

Too, if a distributor tries to allocate all overhead from multi-department, multi-store operations to specific product lines, it may be accused of making arbitrary allocations that cannot be fully justified.

If chain management does allocate overhead either to stores or departmental operations involving several products, it may still be charged with a failure to net out profit contribution by product and brand. Even though contribution measures may account for turnover, management does not know the "actual" profitability of a given private label line.

The charges listed above that might be directed at a chain selling appliances under its own brand are well-founded. Comparative profitability is difficult to determine in large general merchandise chains, particularly when a company is committed entirely to its own brands in certain product lines. Every feasible method of profit measurement is lacking in some respect. Many companies interviewed, however, were aware of the limitations involved, and had made periodic attempts to determine comparative profitability.

Some examples in the general merchandise chain field

One general merchandise chain contacted relied on gross dollar contribution by department as the measure of profit performance. This measure had been adopted after years of operation under a system which attempted to determine net profits. As the organization grew, the costs of maintaining this net profit measure became too high in the view of management. Management's belief was that the allocation of such costs as shared central buying, merchandise planning, occupancy, and distribution overhead had become so arbitrary they no longer warranted allocation on a departmental, or a product basis.

Another general merchandise chain relied on a net measure of profit contribution by department similar to the profit measurement used under a prior commitment to manufacturers' brands. While management realized many artificialities existed in the allocation of costs, the resultant information was thought useful nonetheless.

Most distributors believed dollar contribution to departmental profits to be the most feasible way to measure the profit performance of their own brands of consumer durables. The degree to which estimates were "gross" or "net" depended largely on the complexity of the operation and the company's judgment of the need to allocate overhead costs.

How important is comparative profitability in durables?

Short-term profit comparisons between private and manufacturer brands do not appear to be a major factor in the decision to offer private labels consumer durables. It was found that a majority of executives responsible for distributors' brand programs in durables had been satisfied with the profit performance of manufacturers' brands. Both profits and turnover, on a day-to-day basis, had been adequate before the distributor initiated his private brand program. Thus, the decision to develop a private brand of durables was rarely influenced by a relatively low profit-ability of manufacturers' brands.

Measuring Profitability in Nondurables

The relative profitability of private and national brands in non-durables, however, was an important factor in brand policy determination.

Three general methods of determining the profitability of private as compared with manufacturers' brands were identified during the interviewing: 1) markup; 2) gross dollar profit contribution and turnover; and 3) retail sales or warehouse shipment analysis.

Markup as a percent of price was the most talked about, most criticized, and least relied upon of the three measures. Distributors recognized the severe limitations of comparisons of private and manufacturers' brand markup, and they criticized those that used this approach. A distributor's decision to offer private brands in nondurable product lines is not often made on the basis of percentage markup. A wide spread between potential markup on a private brand compared with a comparable manufacturer's brand was found, however, to serve as a signal for a closer look at the situation.

The method most commonly used by distributors for evaluating relative profitability was a combination of gross profit dollars and turnover. This approach to profit measurement compares the performance of private labels with comparable manufacturers' brands in an effort to determine the brand mix that can generate greatest gross profit in dollars.

Retail sales or warehouse movement analysis is a more systematic way of making this comparison. Instead of analyzing profitability on a selected product basis, computerized sales analysis provides systematic and continuous data on relative profitability; not only between brands but also among product lines.

While computerized retail sales analyses are being used by more and more chains, it is hard to say how widely they will come into use in brand policy determination. Both retail sales and warehouse movement analyses, however, focus on gross profit contribution. Rarely are attempts made by chains to allocate overhead to different products or brands. Even the more direct operating costs are rarely allocated on the basis of brand. While many chains try to account for the more apparent costs of private branding, no systematic methods were used by contacted distributors to isolate net profit by brand.

A Practical View of Profit Measurement

Profit measurement is a degree problem, rather than a matter of either gross or net profit. This view is summarized in Exhibit 41. This illustration compares the McKinsey[2] concept of Direct Product Profit with the problem of profit measurement faced by distributors in brand policy determination. Direct Product Profit is the

EXHIBIT 41

Measuring Relative Profitability of Private and Manufacturers' Brands in Nondurables

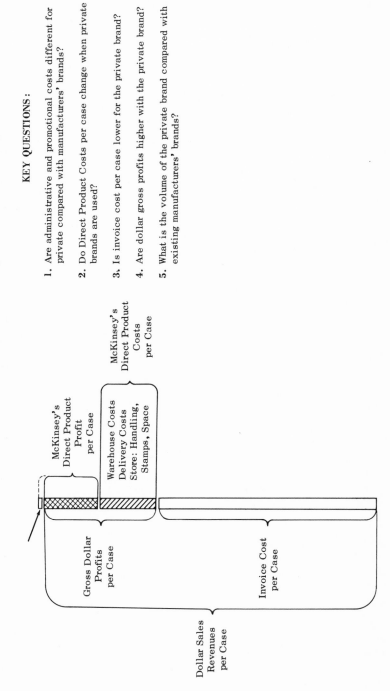

KEY QUESTIONS:

1. Are administrative and promotional costs different for private compared with manufacturers' brands?

2. Do Direct Product Costs per case change when private brands are used?

3. Is invoice cost per case lower for the private brand?

4. Are dollar gross profits higher with the private brand?

5. What is the volume of the private brand compared with existing manufacturers' brands?

residual left over after accounting for such Direct Product Costs as warehouse, delivery, and store costs and subtracting them from available gross profit dollars in a product category.

Direct Product Profit is an important step in the direction of net profit measurement, since major Direct Product Costs are assigned to product lines. Yet the concept is of only limited value in brand policy determination, since two important elements of merchandising costs—administrative and promotional costs—are not counted. Accounting for these costs is an old problem in comparing private and national brand profitability. The Direct Product Profit measure was not developed to provide a solution.

On the right side of Exhibit 41, five "Key Questions" relating to private brand profit measurement are listed. Most widely used measures of profit performance can answer questions three, four, and five, but not one and two. So it is not surprising that most large private brand distributors were found to use accounting systems that provide data on costs, gross profit, and volume by brand. This information was typically used in evaluating comparative profitability in brand policy determination.

The unknowns

Distributors interviewed were fairly sure of private brand profitability, based on the more easily identified elements of the cost-revenue relationship. In addition, most of them came to more or less intuitive decisions about the first two "Key Questions" in Exhibit 41.

1. Are administrative and promotional costs different for private labels as compared with manufacturers' brands?
2. Do direct product costs per case change when private brands are used in a given category?

For example, the Merchandising Vice-President of one chain said:

> It doesn't cost us any more to sell our labels and move them through the stores than it does the national brands. In fact, I think we often do a better job with our own brands. It doesn't make sense to say that it costs us a lot more to promote private brands. This is only a part of our business, and costs on it are not out of line.

Another executive commented: "We found if the private brand gives us superior gross profit dollars, it will end up giving us superior net profit dollars. This approach is criticized a lot, but it has worked well for us."

Most private brand policies among large distributors are not based solely on markup percentages, but neither are they based on a careful accounting of all the costs associated with selling private brands.

Profit measurement most often includes gross dollar profit and turnover. This is essentially a middle course. Distributors know that markup alone is a poor measure since it ignores volume considerations. At the other extreme careful accounting for all the costs associated with handling private labels is practically impossible.

Summary on Profit Measurement Practices

General merchandise chains were not too concerned with comparative short-term profitability in brand policy determination for consumer durables. On the other hand, all distributors were seriously concerned with relative profitability among brands of nondurables. Most companies appeared to have enough accounting information to make what they believe to be adequate profit comparisons among private and manufacturers' brands.

THE DETERMINATION OF BRAND POLICY

Two distinct sets of operating circumstances were identified which cause different factors to come into play in brand policy determination. First, when circumstances indicate that entry into private branding would be relatively easy, distributors place emphasis on short-term or tactical considerations in brand policy determination. On the other hand, when operating conditions indicate that developing a private brand would be relatively complicated and expensive, distributors emphasize longer-term or strategic considerations.

The analysis proceeds in this way: 1) significant differences in the operating conditions or circumstances which affect determination of brand policy are listed, 2) two major types of distributors are singled out as the focus of analysis, 3) tactical considerations in brand policy determination are developed, and 4) strategic considerations are identified.

Conditions Where Tactical Considerations Dominate

The emphasis is placed on tactical factors when distributors face a decision to add private brands under the following conditions:

1. Limited dollar commitment to distributors' brands, or low threshold volume requirements with brand policy determined on a product-by-product basis.
2. No major changes required in normal merchandising operations caused by addition of private brand. Or, management personnel, merchandise planning, promotional programs, and distribution systems do not require major alteration to

handle a new private brand program in a given product category.
3. After-purchase service not involved.
4. Supplier contracts can be short term, and may be terminated without parts and warranty complications.

Conditions Where Strategic Considerations Dominate

If taking on a private brand involves 1. a comparatively large dollar commitment, or high threshold volume, 2. major changes in merchandising operations, 3. after-purchase service, and 4. long-term involvement with suppliers, strategic factors tend to dominate brand policy determination.

Where tactical, or short-term considerations dominate, brand policy determination is similar to solving a product mix problem. Here, the policy most often adopted is a mixed brand policy, under which distributors sell both private and national labels in the product categories involved. Where longer term, or strategic factors dominate, brand policy is closely related to distribution policy, and distributors are normally committed either to their own brands or to manufacturers' brands.

Focusing the Analysis on Types of Distributors

Analysis of the tactical and strategic considerations that lead distributors to adopt their own brands is accomplished most easily by focusing first on special merchandise chains and then turning to general merchandise chains.

Special merchandise operations (such as supermarket chains) are used to illustrate how tactical considerations fit into brand policy determination. The operating conditions outlined above cause special merchandise chains to give primary emphasis to tactical considerations in brand policy decisions involving nondurables.

General merchandise chains, on the other hand, were found to base their private brand policies in consumer durables on strategic considerations because of the different sets of operating conditions identified earlier. As a result, general merchandise chains are used to illustrate how strategic elements come into play.

TACTICAL CONSIDERATIONS IN BRAND POLICY DETERMINATION

Distributors tend to view the decision to add a private brand nondurable as a tactical one. Major changes are not required in merchandising programs by adding a private brand. Hence, management can quickly estimate its impact and profitability.

Seven short-term considerations were identified as important in brand policy determination. They are directly related to extra product category profits through addition of a private brand. These considerations are:

1. category sales volume
2. immediate profit potential
3. invoice cost of private relative to manufacturers' brands
4. strength of leading brands
5. the degree of success achieved by other distributors in merchandising private brands in the category
6. nature of the product
7. day-to-day merchandising needs.

These factors emerged from the interviews as the primary short-term factors taken into account by distributors in brand policy determination. Comments relating to the importance of these factors came from discussions with all types of distributors. For example:

> Any time we find a product with high volume and profit potential, we try to see if we can put our own brand in the category.

> There's not much sense kidding ourselves about the importance of superior profits as the important factor. Unless a product can truly contribute profits above what a national brand offers, there is not much reason for going into private labels.

These statements were made by executives of two of the largest special merchandise chains in the country. Distributors did not overlook longer-term considerations, such as developing consumer franchises, but they seemed to view these as secondary.

In some companies, management viewed longer-term considerations as goals which provided some direction for the overall private brand program in nondurables. Decisions to add or drop a private brand, however, were typically made on a product-to-product basis, with judgments centering on short-term profit performance and other short-term considerations.

The Distributors' Brand Profit Differential

A summary measure of relative profitability was developed for this study which is believed to be useful in explaining the rationale of a mixed brand policy. It is called the "Distributors' Brand Profit Differential," and represents a way of formalizing the process of brand policy determination in situations where short-term considerations dominate. Many readers will identify this measure as a simple adaptation of distribution cost analysis to the problem of brand policy determination within product categories.

The Distributors' Brand Profit Differential is defined as the profit advantage (or disadvantage) that results from offering a private brand in the sales mix of a given product category. The Profit Differential has several important characteristics.

First, it is based on standard accounting data, and does not require computerized processing.

Second, the Distributors' Brand Profit Differential takes into account several factors that distributors believe to be important in brand policy determination.

Third, it isolates the relative profitability of all brands offered in a product category, and allows for explicit recognition of the potential costs that may be added with a private brand. Profits for each brand are viewed in the context of total product category profit.

Fourth, the measure is equally applicable to explaining corporate brand policy in merchandising situations where tactical factors dominate, and identifying the reasons for the brand mix adopted in a given product line by individual stores in a chain.

Measuring the profit differential

The Distributors' Brand Profit Differential is measured first in its most basic form, using cost, volume, and profit information normally available in distributors' accounting systems. Then, where justified, other assignable costs and revenues are added to initial estimates. Thus, a measure before assigning costs is presented first, and followed by a discussion of estimating the differential after cost assignment. This approach reflects the attitude and informal procedure of distributors in evaluating private brand profit performance.

Initially, a private brand's share of profits may be computed as the percent of total gross product profits earned by the distributors' brand in a given period of time, or:

Private Brand Gross Profit Dollars
Total Gross Profit Dollars in Product Category

The private brand's share of costs is estimated by the percent of total case volume accounted for by the distributors' brand in a given period of time, or:

Case Sales of Private Brand
Total Case Sales in Category

This measure of a private brand's share of costs within a given product category is based on two assumptions. First, it costs at least as much to handle and sell a private brand as a manufacturers' brand within the same product category. Second, handling and selling costs vary directly with unit (case) volume.

The initial estimate of a Distributors' Brand Profit Differential is the percent difference between the private brand's contribution to gross product profits and its participation in costs (measured by share of case volume). But, there are sometimes known or assignable costs and revenues which may be included to improve the original estimate.

Assigning costs and revenues

Information on direct handling costs may be available, and if so these costs would be assigned to brands in estimating the Profit Differential. For example, warehouse, delivery, handling, and stamp costs may be charged against each brand on a per case basis. Direct costs will normally be about the same for any brand in a given product category. In this event, each brand would be assigned the same direct cost per case.

There are some elements of selling costs, as opposed to handling costs, that may not vary directly and proportionately with unit volume. For example, sales promotion and advertising costs may be higher for the distributor's own brand. Extra administrative time or separate quality testing and control may be required. Where there are extra costs that can be estimated and assigned to the private brand, they would be used to adjust the Distributors' Brand Profit Differential by reducing dollar profits earned.

Manufacturers' brands, on the other hand, often carry extra revenues such as cash discounts and special promotional allowances. This "extra profit" can also be included in the estimated Profit Differential to reflect actual revenues.

The approach used in estimating the Distributors' Brand Profit Differential is an interpretative one, based on the way private branders appear to view brand policy determination where tactical factors dominate. A private brand proposal, or reevaluation of current policy, is not judged on a simple comparison of markup percentages by brand. Nor is it typically based on comparing private brand profitability with either the best or the worst profit performer in a category. Interest is in the best balance among brands; in the sales mix that generates the highest product category profit. Private brands are considered when they appear to offer a significant profit advantage.

Some illustrations of the profit differential

Examples of the Distributors' Brand Profit Differential in four product categories are presented in Exhibits 42 and 43. They are based on an analysis of cost, volume, and profit data from cooperating companies.

EXHIBIT 42

Profit Differentials Among Brands in Two Nondurable Product Lines*

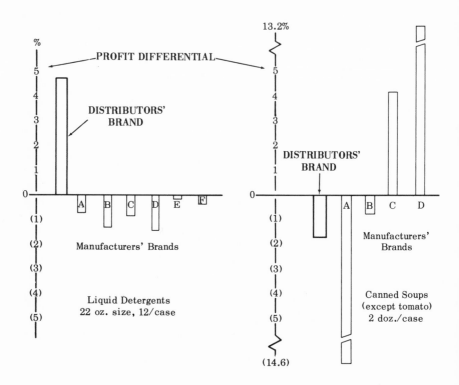

*Used for illustration only. Not representative of relative profitability in each product category. Estimates of the Profit Differential are after assignment of direct handling costs.

These illustrations show that the Profit Differential may be either positive or negative, ranging in either direction as much as 10 or 15 percent. For example, a striking contrast appears in Exhibit 42. The Differential of liquid detergents, is almost five percent. The private brand accounted for 13.6 percent of the direct profit earned in liquid detergents but was estimated to account for only 8.9 percent of product costs. The difference of 4.7 percent, is the Distributors' Brand Profit Differential. For the six manufacturers' brands the share of case volume in each is greater than their share of direct profits, so no positive Profit Differential exists.

Canned soups (excluding tomato) present a different picture. Here, given the mix of sales, invoice costs, selling prices, and brands, no positive Profit Differential is associated with the

EXHIBIT 43

Profit Differentials Among Brands in Two Nondurable Product Lines*

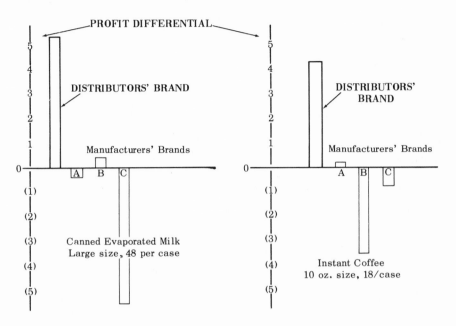

*Used for illustration only. Not representative of relative profitability in each product category. Estimates of the Profit Differential are after assignment of direct handling costs.

private brand. It accounts for 3.0 percent of case volume (and at least three percent of handling and selling costs), while it contributes only 1.3 percent to direct profit in the category. On the other hand, two of the four manufacturers' brands available in this category, show a comparatively large positive Profit Differential.

How changes affect the profit differential

Using the Distributors' Brand Profit Differential as a framework for viewing the effect of profitability, an understanding of why distributors adopt private brands can be gained by analyzing the impact of 1) changes in private brand volume, 2) direct cost assignments and 3) cost and revenue changes. These effects are traced using the product illustrations presented earlier in Exhibits 42 and 43.

Private brand sales volume

The estimated Distributors' Brand Profit Differential can be
changed in magnitude by increasing or decreasing private brand
volume within a category, but it cannot be changed from negative
to positive by changes in volume alone.

For example, in the canned soup illustration presented earlier
the negative Distributors' Brand Profit Differential is based on a
sales mix where the private brand accounts for 3.0 percent of
case volume. As shown in Exhibit 44 if this 3 percent were increased to 18 percent (with total sales unchanged) it still would
not turn the negative Profit Differential into a positive one. In
fact, increasing private brand volume from 3.0 percent to 18.0
percent of total canned soup sales would increase the disadvantage
associated with it, by reducing overall product category profitability. The result shown in Exhibit 44 is a change in the magnitude
of the Differential from −1.7 percent to −10.0 percent.

EXHIBIT 44

Effect of Increasing Private Brand Volume on Distributors' Brand Profit Differential*

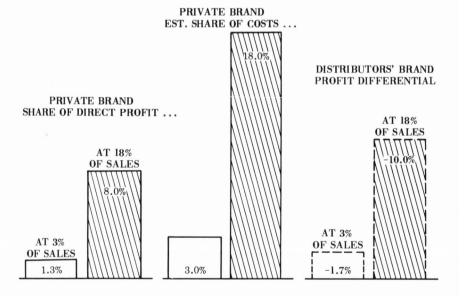

*In this illustration, based on canned soups, product category volume is assumed to re-
main constant. Figures are not presented as representative of comparative profitability in
the category.

By the same token, with a positive Distributors' Brand Profit Differential in a category, like that shown earlier for instant coffee, increasing private brand volume will not reduce the advantage, or make it negative. With the Profit Differential of 4.2 percent shown previously in Exhibit 43, increases in private brand volume will substantially increase the Differential and departmental profitability as well.

The relationship between volume and the Profit Differential stated above is one that often leads distributors to push private brands to a larger share of category volume. Of course, pushing a private brand in this way can begin to strain the assumptions of direct and proportionate cost participation among brands. If the private label receives an increasingly disproportionate amount of shelf, promotional, advertising, and administrative effort appropriate cost assignments would have to be charged against it. Or if manufacturers' brands carried special promotional allowances that are not available with the private brand, this element would be assigned to the estimated Profit Differential.

Accounting for direct handling costs

Estimates of the Distributors' Brand Profit Differential in a product category can be improved by assigning direct handling costs to each brand. This procedure converts the estimated Differential from a gross profit to a direct profit basis. Since handling costs, like warehouse and delivery costs, normally vary with case volume in a given product category, the effect on the Differential of assigning these costs will depend primarily on the dollar margin per case by brand.

Brands with longer dollar margins—which is characteristic of private labels in packaged foods, household supplies, and proprietary drugs—are favored by proportionate allocation of direct costs. Or, accounting for direct handling costs can often make private brands more, rather than less, attractive from the profit standpoint. One illustration of this is shown in Exhibit 45.

In this illustration, the Distributors' Brand Profit Differential for instant coffee is +3.2 percent; based on the difference between the private brand's share of gross profits and its estimated share of costs. When direct handling costs are assigned to each brand, the Distributors' Brand Profit Differential increases to +4.2 percent; based on the difference between the private brand's share of direct profits and its estimated share of costs.

Several aspects of this illustration bear closer examination (the following details are charted in Exhibit 46):

a. The percent markup on price for the private label, at 20 percent, is higher than any brand in the instant coffee category.

EXHIBIT 45

Effect on the Distributors' Brand Profit Differential of Assigning
Direct Handling Costs to Each Brand*

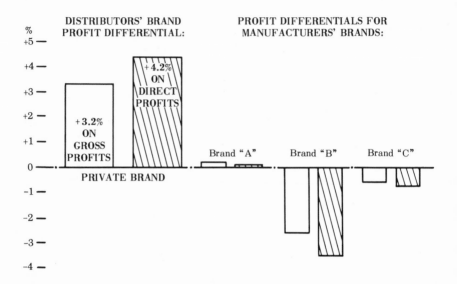

*Based on Instant Coffee example presented earlier, 10 oz. size, 18/case. Direct Profits
follow the McKinsey definition of Gross Dollar Profits less direct handling costs. The
figures are represented for illustration and are not representative of comparative profitability in the category.

   b. The private brand instant coffee is the poorest performer in
       terms of volume with only 5.5 percent of unit sales, while
       one manufacturers' brand is a clear leader with over 70
       percent of sales.
   c. A retail price (and revenue) on the private brand of slightly
       more than $23 per case is much lower than the other three
       labels available.
   d. At about $18.50, invoice costs per case are far lower for
       the private label than for any of the competing manufactur-
       ers' brands.
   e. Dollar margins on the private label, at $4.64 per case, are
       much longer than is true of the three manufacturers'
       brands.

   The combination of merchandising data on each brand shown in
Exhibit 46 results in a Distributors' Brand Profit Differential of
+3.2 percent, based on gross profits. Or, the private label generates 8.7 percent of instant coffee gross profits and roughly 5.5

121

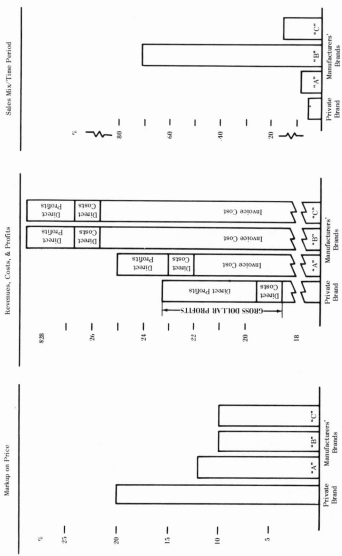

EXHIBIT 46

Operating Results by Brand of Instant Coffee*

*So direct comparisons may be made, all data are for 10 oz. size, 18 units per case. Estimates developed from cost, volume, profit data supplied by cooperating companies. This material is used for illustration, and is not presented as a general picture of relative profitability.

percent of the handling and selling costs. The difference between these last two percentage figures is the Profit Differential in this illustration. Because of the longer dollar margins on the private label, assigning a direct handling cost of 85 cents per case to each brand, favors the distributors' own label by increasing the Differential to +4.2 percent, based on direct profits.

Assigning other costs and revenues

The strongest effect on Profit Differentials comes from assigning additional known costs (or revenues) to each brand's dollar profit per case. Rather large changes are necessary, however, in the cost or revenues per case on a private brand to alter the Distributors' Brand Profit Differential significantly. In addition, even large increases in the profit per case on one of the manufacturers' brands in a category can have relatively small effects on the Distributors' Brand Profit Differential in the same category.

To illustrate the point, take the instant coffee example for which detailed operating data were shown above. Suppose that an additional selling cost of 50 cents per case is charged against the private brand on top of direct handling costs indicated in Exhibit 46. This will reduce direct profits per case by about 13 percent. At the same time, suppose every case sold under manufacturers' brands "A," "B," and "C" receive an added profit of 50 cents in special promotional allowances and cash discounts. This amounts to increasing the direct profit per case on all three manufacturers' brands by roughly 17 percent. If the sales mix in the given time period does not change, these combined allocations will reduce the Distributors' Brand Profit Differential from +4.2 to +1.3 percent on direct profit. But even changes this large do not eliminate the positive Profit Differential.

The size of cost/revenue assignments necessary to accomplish this result is suggested in the following:

a. To reduce the estimated Profit Differential of +4.2 percent for instant coffee to zero, cost or revenues per case on the private label would have to change by $1.68. This means an additional cost loading of about 45 percent of per case direct profit, or some 6.0 percent of per case revenues for the private brand.

b. A similar result could be achieved by increasing the profitability of the manufacturers' brands. But to do this, say with the leading Brand "B" in Exhibit 46, its direct profit would have to be doubled by a sharp reduction in invoice costs, increases in allowances, or price change.

In short, where private brands gain a strong edge from lower invoice costs and longer dollar margins, even with a substantially lower retail price and limited sales volume, the Profit Differential is difficult to erase by working with only one element of the merchandising mix or brand at a time. The Profit Differential can be relatively insensitive to increases in costs assigned to the private brand, or to increases in profits assigned to manufacturers' brands.

Some guidelines for the distributors' brand profit differential

Distributors were not found to be using the Profit Differential as an explicit way to judge profit potential. The concept is a way of formalizing how they seem to view a major element of brand policy determination where comparative profitability is a crucial factor. Some general guidelines can be suggested from the cost, profit, and volume data supplied by cooperating companies. These are shown in Exhibit 47.

EXHIBIT 47

Some Guidelines for the Distributors' Brand Profit Differential

If the Estimated Distributors' Brand Profit Differential is:	Distributors Would Probably Follow This Brand Policy:
Negative	Manufacturers' Brands
Between 0.0 and 2.0%	Mixed Brand Policy (Private Brand Potential)
Larger than 2.0%	Mixed Brand Policy (Tendency to Push Private Brand)

If the percent Profit Differential that results from comparisons with manufacturers' brands is negative, it is not likely the private brand can be justified on the basis of its profitability even though it may yield some dollar profit. If the Differential is somewhere between 0.0 and 2.0 percent, a private brand profit potential exists.

As the Profit Differential takes on larger values, say 5.0 to 10 percent, there is a strong profit potential, and a tendency for distributors to push the private brand to a greater and greater share of product category sales. This tendency is exaggerated by the fact that a positive Profit Differential enlarges with increased volume, unless checked by assignment of added costs that might result.

Other Tactical Considerations

Two of the short-term considerations identified earlier do not fit directly into the notion of a Distributors' Brand Profit Differential but do have a significant effect on brand policy determination.

The first of these is the nature of the product involved. Distributors generally are reluctant to develop private brands in specialty products—particularly ones where the manufacturers' brand is well established and based upon such things as unique recipes or formulas like some prepared foods, toiletry, and cosmetic items. This is also true of products with special demand characteristics, where consumer tastes are highly changeable and the demand is erratic, as with ready-to-eat cereals. For products of this sort, distributors would probably not go into private brands, even if the profit potential were high.

A special product characteristic does have some effect on the estimated Profit Differential, although it is difficult to determine. Products with unique demand or physical characteristics are often not priced attractively enough from suppliers to yield the distributor sufficient profit potential.

The second consideration which does not fit neatly into the Distributors' Brand Profit Differential measure is merchandising need. Distributors will sometimes adopt a mixed brand policy even though they do not believe the profit potential warrants it. For example, distributors may need to fill a price or quality gap in a product category and will do this by offering a private brand. However, even this may be related to profit potential, since a wide gap in the merchandise line is likely to yield enough of a cost, price difference to result in a substantial Profit Differential.

Distributors may also offer a private brand in a product line because they believe their customers expect to have the choice available, or they may do it in an effort to match the assortments offered by competitors.

However, the least significant of the tactical considerations seems to be the existence of a merchandising need. If no particular need exists, and the other considerations are favorable, the private brand may be developed anyway.

The most important of the tactical considerations, regarding a distributor's expansion of sales under a private brand, would be the Distributors' Brand Profit Differential. Where it is large, and continues to grow, the private brand will take a larger share of volume in any given category.

STRATEGIC CONSIDERATIONS IN BRAND POLICY DETERMINATION

Under certain conditions, tactical considerations are not sufficient to induce a distributor to develop a private brand. Longer-term or strategic factors tend to dominate brand policy determination when private branding requires 1) a large dollar commitment, or high threshold volume, 2) major changes in merchandising programs, 3) after-purchase service, and 4) long-term involvement with suppliers. Where these strategic considerations are relevant, brand policy determination becomes closely related to distribution policy.

These four conditions are most relevant to durable goods like household appliances, and certain semidurables, like replacement tires. Since general merchandise chains are the principal force in private branding under conditions where strategic factors dominate brand policy, they are used to illustrate how these factors relate to brand policy determination.

The case study presented below is a composite of 24 intensive interviews. While it does not faithfully mirror the operations or the exact rationale of any one company, it does closely reflect the strategic factors that led several general merchandise chains into private branding.

Why Private Brands?

This general merchandise chain operates some 100 retail stores in ten different regions. The first outlet was opened in the late nineteenth century and today the chain is recognized for "value." Stores are well established in over 50 different communities, principally in the middle and eastern portions of the United States. The typical outlet offers over 14 major lines of hard and soft goods. Among the hard goods, replacement tires and automotive equipment were taken on in the early 1920's, but household appliances were not an important part of the total merchandising effort until the middle 1930's. Since the initial development of these programs, the appliance and tire departments have become franchise dealers for the sale and service of three different manufacturers' brands of appliances, and two brands of replacement tires. Both tire brands, however, were owned by the same manufacturer.

Appliances were sold in 75 of the 100 outlets and tires, batteries, and automotive after-market equipment in 60. These 75 stores tended to be concentrated in ten of the larger metropolitan areas. The chain's annual volume in appliances was roughly $45 million, while replacement tire volume was just under $3 million. Profits had been reasonable good over the last several years as compared with other chain's national brand merchandising programs.

Soon after management made a "confidential" request of one major supplier in each of the two industries to consider the production of a distributors' brand for the chain, it became evident that a number of other manufacturers were interested. Approximately 40 different companies from both industries approached the chain with proposals for producing private label products. Some manufacturers even proposed taking full responsibility for physical distribution and billing of private brand output to individual outlets.

Despite persuasion, promises of increased special promotion allowances and decreased delivery time, as well as some outright threats from existing suppliers, the chain management continued on what one appliance manufacturer referred to as its "collision course with disaster"—development of new private brands. The final result was the initiation of two new merchandising programs under private brands of appliances and tires which excluded manufacturers' brands completely.

Why did this chain organization give up established national brands in favor of developing its own labels in appliances and tires? Among the problems the chain's executives associated with high volume operations in manufacturers' brands of appliances and tires, the following considerations were the most important in persuading them to give up manufacturers' brands and develop programs under their own brands.

Conflict in buying requirements

With manufacturers' brands in appliances and tires, the large corporate chain organization was acting more like a loosely-knit group of 100 independent dealers.

Even though the chain maintained central offices for administration, merchandise planning and control, and accounting, it bought both tires and appliances from traditional wholesalers in ten different markets. Some these were manufacturer-owned distribution points while others were independent wholesalers. Individual stores or regional groups of stores bought from these wholesale sources and were billed by them. Shipment to the store was often made directly from the manufacturer, but a commission on sales was still credited to the traditional distribution point.

For each of these regions, the chain was forced to maintain separate, fully trained merchandise managers and buyers in each of the two product lines. If regional merchandise planning and purchasing departments had not been maintained, these functions would have had to be handled by store managers or sales personnel—an unsatisfactory alternative. Chain management believed the situation resulted in an undesirable duplication of personnel and a loss of planning efficiency.

The chain's annual volume of over $40 million in appliances and just under $3 million in replacement tires represented a substantial amount of buying power. However, it was not using this power effectively. Total purchases in each product line were broken down into ten smaller purchased volumes for each region. The chain was not earning discounts proportionate to actual chain-wide purchases. Management was fully aware of the loss of volume discounts and efficiency brought about by segmented purchasing.

Dealing with ten different suppliers representing the same manufacturer frequently resulted in ten different prices the chain had to pay for the same merchandise at any given time. This resulted in differences in margins and contributions on the basis of differences in purchase price which were not related to the effectiveness of merchandising operations in a region.

Not only did the chain suffer losses in volume discounts, but it was unable even to use the existing distribution systems effectively, because it could not cross distributor franchise lines so that price advantages in one region could benefit the chain in another.

Efficient use of advertising

With manufacturers' brands the company was involved in an advertising program that in the judgment of management involved wasted expenditures, created unnecessary administrative problems, and carried excessive costs.

Because roughly 60 percent of each of the tire and appliance manufacturer's investment in advertising was directed toward a national audience, chain executives considered much of this wasted. In some markets, where stores of the chain were highly concentrated, the national coverage was too thin. In other areas, where the chain had no outlets, the coverage was too heavy. There was a substantial amount of cooperative advertising money available to the chain but management was concerned about the 60 percent of its suppliers' advertising over which it had no control. While chain management believed these advertising expenditures generated sales, it felt that demand was being created in many communities where the chain had no outlets, yet it paid a share of the cost of advertising in these areas.

In areas where national coverage was thin, the chain had considerable amounts of cooperative advertising money available to it. Cooperative advertising allowances, however, were typically administered by the traditional wholesalers in each of the ten regions in which the chain had outlets. This meant that regional merchandise managers of the chain were responsbile for the accounting and expenditure of cooperative funds received from regional wholesalers. Central planning of advertising was difficult under these conditions. Tearsheets and other material needed to validate use of cooperative allowances were required from each store. These were also handled on a regional basis and sent to each regional wholesaler as a part of the administrative procedure. This caused what management believed to be unnecessary and costly administrative problems in advertising.

A further annoyance to management was that manufacturers paid from 20 to 50 percent more for their advertising coverage than the chain would have had to pay for similar coverage. This was because of the higher costs of national as compared with local advertising in newspapers. The chain could, if it did its own advertising, concentrate on newspapers in regions in which its stores were located, and get the same amount of coverage at a significantly lower cost than manufacturers would have to pay for less selective advertising in magazines and broadcast media.

Is the field service necessary?

Manufacturers and their wholesalers maintained large sales forces whose efforts were directed at "servicing and assisting franchise dealers in their merchandising operations." Chain management said, "we don't need this assistance, but we can't get rid of it." Centralized merchandise planning departments performed these tasks. Moreover, chain management felt the assistance from manufacturer salesmen was often "annoyance" at best and "costly interference" at worst.

Sales personnel representing different appliance manufacturers and competing brand salesmen from the same tire manufacturer made frequent sales calls on individual stores. Management believed these salesmen's primary objectives too often involved inducing store salesmen to push a given model or line under one brand. To accomplish this, "spiffs" and other forms of bonuses were commonly used.

Chain executives believed that appliance and tire manufacturers' sales personnel seemed to have little regard for predetermined merchandising objectives as developed by central planning operations. Even salesmen representing competing brands owned by the same tire manufacturer had conflicting sales objectives. Management admitted that manufacturers' salesmen could not be expected to have a complete understanding of corporate merchandising plans, but argued they generally gave no consideration to the fact that such plans existed and that their actions might conflict with the overall objectives.

Chain management believed they should not have to pay for assistance of this sort at the local level, even if the override paid to traditional wholesalers for maintaining the sales force was relatively small for chain store sales.

"We don't need the incentives."

There were also distribution expenses which the chain organization had to bear, though they served no useful purpose, according to the judgment of the chain's management.

Bonus systems were so firmly entrenched in wholesale distribution they could not be avoided.

Each chain regional merchandising office accumulated large stocks of trading stamps, free gifts, and vacation trips which were nonnegotiable volume incentives. These incentives, management argued, had no value to the chain and might have been eliminated and applied as reductions in price. Apparently, the traditional distribution system could not be altered to accomplish this.

Reliability in distribution

Chain management suggested that the traditional distribution network could not be relied upon to provide merchandise at the time and place it was required.

Investments in regional and store inventory were either kept above estimated turnover requirements with accompanying higher insurance, warehousing, and handling costs, or stores experienced frequent stockouts because shipment and delivery could not be relied upon.

Orders were placed and billed through traditional wholesalers or company-owned distribution points, although shipments often came directly from the supplying factory. Because delivery was not dependable, and the chain assumed much of the warehousing function, management believed that this additional step in distribution was costly, that it contributed to uncertainty, and that it resulted in a much less responsive system.

"Why so many product variations?"

Chain management also felt that the proliferation of product lines by competing suppliers coupled with national advertising of these items compelled stores to stock and service a much broader line of products than was necessary for efficient merchandising. Moreover, such breadth in product lines with an offering of several competing brands complicated the task for store salesmen who were supposed to specialize in specific groups of closely related products.

Parts, warranty, and service costs multipled with additions to product lines. Several brands within one product line required duplication in service training and parts inventories.

Service and warranty costs tended to be much higher on new product offerings. The chain was not given the choice of waiting until the durability and quality of new products was known, or in developing their own assurance of quality. The substantial increase in adjustment rates on tubeless tires in the first two years of use was cited by management as one example of "putting new products on the market before they're ready."

"We need flexibility in merchandising."

Merchandising programs based on manufacturers' brands did not provide chain management with the opportunity to adjust product line offerings to meet their estimates of market requirements. For example, even though customer purchases and market conditions might indicate the need for a merchandising program based on low-end price models in a particular item, the product might not be available in adequate quantities. Or, the manufacturer might be unwilling to supply this merchandise under his own brand.

Focus of the Conflict

From the viewpoint of management of this chain organization, the producers of these manufacturers' brands of appliances and tires seemed unable to supply products by methods believed essential to the long-term success of its high volume merchandising programs. Manufacturers, in supplying products under their own brands, were unable or unwilling to treat this multiple-store, multiple-product merchandiser as a single, large, corporate organization. Instead, suppliers apparently insisted on dealing with the company as if it were composed of ten smaller franchised dealers. Only by contracting for the purchase of appliances and tires under its own brands, and thus changing its distribution policy, was the chain able to deal with manufacturers in what management believed to be the most efficient manner.

The following guidelines emerge as the desirable elements of a mass merchandiser's operations:

1. Centralized, total volume purchasing.
2. Centralized product line planning.
3. Central merchandise planning with uninterrupted local implementation.
4. Central planning of promotion and advertising with local implementation at local space and time rates. Elimination of the overhead and administrative complexities of cooperative advertising allowances.
5. Single or noncompeting brand merchandising in appliances and tires.
6. Concentration on relatively narrow product lines, with the capability to adjust product offerings to fit changing market requirements.
7. Sales personnel specialized by product line.
8. Direct, dependable delivery with a minimum of investment in inventory.
9. Retail outlets closed to outside interference from competing lines.
10. Centralized, consistent, recommended pricing implemented at local levels.
11. Elimination of merchandising services not required by a large volume chain operation.

These considerations resulted from a basic conflict between the way the manufacturers wanted to do business, and the objectives of the large chain. However, private brands are not, at least in principle, necessary to meet these objectives. Each can be summarized in three long-term, or strategic considerations:

1. Control over marketing planning and performance.
2. Central planning for merchandise operations.
3. Selective use of manufacturers' capabilities.

Not one of these considerations are unique to private brands, in the sense that distributors could not satisfy their requirements with programs built on manufacturers' brands if they so desired. But, in the context of traditional methods of distribution, and because of the high threshold volume requirements, general merchandise chains have turned to a full commitment to private brands as the best way to overcome the problems they associate with distribution of manufacturers' brands.

Using the Best of a Supplier's Talents

Comments on the selective use of manufacturers' capabilities are especially important in showing how distributors view their private brand programs. Typically, management does not want to lose access to the special knowledge and certain unique capabilities of its suppliers—even with a full commitment to private brands. Particularly important to distributors in this regard are manufacturers' product research and development activities.

Even large distributors with their own brands in many lines expressed a reluctance to take on private brands of consumer durables. Private branding in durables was viewed as a costly and hazardous business by many of these companies; an undertaking not worth the financial and management commitment necessary unless manufacturers' brand programs became unable to serve as the basis for the distributors' long-term growth. This common thread ran throughout most of the interviews with distributors of consumer durables, whether they followed a manufacturers' brand policy or had already developed their own brands.

Essentially general merchandise chains look for control over merchandise planning and performance, while continuing to rely on the supplier for those services he can perform most effectively. It seems as if these large volume merchandisers are able to be selective in the support provided by a supplier, only by competing with him by selling private brands. By remaining part of a manufacturer's marketing operations, a distributor apparently must take what the supplier believes best suited to the customer's needs. Several executives suggested that while their chain organizations seek control over their operations through private brands and the opportunity to be selective in determining the nature of supplier support, they do not want to separate themselves from national brand manufacturers. If this were an important goal, the logical result would be vertical integration through manufacturing and this was not found to be a long-term objective of most private branders.

It seems unlikely that manufacturers fail to recognize that some of these factors discussed may constitute serious limitations in national brand appliance or tire marketing programs. Yet, few manufacturing executives suggested that an important reason for the development of private brands might be the failure of manufacturers' brand programs to adapt to the unique, high volume, interregional operations of mass merchandisers and special merchandise chains. The reasons put forth by most manufacturers were concerned with those factors unique to private branding, like exclusivity, and freedom from direct price comparison. These were found to be important in the decision to adopt a distributors' brand policy, but only one of several crucial elements of the situation.

Special Advantages of Private Brands

The final strategic consideration of the chain is the development of a long-term store/brand consumer franchise. Control over centralized merchandise planning, local implementation, and selective use of suppliers' talents are given additional dimension through the benefits of exclusivity and a strong store/brand image. It is difficult for manufacturers' brands to satisfy large distributors' needs on this count. While a sale of a national brand of appliance, TV, or replacement tire may yield a reasonable profit, chain management believed it did not contribute to long-term success.

The following considerations, long viewed as dimensions of a private brand operation, were also noted as part of the picture by distributors contacted in this study:

1. Each time a sale is made, the purchaser becomes a potential long-term customer. If the customer is satisfied, this satisfaction can be repeated only by repurchasing the exclusive private brand.
2. Products sold under the private brand cannot be directly compared with merchandise available from competitors.
3. Merchandise offerings can be what the distributor believes to be the best mix for a given market (on the basis of quality and features), with assurance that competition cannot duplicate successful programs.
4. Since quality and features developed for the private brand are not subject to direct comparison in an objective fashion by consumers, predetermined retail price points are not affected as much by loss leader competition from distributors selling national brands. Price lines carefully

developed around quality levels and product features are not broken by competitors' pricing tactics.

The result of these advantages in merchandising consumer durables is that the development of a store/brand consumer franchise becomes a fourth strategic factor leading to a private brand policy by general merchandise chains in consumer durables.

Strategic Factors Leading to a Private
Brand Policy

At some stage in the growth of multi-line, inter-regional merchandising operations, programs built around manufacturers' brands may become too inflexible to meet the organization's changing requirements. This growth stage is well beyond the private brand threshold volume requirements in a product line, and seems to be reached when management believes its greatest long-term advantage rests in a program that offers:

1. control over marketing planning and performance,
2. central planning of merchandising operations,
3. selective use of manufacturers' capabilities, and
4. store/brand franchise development.

General merchandise chains were not found to overlook the tactical or short-term considerations noted earlier, but the emphasis was clearly on longer-term factors. Short-term volume and profit gains were not crucial; manufacturers' brands were satisfactory on these counts. Neither was it of paramount importance to balance the merchandise offering with both kinds of brands. The focus of brand policy determination was on the strategic variables.

A BROADER VIEW OF BRAND POLICY
DETERMINATION

From the standpoint of developing a reasonable brand policy, both the tactical and the strategic factors outlined below should be involved. In varying degree, they were found to be of importance to most distributors.

TACTICAL CONSIDERATIONS
(emphasized in nondurable lines)...

Large Dollar Sales Volume in the Product Category
Estimated Private Brand Sales Which Exceed Threshold
    Volume Requirements

Distributors' Brand Profit Differential (Positive)
Standardized Product (From Standpoint of Both Demand and
    Physical Characteristics)
Short-Term Merchandising Need

STRATEGIC CONSIDERATIONS
(emphasized in durable lines)...

Need for Control over Marketing Planning and Performance
Central Planning and Local Implementation of Merchandising
    Operations Withoug Interference from Competing Brands
Lack of Flexibility in Suppliers Marketing Programs and Need
    for Selective Use of Their Capabilities
Store/Brand Franchise Development Key Element in Success-
    ful Merchandising

The emphasis given short-term considerations by special merchandise chains, compared with the stress on longer-term factors by general merchandise operations, is largely the result of basic differences in operating conditions. It is easier to decide to take on private brands in one product line or another without major changes in merchandising and promotional programs, than it is to change the orientation of a company. Where major changes are involved the action is not taken lightly, hence, the more compelling strategic reasons prevail.

Overemphasizing either tactical or strategic considerations can be dangerous. For example, too much faith in brand policies based on tactical factors, such as short run profit gains in one product line or another, can result in an overemphasis of private brands.

On the other hand, excessive concentration on the broad, strategic considerations can also lead to overextended private brand programs. Failure to give systematic attention to the short-term profit potential of both private and national brands where a mixed brand policy can easily be adopted might reduce merchandising flexibility and weaken long-term market standing.

The balanced viewpoint for any distributor is a careful review of both the tactical and strategic considerations which shape brand policy.

Appendix A

Research Methods

THE RESEARCH METHODOLOGY consisted of four phases: Preliminary Investigation, Field Research, Collection of Private Brand Data, and Analysis.

PRELIMINARY INVESTIGATION

The preliminary investigation evolved around the study's primary objective of identifying and analyzing the variables taken into account by manufacturers and distributors in developing their brand policies.

For the purpose of assessing the research requirements, an examination of available published and unpublished research was made. It was found that little substantive work in the area of private branding was publicly available.

Prior to the development of specific research hypotheses, members of the project team conferred with Professors Malcolm McNair and William Applebaum of the Harvard Business School. The research and business experiences of both professors provided a valuable foundation for the design of the study.

The next stage of the preliminary investigation entailed the development of hypotheses which served as the focus of the total research effort. Fifty hypotheses were generated, dealing with possible factors influential in the development of private branding. Several techniques and sources were used in order to develop these hypotheses. For example, staff personnel screened and selected approximately 500 documents from such sources as trade papers, journals, books, speeches, and company reports. An abstract was prepared for each of these documents. Although the literature search was conducted initially to guide the hypotheses development, comprehensive monitoring of published and unpublished documents continued throughout the course of the research.

In addition, executives from the Marketing Science Institute's supporting companies reported to interviewers their experiences relating to private brands. Their comments resulted in ideas and guidelines for developing hypotheses, as dis an interchange of ideas between the authors and other members of the MSI research staff.

FIELD RESEARCH

Interviews with 48 trade associations served the important purpose of obtaining:

1. An overview of the structure and problems of each of the industries studied;
2. Insights regarding the role of private branding in specific industries;
3. Cooperation in conducting research in the industries represented by the trade association; and
4. A list of appropriate companies and executives for interviewing.

Selection of Companies in the Study

Trade associations suggested the names of companies and executives to be interviewed on the basis of the following criteria:

1. Product category. Manufacturers were selected on the basis of product category, while distributors were selected to represent different retailing and wholesaling institutions, such as the independent retailers, corporate chains, and department stores.
2. Brand policy of the firm. Manufacturers and distributors were selected to represent each of the three brand policy options in a given product category.
3. Degree of commitment to a given brand policy. Manufacturers and distributors were specifically sought if it were known that the company was undergoing (or had undergone) a change in brand policy. Some companies were regarded as outspoken opponents or proponents of private branding. Firms representing each of these opposing views were included in the sample where possible.
4. Sales volume. For each product category, manufacturers and distributors were selected to cover the range from small to medium and large organizations on the basis of sales volume.

Number and Type of Company Interviews

A total of 199 executive interviews were conducted in 189 manufacturing, distributing, agency, and media organizations. A breakdown of the interviews conducted is shown in Exhibit 48.

EXHIBIT 48

Number of Corporate Interviews

Market Level	Number of Respondents	Number of Firms
Manufacturers	115*	112
Distributors	77**	72
Advertising Agencies and Media	7	7
Total	199	191

*Three respondents were interviewed in one company, two in another.
**Two respondents were interviewed in each of two companies, four in one other.

The number and percent of executive interviews conducted are presented in Exhibit 49 by corporate rank and type of company. Of the total 199 respondents, nearly 80 percent held the title of chairman, president or vice president.

Interviewers

The authors conducted over one-third of the interviews and then personally selected and trained an outside field force to conduct the remaining interviews. Thirteen business school professors and one marketing research consultant were used as interviewers. They were selected on the basis of their experience in communicating and working with top business executives. An instruction manual was prepared for each interviewer.

The Executive Interviews

The objective of each interview was to draw as much information as possible from each executive concerning his company's brand policy and obtain any data useful for evaluation of results (e.g., profitability). No attempt was made to ask precisely the same questions of each executive.

In effect, the interviews became small scale case studies of brand policies and marketing programs. The interviews averaged

EXHIBIT 49

Composition of the Sample by Corporate Rank and Type of Company

Corporate Rank of Respondent	Manufacturers		Distributors		Advertising Agencies and Media	
	Number of Interviews	Percent of Subtotal	Number of Interviews	Percent of Subtotal	Number of Interviews	Percent of Subtotal
Chairman of the Board	2	1.7	2	2.6	1	14.3
President	27	23.5	32	41.5	–	–
Vice President	61	53.0	28	36.4	2	28.6
Merchandising Manager	–	–	8	10.4	–	–
Director of Marketing	5	4.4	–	–	–	–
Product Manager	3	2.6	–	–	–	–
Director of Corporate Planning/Research	10	8.7	2	2.6	–	–
Director of Advertising	5	4.4	–	–	4	57.1
Other	2	1.7	5	6.5	–	–
Subtotal	115	100.0%	77	100.0%	7	100.0%
Total Number of Interviews	199					

just less than three hours in length—with a few as short as one hour, and a few as long as five hours. Although the general areas covered in each interview were constant due to use of an interview guide, specific questions developed during the course of a discussion. Pilot interviews had revealed that executive officers could not be forced into a mold of structured questions. More important, structured questions tended to elicit short, often shallow answers. Initial questions in each area proved not to be as useful in drawing information from a respondent as were the series of probes directed at initial answers. Only an unstructured interview guide would serve this purpose.

The executive interview guide which developed after considerable testing was a bit unorthodox. Its format was dictated by the fact that executives' comments could not be directed effectively along a predetermined path. A respondent might, and often did, jump from one subject area to another with little regard for planned sequence. To interrupt this pattern would be to lose useful information and perhaps the entire interview. On the other hand, to allow free rein to respondents required an interview guide format which made possible immediate detection of areas already covered in earlier portions of a discussion.

The format finally adopted, and used throughout the interviews included in this research, served both purposes. Questions could be developed on the spot and material already covered could be easily identified, while maintaining uniformity of general content.

The substantive content of the interview responses and the cooperation of respondents were judged satisfactory. The refusal rate among executives contacted was approximately 17 percent.

Interview Guides

The hypotheses discussed above served as the basis for constructing the interview guide. Guides were prepared for each of the following types of respondent organizations: manufacturers, distributors, advertising agencies and print media. For example, the manufacturer guide consisted of the following major sections:

1. Historical development of private branding: a description of the history of private branding in the respondent's industry and company.
2. Manufacturer's brand policies: the reasons for existing company brand policy, and the results of a given policy in terms of financial and competitive success.
3. Views on distributor brand policies: manufacturers' opinions on the reason for and results of distributors' branding policies.
4. Views on consumer attitudes toward private branding: opinions of how and why consumers distinguish between

private and manufacturers' brands when buying given consumer products.
5. Effect of governmental regulation: the impact of governmental regulation on brand policy.

The distributor guide paralleled closely that of the manufacturer but was oriented to the operations of wholesalers, retailers,
and buying organizations. The guide used for agency and media
interviews also paralleled the manufacturer guide.

COLLECTION OF PRIVATE BRAND DATA

Private brand market share data were obtained for a selected
number of products in each of the consumer product categories
included in the study. These data generally covered the period
from 1955 to 1965. The following is a list and description of the
data obtained for each of the product categories.

Packaged Foods and Household Supplies

A. C. Nielsen Company supplied manufacturers' share of market
data based on dollar sales of major advertised brands for approximately 70 packaged food and household supply products, and
it was agreed that the figures for specific products be unidentified
in the report. For most products the period of time covered was
from 1961 through 1965. In addition, data covering distributors'
brands were provided on a unit basis for 24 product classifications.

Drugs and Toiletries

Share of market data for major advertised manufacturers' brands
and remaining brands for 21 toiletry and proprietary drug items
were also obtained from A. C. Nielsen Company. Here, too, it
was agreed that the figures for specific products remain unidentified. The general period of time covered each year from 1961
through 1965. The market share data were based upon dollar
sales in grocery and drug stores monitored by Nielsen.

Gasoline

The manufacturers' and private brand shares of market for
gasoline were measured in terms of net highway gallonage data.
The authors estimated manufacturers' and private brand market
shares from data supplied by a major oil company and the Look

magazine gasoline survey.[1] The major oil company's market share data for 1954 and 1960 and the Look magazine brand share data from 1961, 1962, and 1964 served as the basis for the estimates. The authors' estimates were checked by the marketing research department of a major oil company.

Footwear

Manufacturers' and private brand data were based upon the total unit output (nonrubber conventional footwear) of the 70 largest shoe manufacturers in the United States. The 70 largest shoe manufacturers were determined on the basis of pairage production. The years covered by the data were 1955, 1960, and 1964. The estimates were developed for this study by Mr. Iver M. Olson, Vice President for Market Research of the National Footwear Manufacturers' Association, Inc.

Replacement Tires

Estimates of manufacturers' and private brand share of unit volume in replacement tires were developed by the authors on an annual basis from 1930 through 1965. For the period from 1930 through 1948, the data used were compiled and published by Dr. Warren Leigh, consultant to the tire industry. Estimates for 1949 through 1965 were based on Look magazine's tire surveys[2] with adjustments made by the authors to correct for special conditions revealed by information supplied by cooperating tire manufacturers and distributors.

Household Appliances and Television Sets

Estimates of manufacturers' and private brand market share for eight appliances and TV sets were prepared by the Starch Marketing Data Service. The nine product categories were:

1. Electric refrigerators
2. Automatic washing machines
3. Clothes dryers
4. Home freezers
5. Air conditioners
6. B&W television sets
7. Portable and stand mixers
8. Electric toasters
9. Steam irons

Because the last three categories experienced similar patterns of private brand sales over the decade, they were grouped together. The same was true of dryers, freezers, air conditioners; estimates for these three categories were also grouped.

The data were based upon a known probability, multistage area sample of private households in the United States. The data represent appliance and television ownership or purchases for each of the nine product categories and were developed from a pooling of sample results for two successive years spread evenly over the decade from 1953-54 to 1963-64. Each of the two-year sample points include a pooled sample of over 45,000 households.

To protect its clients and provide meaningful data for the study, the Starch Marketing Data Service converted its estimated manufacturers' and distributors' brand market share data into index numbers with 1953-54 as the base. These data appear in Appendix D. The maximum sampling error for the original percentages was less than ± 2.5 percent for all categories. When converted to index numbers, the maximum sampling error was less than ± 20 points.

ANALYSIS OF DATA

The data were grouped and analyzed on the basis of the following general categories:

1. Aggregate Economic Factors
2. Manufacturers' Branding Policies
3. Distributors' Branding Policies

The literature abstracts, private brand data, completed interview guides, and each of the originally prepared 50 hypotheses were classified into these three categories. This organization served as the basis for data analysis and report writing.

Appendix B

Technical Matters

DEFINITIONS OF THE MAJOR PRODUCT LINES

The following pages contain detailed definitions of each major product line, or industry examined in this study. All data related to sales volume (in dollars or units) and other industry-wide measures are given consistency throughout the report because they are based on the definitions presented here.

The first five classifications are for the product lines referred to as "nondurables." The next three cover the lines referred to as "semidurables" and the final two classifications list the lines of "durables." Each definition is based on accepted trade practice.

MEASURES OF EXCESS INDUSTRY CAPACITY

Conceptually, the basic definition of aggregate excess capacity in an industry is the difference between "potential" unit output and "realized" unit output under standard operating conditions. There are three ways of approaching the measurement problem:

1. Maximum potential unit output less realized unit output
2. Maximum historical output less realized unit output
3. Expected unit output less realized unit output

Realized unit output data are readily available, even for narrowly defined product lines. In this report, the indices of Industrial Production generated by the Federal Reserve Board (FRB) were used as annual estimates of realized output. The Federal Reserve Board presents consistent series of unit output indices from 1947 through 1964 for what it calls "sub-thirty industries." This term refers to specific products such as washing machines, concentrated milk, and nonrubber footwear, and

Packaged Foods[*]

Items	Items

Baked Goods:
  White Bread
  Rolls
  **Crackers
  **Cookies (Chocolate chip and sand-
    wiches)
  Biscuits
  **Potato Chips
  Other Tidbits
 	
Dairy Products:
  **Cheese Slices
  Packaged Ice Cream
  Butter (for home consumption)
  Fresh Milk (for home consumption)
  **Margarine
 	
Baking & Flour Products:
  Cake Mixes
  **Pancake/Waffle Mixes
  **Flour
 	
Beverages:
  Cocoa
  **Regular Coffee
  **Soluble Coffee
  **Tea (Bags & instant)
  Prepared Food Drinks
  **Soft Drinks (all types)
 	
Canned Foods:
  **Baby Foods (Junior & strained)
  Seafoods
  **Fruits (five different items)
  **Juices (Pineapple, tomato, &
    vegetable)
  **Meats, Spiced
  **Milk, Evaporated
  Poultry
  **Soups
  **Vegetables
  Dinners
 	
Pet Foods:
  **Wet Dog Foods
  **Wet Cat Foods
  **Dry Dog/Cat Foods
  Bird Foods
	Cereals:
	  **Cold Cereals (Ready-to-eat)
	  **Hot Cereals
	  **Infant Cereals
	  **Rice, Prepackaged
	
	Condiments:
	  Barbecue Sauces
	  Catsup
	  Condiment Sauces
	  Prepared Mustard
	  Pepper
	  **Salt
	  Spices
	
	Desserts & Flavorings:
	  Gelatin
	  **Prepared Puddings (instant & tapioca)
	  Flavoring Extracts
	  Marshmallow Creme
	  Molasses
	  Sugar
	  **Syrup, Maple
	  **Toppings
	
	Dressings and Spreads:
	  Cooking & Salad Oils
	  Lard
	  **Shortening
	  Vegetable Shortening
	  **Mayonnaise
	  **Salad Dressings
	  Vinegar
	  **Peanut Butter
	  Citrus Marmalade
	  Fruit Butter
	  Preserves
	  Jellies
	
	Frozen Foods:
	  **Meat, Fish, Poultry
	  Precooked Foods
	  Vegetables
	  Fruits
	  Juices

[*]Definition of the "packaged foods" product line is based on the format used by *Food Topics* in their "18th Annual Study of What Consumers Spend," September, 1965, pp. 16-20.

[**]The A. C. Nielsen Company made data available on share of the market by type of brand for each of these products. It was agreed that figures would not be identified with specific products in this report in order to protect Nielsen's client interests. As a result, summary measures of the detailed data are presented in Appendix D.

Household Supplies*

Items	Items
Dry Cleaners: 　Home Dry Cleaning Fluids 　Spot Cleaning Liquids	*Paper Products*: 　**Cleansing Tissues 　Paper Cups 　Paper Plates
Laundry Supplies: 　**Bleaches, Household 　Bluing 　Laundry Starch	**Paper Towels 　Sanitary Napkins 　**Toilet Tissue 　Freezer Paper
Soaps & Detergents: 　**Cleansers 　Laundry Bar Soaps 　Soap Flakes, Chips, Pwd. 　**Synthetic Detergents 　Toilet Soaps	Garbage Bags 　**Paper Napkins 　Sandwich Bags 　Shelf Paper 　**Waxed Paper *Nonpaper Wrapping Products*:
Other Cleaners & Cleansers: 　Cellulose Sponges 　Drain Pipe Solvents 　Household Ammonia 　Household Floor Brooms 　Rug Cleaning Powders 　Steel Wool & Wire Spgs. 　Toilet Bowl Cleaners 　Wall & Floor Cleaners 　**Window Cleaning Liquids 　Other Cleaning Supplies	**Household Aluminum Foil 　**Plastic Wrap *Waxes & Polishes*: 　Automobile Polishes 　Furniture Polishes 　**Floor Wax 　Self-polishing Floor Wax *Misc. Household Supplies*: 　Electric Light Bulbs 　**Household Deodorizers
Home Canning Supplies: 　Caps, Lids, Bands 　Jars 　Rings	Disinfectants 　Tints & Dyes 　Boxed Matches 　Shoe Polishes 　Rubber Gloves
Household Pesticides: 　Aerosols 　Liquids 　Pastes & Solids	

*Definition of the "household supplies" product line is based on the format used by *Food Topics*, *op. cit.*, pp. 20-21.

**The A. C. Nielsen Company made data available on share of market by type of brand for each of these products. It was agreed that figures would not be identified with specific products in this report in order to protect Nielsen's client interests. As a result, summary measures of the detailed data are presented in Appendix D.

represents a more detailed enumeration of the "thirty components" of the Federal Reserve Board Index of Production. Estimates of output are published by the FRB as annual averages, and most figures are not available on a quarterly basis.

Approach number one above, requires estimates of maximum potential unit output. For these estimates, detailed information is needed on productive facilities in place, and the productive capacity of these facilities. The data needed for this method, however, are difficult to obtain from published sources. Corporate annual

Proprietary Drugs and Other Health Aids*

Items	Items
Vitamin Concentrates:	*External Antiseptics*:
Prescriptions	Liquids
Others	Aerosol
	Salves, Jellies, Pastes
Cough & Cold Items:	Powders
Cough Drops, Lozenges, Gums	Iodine
Cough Syrups, Elixirs	
Salves & Ointments	*Antacids*:
**Cold Tablets	Tablets, Pills, Gums
Antihistamines	Powders
Nose Drops, Nasal Sprays, Inhal.	Liquids
Room Decongestants	Milk of Magnesia Tablets
All Others	
	Other Packaged Medicaments:
Laxatives:	Burn Remedies
Tablets, Pills, Gums, Lozenges	Suntan Lotions & Oils
Milk of Magnesia Liquids	Eye Lotions & Washes
Mineral Oils	Lip Protectors
Mineral Oil Emulsions	All Others
Other Laxatives	
	Surgical Elastic Goods
Internal Analgesics:	
**Aspirin	*Home Health Rubber Products*
**Aspirin-Salicylate Compounds	
Arthritic & Rheumatic Pain Rel.	*Heating Pads & Lamps*
Others	
	Sickroom Equipment
Tonics & Alternatives:	
Liquids	*First Aid Products*:
Tablets, Pills, Lozenges	Adhesive Tape
Yeast Tablets, Powders	**Cotton Swabs
	Gauze Bandages & Dressings
External Analgesics:	Adhesive Bandages
**Salves, Ointments, Balms	First Aid Kits
Liniments	
Rubbing Alcohol	*Foot Products*:
Others	Foot Powder
	Salves & Ointments
Baby Needs:	All Others
Milk Modifiers & Formulas	
**Baby Powder	*Feminine Needs*:
**Baby Lotions	**Sanitary Products
Nursing Bottles	Hygiene Medicaments
Nipples	Other Feminine Needs
Pacifiers	
Bottle Sterilizers & Warmers	*Pet Health Products*
Food Warmers	
Disposable Diapers, Liners	
Cotton Swabs	
All Other Baby Needs	

*Definition of the "proprietary drugs and other health aids" product line is based on the format used by *Drug Trade News* in their "Summary of 1964 Sales of Drug Store Products," August 2, 1965, pp. S4-S8.

**The A.. C. Nielsen Company made data available on share of market by type of brand for each of these products. It was agreed that figures would not be identified with specific products in this report in order to protect Nielsen's client interests. As a result, summary measures of the detailed data are presented in Appendix D.

Toiletries[*]

Items	Item
Oral Hygiene Supplies:	*Shaving Accessories*:
Tooth Paste	**Razor Blades
Tooth Powder	Razors
Denture Cleansers	Razor Blade Sharpeners
Denture Adhesives	Razor Strops
**Tooth Brushes (Nonelectric)	Lather Brushes
Dental Floss	Men's Toiletry Sets
**Mouth Washes & Gargles	*Hand Preparations*:
Hair Preparations:	Hand Lotions & Creams
**Shampoos	Nail Polish & Enamel
Dandruff Rinses	Nail Enamel Removers
Hair Coloring Preparations	Cuticle Softeners
Hair Medicaments	*Manicure & Pedicure Implements*
Men's Hair Tonics	
Hair Dressings	*Face Creams*:
Cream Rinses	Cleansing Creams
Waveset Preparations	Lubricating Creams
Depilatories	Foundation Creams
Spray Hair Fixatives	Other Cosmetic Creams
**Home Permanent Kits & Refills	*Makeup Preparations & Accessories*
Hair Accessories:	Makeup Bases
Hair Brushes	Pressed Cake Powder
Combs	Loose Face Powder
Hair & Bobby Pins	Face Lotions & Astringents
Pin Curl Clips & Curlers	Liquid Facial Cleansers
Hair Nets	Talcum & Body Powder
Shaving Preparations:	Powder Puffs
**Shaving Cream	Lipsticks
Shaving Soaps & Sticks	Rouge
**Aftershave Lotion	Mascara
**Preshave Lotion	Eyebrow Pencil
Men's Talcum	Eye Shadow
Styptics	Compacts
Fragrance Preparations:	*Bathroom Accessories*:
Perfumes	Brushes
Toilet Water & Cologne	Sponges (all types)
Bath Salts, Tablets, Oils	Bathroom Scales
Purse Atomizers	All Other Accessories
External Personal Deodorants:	
All Types of Personal Deodorants	

[*]Definition of the "toiletries" product line is based on the format used by *Drug Trade News*, *op. cit.*, pp. S8-S10.

[**]The A. C. Nielsen Company made data available on share of market type of brand for each of these products. It was agreed that figures would not be identified with specific products in this report in order to protect Nielsen's client interests. As a result, summary measures of the detailed data are presented in Appendix D.

reports provide only a rough measure of total plant and equipment (because of depreciation provisions and changing costs over time), and data on specific product lines are seldom presented.

Gasoline

Product	Definitional Criteria
*Refined Gasoline	1. Noncommercial purchases for private use—excluding purchases by private taxicab owners 2. For use on the "highway"

*Private and manufacturers' brand share data are presented in Appendix D.

Footwear*

Product	Definitional Criterion
**Footwear, All Types	Nonrubber

*Specification of the different items contained within the footwear market may be found in *Facts and Figures on Footwear—1964 Supplement* (New York: National Shoe Manufacturers Association, 1965). In this report, no distinctions are made between different sizes and styles of footwear.
**Private and manufacturers' brand share data appear in Appendix D.

Tires*

Product	Definitional Criteria
**Tire Casings (all types)	1. For use on passenger cars 2. Purchased as replacement units by private final customers

*In this report, no distinctions are made between styles and size of replacement tires.
**Private and manufacturers' brand share data appear in Appendix D.

The second approach, requiring an estimate of maximum historical output, can be based on available realized output data. However, this method assumes that past peaks in output are good measures of current maximum capacity. Since ongoing capital expenditures as well as operating conditions (overtime, added shifts, etc.) affect historical output, this assumption may not always be correct, and judgmental revisions must subsequently be made.

Estimating expected unit output, a requirement of the third approach mentioned above, is simply an analytical judgment of capacity based on some system of data inputs. All capacity estimates are expected unit output estimates, with varying data input bases. Some estimates start with data in productive facilities, while others use historical output data as a base.

Electric Housewares*
(Portable Appliances)

Product	Definitional Criteria
Bed Coverings (electric) Blenders Broilers (all types) Can Openers (all types) Coffeemakers Cornpoppers Frypans Griddles Hair Dryers Heating Pads Hotplates **Irons (steam/spray) **Mixers (stand/portable) Polishers (floor) Sharpeners (knife) **Toasters (automatic-electric) **Toothbrushes Vacuum Cleaners Waffle Irons-Sandwich Grills	1. Portable household equipment 2. Using electric power 3. Purchased as independent units for private use by consumers

*Definition of the "electric housewares" product line is based on the format used by *Merchandising Week*, in their "1965 Statistical Report," January 25, 1965, pp. 24-25.
**Indices of private and manufacturers' brand share appear in Appendix D.

Household Appliances*

Product	Definitional Criteria
**Air Conditioners (room) **Automatic Washing Machines **Clothes Dryers (gas & electric) Dehumidifiers Dishwashers (all types) Disposers (food waste) **Freezers Ranges (gas & electric) **Refrigerators (electric)	1. Stationary household equipment 2. Purchased as independent units for private use by consumers

*Definition of the "household appliances" product line is based on the format used by *Merchandising Week*, *op. cit.*, pp. 22-23.
**Indices of private and manufacturers' brand share appear in Appendix D.

There are several published estimates of excess capacity. One method relies on an estimate of constant dollar book value of fixed capital (National Industrial Conference Board), another uses capital accumulation data (Fortune), and another conducts a plant and equipment survey (McGraw-Hill Department of Economics). Since for this study, capacity data were needed for individual

Consumer Electronics*
Products
Phonographs (all types) Radios (all types) **Black & White Television Sets (all types) Color Television Sets

*Definition of the "consumer electronics" product line is based on the format used by *Merchandising Week*, *loc. cit.*
**Indices of private and manufacturers' brand share appear in Appendix D.

product lines rather than entire segments of the economy, published estimates were too broadly defined to be of use. The approach used in this study was based on techniques used in the Wharton Index of Capacity Utilization. This index uses historical output data as a base. The estimating procedure for the Wharton Index is as follows:

> Briefly the method involves marking off cyclical peaks for each of thirty component indexes of the Federal Reserve Board Index of Industrial Production and fitting linear segments between successive peaks.[1]

The procedure employed in this study to estimate excess capacity in a specific industry is illustrated in Exhibits 50 (soluble coffee), and 51 (electric refrigerators). Excess capacity was defined as the difference between expected annual unit outputs and realized annual unit output. A projection of historical unit output was used to estimate expected unit output, much the same as in the method used for the Wharton Index of Capacity Utilization. The Wharton Index procedure was followed because:

1. It is applicable to specific products
2. Necessary data are available, and
3. It is a reasonable way to measure excess capacity

Three principal differences, however, exist between the method employed for the Wharton Index and those used to estimate excess capacity in this study. First, because quarterly data are not available for what the FRB refers to as "sub-thirty industries," annual output averages were used in place of quarterly peaks.

Second, the difference between expected output and realized output (estimated excess capacity) was not converted into a capacity utilization scale, but used simply as an index of excess capacity.

Third, examining small industry segments led to considerably more variation in each industry index of production than experienced in the indices of the thirty major components used in the

EXHIBIT 50

Illustration of Method Used to Estimate Excess Industry Capacity:
Soluble Coffee Industry

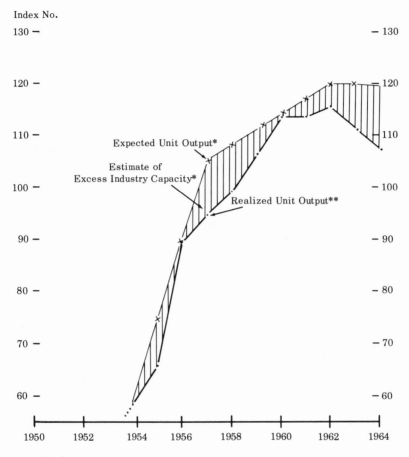

Index No.

*Authors' estimates.
**Index of Industrial Production, 1957- 59 = 100.

Wharton Index. With this increased variation, reasonable capacity
estimates required judgmental correction of expected output. In
those industries where output changed rapidly for two or three
years the linear projection technique used by Wharton was not
always followed. Instead, expected unit output was projected at
the same rate for one or two additional years and then projected
to the next cyclical peak. This was done in the belief that productive capacity is seldom eliminated at the same rate as that of
actual output decline (at least until a definite trend becomes

EXHIBIT 51

Illustration of Method Used to Estimate Excess Industry Capacity:
Electric Refrigerator Industry

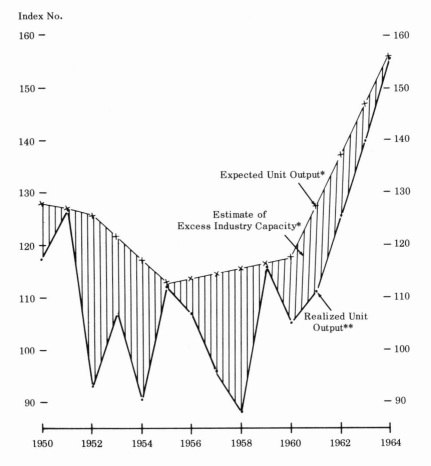

*Authors' estimates.
**Index of Industrial Production, 1957-59 = 100.

obvious to management), and that additions to capacity often exceed actual requirements during times of rapid expansion. The
procedure introduced an upward bias to excess capacity estimates
for years in which realized output declined. The effect on capacity
estimates of this assumed "lagged" response in capacity to changes
in realized output can be seen in Exhibits 50 and 51. The vertical
difference between expected and realized annual unit output is the
measure of estimated excess capacity for each year.

Estimates of excess capacity were made for 26 specific durable, semidurable, and nondurable products for which distributors' brand share data were available. The 26 products were divided as follows: five durable goods, five semidurable goods, and 16 nondurable goods. The time intervals studied were as long as 17 years (1948 through 1964 for automotive tires) and as short as five years (1960 through 1964 for soaps and detergents).

THE LEVEL OF PROSPERITY

In this study, the level of prosperity was defined as the cyclical behavior of fifteen roughly coincident indicators compiled by the National Bureau of Economic Research (NBER), and made available on a current-month basis in the Department of Commerce publication Business Cycle Developments.

In the introduction to the monthly Business Cycle Developments, the following comment is made:

Intensive research by the National Bureau of Economic Research (NBER) over many years has provided a list of those significant series that usually lead, those that usually move with, and those that usually lag behind cyclical movements in aggregate economic activity. The series have been grouped and classified by the NBER as "leading," "roughly coincident," or "lagging" indicators.[2]

The "roughly coincident" indicators, following the numbering system used in Business Cycle Developments,[3] together with their sources, are listed below:

40. Unemployment rate, married males, spouse present—Department of Labor, Bureau of Labor Statistics
41. Number of employees in nonagricultural establishments—Department of Labor, Bureau of Labor Statistics
42. Total nonagricultural employment, labor force survey—Department of Labor, Bureau of Labor Statistics, and Department of Commerce, Bureau of the Census
43. Unemployment rate, total—Department of Labor, Bureau of Labor Statistics, and Department of Commerce, Bureau of the Census
45. Average weekly insured unemployment rate, State programs—Department of Labor, Bureau of Employment Security
46. Index of help-wanted advertising in newspapers—National Industrial Conference Board
47. Index of industrial production—Board of Governors of the Federal Reserve System
49. Gross national product in current dollars—Department of Commerce, Office of Business Economics

50. Gross national product in 1958 dollars—Department of Commerce, Office of Business Economics
51. Bank debits, all standard metropolitan statistical areas except New York—Board of Governors of the Federal Reserve System
52. Personal income—Department of Commerce, Office of Business Economics
53. Labor income in mining, manufacturing, and construction—Department of Commerce, Office of Business Economics
54. Sales of retail stores—Department of Commerce, Bureau of the Census
55. Index of wholesale prices, all commodities other than farm products and foods—Department of Labor, Bureau of Labor Statistics; seasonal adjustment by Bureau of the Census
57. Final sales—Department of Commerce, Office of Business Economics.

From these individual indicators, the NBER determines "the approximate dates when aggregate economic activity reached its cyclical high or low levels."[4] These are designated business cycle peaks and troughs. For this study, selection of each period of low prosperity was based on the estimates of economic peaks and troughs as designated by the NBER and presented in Business Cycle Developments. Basically, a period of low prosperity was defined for this report as the time interval beginning midway between a peak and trough and ending midway between the trough and the succeeding peak.

The pattern of fluctuation of each indicator varied considerably with each major economic cycle, making it necessary to refine the basic estimates of periods of low prosperity. This was accomplished by an analysis of the movements of the more sensitive "roughly coincident indicators" and an adjustment in the estimated peak-trough midpoint. The result was a close approximation of the actual lower half of each business cycle as the period of "low prosperity." Time intervals on the upper half of each cycle were called periods of "high prosperity."

The index of help-wanted advertising in newspapers, compiled by the National Industrial Conference Board, was the only individual business indicator used for comparative purposes in the section on the measurement of levels of prosperity. This "roughly coincident indicator" was selected because of the following characteristics:

1. "The help-wanted index has been extremely sensitive to changes in general business conditions. All the economic cycles of the past 40 years have had their counterparts in the movements of the help-wanted index, and the relatively large swings in the index."[5]

2. The index is highly correlated with, but more sensitive than levels of unemployment and personal income. "...(T)he amplitude of the help-wanted index has been considerably larger than the amplitude of general measures of economic activity."[6]

3. It has been established that the help-wanted index "has reached a peak in the last three cycles several months before the high point in general business activity,"[7] and, thus, has potential as a lead indicator of the level of personal income and unemployment.

4. The index has experienced no secular growth trend. This means that, using this indicator, the identification of economic peaks and troughs is considerably simplified.

5. The index is currently available and directly comparable with the indices of distributors' brand market share used in this analysis.

Four comparisons of grocery product private brand market share with the NICB Index are presented in Exhibit 52 to supplement the comparisons developed in Chapter III.

RESPONSES OF NATIONAL ADVERTISING TO PRIVATE BRANDS

National advertising estimates for each product line were developed by adding up published expenditure data on individual brands in four different media. Initial examination of the data revealed that advertising expenditures by a relatively small percentage of manufacturers in an industry accounted for a large proportion of total advertising. Thus, since the same brands had to be used in each medium for a given product line to maintain consistency, only expenditures on leading manufacturers' brands were included in the estimates.

Comparisons of changes in advertising and private branding to supplement those which appeared in Chapter III are presented on the following pages. In all product lines, linear projections between periodic estimates of national advertising were used as trend lines. Each estimate was an average of expenditures in two successive years, such as 1963 and 1964.

Four media were used to develop estimates of national advertising expenditures at selected points in time for 12 product lines. These were newspapers, spot television, network television, and magazines. Data on radio advertising were not included because they were not available by individual product. Sources of the advertising expenditure data by media are listed below:

EXHIBIT 52

Changes in Prosperity and Private Brand Share in Selected Nondurable Product Lines
(Continued from Chapter III)

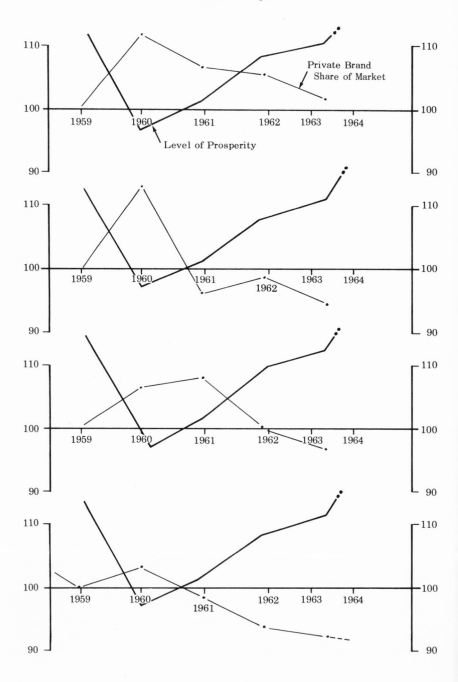

Newspapers

Newspaper advertising expenditures were obtained from Advertising Age, which annually publishes the data by company and product.

Television

Expenditures for television advertising were divided into two categories—spot and network. The sources of data on spot television expenditures were:

Annual Rorabaugh Report on Spot Television Advertising Expenditures. Published by N. C. Rorabaugh Co., Inc., New York, N. Y. (1960 and 1963).

1964 Spot TV Expenditures for Selectronic Marketing, Published by Television Bureau of Advertising, Inc., New York, N. Y.

Expenditures on network television were obtained from:

LNA-BAR Network Television Advertising Expenditures. Published by Miller Associates, Inc., Norwalk, Conn. (Various years from 1953 to 1964.)

Magazines

Expenditures on magazines were obtained from:

National Advertising Investments. Published by Leading National Advertisers, Inc., Norwalk Conn. (Various years from 1953 to 1964.)

MEASURES OF THE PRODUCT LIFE CYCLE IN 24 LINES

Product life cycles for all but three of the 24 product lines were estimated from data on retail value of shipments adapted from Food Topics and Merchandising Week, adjusted for secular price trends. The three exceptions were electric refrigerators, replacement tires, and footwear. Data on unit volume of shipments were used to estimate product life cycles of these product lines.

Refrigerators posed a special problem. Essentially two products were involved—"single door refrigerators," and "combination refrigerator freezers." Product life cycle estimates

EXHIBIT 53

Changes in National Advertising and Private Branding for a Product Line* Where
Private Brand Share Remains Under 10 Percent

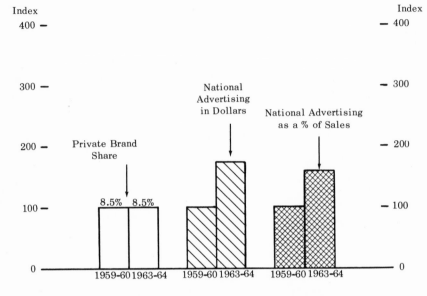

Changes in National Advertising and Private Branding for a Product Line* Where
Private Brand Share Remains Under 10 Percent

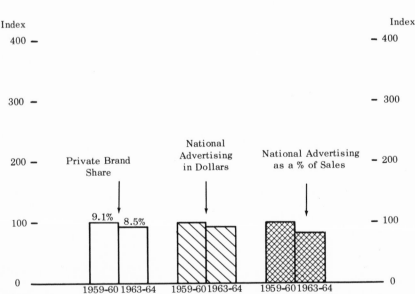

*Product lines unidentified at request of data sources.

EXHIBIT 54

Changes in National Advertising and Private Branding for a Product Line* Where
Private Brand Share Reaches 11 Percent

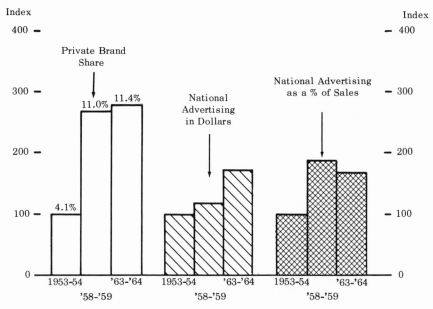

Changes in National Advertising and Private Branding for a Product Line* Where
Private Brand Share Reaches 36 Percent

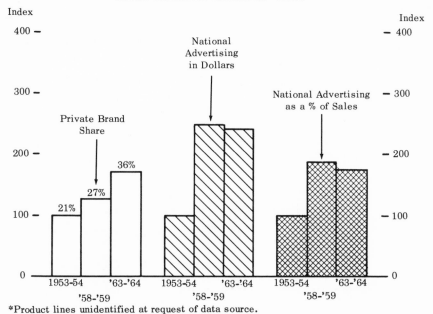

*Product lines unidentified at request of data source.

EXHIBIT 55

Changes in National Advertising and Private Branding for a Product Line* Where
Private Brand Share Remains at 40 Percent

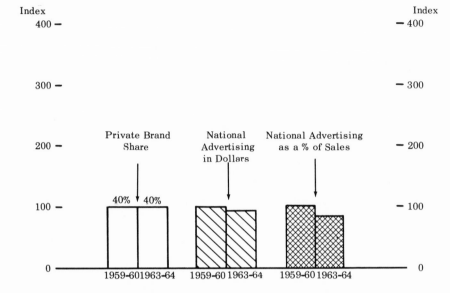

Changes in National Advertising and Private Branding for a Product Line* Where
Private Brand Share Reaches 42 Percent

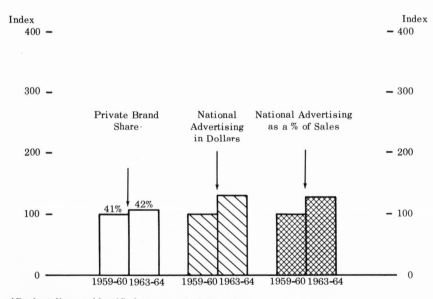

*Product lines unidentified at request of data source.

EXHIBIT 56

Data Used in Estimating Product Life Cycles
(Millions of Dollars)

	Canned Milk Adjusted by Food at Home C.P.I.		Regular Coffee Adjusted by Food at Home C.P.I.		Prepared Pudding Adjusted by Food at Home C.P.I.		Margarine Adjusted by Food at Home C.P.I.	
	A	B	A	B	A	B	A	B
1947	468.6	490.0	1,152	1,220			355.2	315.0
1948	498.9	487.0	1,293	1,390	36.7	35.0	413.7	320.0
1949	466.2	479.0	1,506	1,600	36.2	35.9	314.8	328.0
1950	469.7	468.0	2,113	1,870	36.9	36.5	334.6	337.0
1951	449.4	459.0	2,106	1,990	32.9	37.0	353.3	356.0
1952	445.2	448.0	2,097	2,100	34.8	38.0	362.5	362.0
1953	441.7	438.0	2,192	2,170	38.9	38.5	380.3	380.0
1954	413.3	429.0	2,250	2,250	47.7	39.0	411.1	385.0
1955	411.9	418.0	2,086	2,170	44.9	39.9	412.6	400.0
1956	420.7	408.0	2,351	2,140	45.2	40.5	418.9	418.0
1957	412.3	399.0	2,289	2,090	44.2	41.3	442.9	435.0
1958	386.1	387.0	2,045	2,040	43.5	42.0	442.5	452.0
1959	384.0	378.0	1,809	1,950	42.8	42.9	452.2	462.0
1960	381.6	367.0	1,804	1,900	41.4	43.4	475.4	475.0
1961	370.3	356.0	1,784	1,860	41.9	44.5	492.0	483.0
1962	343.1	347.0	1,720	1,840	44.4	45.5	484.7	484.0
1963	322.5	329.0	1,736	1,800	45.6	46.5	479.6	485.0
1964	307.7	315.0	1,970	1,780	48.6	48.0	465.5	479.0

A. Dollar consumption adjusted by C.P.I.
B. Estimated secular trend.

EXHIBIT 56 (Continued)

Data Used in Estimating Product Life Cycles
(Millions of Dollars)

	Liquid Window Cleaner		Paper Towels		Salt		Vegetable Shortening	
	Adjusted by Soap & Detergent C.P.I.		Adjusted by Toilet Tissue C.P.I		Adjusted by Food at Home C.P.I.		Adjusted by Food at Home C.P.I.	
	A	B	A	B	A	B	A	B
1947			20.0	20.0	46.2	47.5	192.5	162.0
1948	12.4		19.5	20.0	50.8	48.7	162.3	162.0
1949	17.3		22.1	21.0	52.1	49.7	161.8	163.0
1950	16.6	11.1	25.5	23.0	51.9	50.2	164.1	164.0
1951	11.5	11.4	22.9	22.9	48.8	51.1	150.6	165.0
1952	11.9	11.7	25.1	25.1	47.2	51.9	157.3	168.0
1953	12.2	12.0	28.1	28.1	49.5	52.5	188.9	173.0
1954	12.0	12.5	31.1	31.1	51.5	53.0	182.7	182.0
1955	12.1	13.0	36.1	36.1	53.8	53.8	182.8	187.0
1956	12.4	13.6	42.1	42.1	54.3	54.1	211.6	193.0
1957	13.8	14.7	49.1	49.1	56.1	54.8	197.9	195.0
1958	14.0	14.9	54.5	54.5	54.2	54.9	185.6	200.0
1959	15.0	15.5	61.3	61.3	54.9	55.0	187.3	202.0
1960	15.2	15.8	72.7	72.7	55.0	55.1	201.6	201.0
1961				83.0	55.2	55.2		
1962	16.2	16.4	92.7	92.7	56.0	55.2	206.4	198.0
1963	16.7	16.8	101.7	104.0	55.8	55.1	191.8	192.0
1964	17.9	17.5	118.4	116.0	54.0	55.0	179.5	182.0

A. Dollar consumption adjusted by C.P.I.
B. Estimated secular trend.

EXHIBIT 56 (Continued)

Data Used in Estimating Product Life Cycles
(Millions of Dollars)

	Soluble Coffee Adjusted by Food at Home C.P.I.		Cleansing Tissue Adjusted by Cleansing Tissue C.P.I.		Soap and Detergent Adjusted by Soap & Detergent C.P.I.		Bathroom Tissue Adjusted by Toilet Tissue C.P.I.	
	A	B	A	B	A	B	A	B
1947	48.4	53.0	70.1		123.7	110.0	134.7	112.0
1948	55.8	57.0	90.5		124.8	150.0	125.0	124.0
1949	65.6	60.0	95.7		181.2	200.0	137.9	135.0
1950	89.4	70.0	111.0		257.4	250.0	161.7	148.0
1951	88.9	89.0	116.3		302.6	317.0	156.0	160.0
1952	105.9	118.0	121.2		355.6	368.0	164.2	173.0
1953	144.9	160.0	125.6	118.0	471.6	426.0	183.4	179.0
1954	348.9	258.0	130.9	125.0	508.7	490.0	200.4	196.0
1955	368.6	398.0	138.9	133.0	566.6	550.0	219.0	208.0
1956	425.1	440.0	147.2	140.0	623.3	608.0	232.6	222.0
1957	480.6	460.0	156.6	150.0	665.3	660.0	251.6	235.0
1958	465.0	470.0	165.7	160.0	715.0	718.0	260.9	250.0
1959	449.0	471.0	170.8	170.0	772.7	760.0	266.3	265.0
1960	465.1	472.0	180.5	183.0	827.5	810.0	273.5	280.0
1961	486.3	473.0		193.0		860.0		295.0
1962	474.3	479.0	195.6	204.0	895.9	908.0	309.1	310.0
1963	465.5	481.0	208.5	216.0	938.7	948.0	323.3	328.0
1964	516.4	489.0	218.8	229.0	991.0	1,000.0	340.2	346.0

A. Dollar consumption adjusted by C.P.I.
B. Estimated secular trend.

EXHIBIT 56 (Continued)

Data Used in Estimating Product Life Cycles
(Millions of Dollars)

	Baby Powder Adjusted by Consumer Nondurables Less Food C.P.I.		Preshave Lotion Adjusted by Toilet Goods C.P.I.		Aspirin Tablets Adjusted by Aspirin C.P.I.		Bandages Adjusted by Consumer Nondurables Less Food C.P.I.		Deodorant Adjusted by Toilet Goods C.P.I.	
	A	B	A	B	A	B	A	B	A	B
1947	10.6	9.5			41.6	42.0	18.5	18.0	28.7	29.0
1948	9.8	10.5			42.5	42.5	18.1	19.0	32.1	31.0
1949	10.7	11.0			43.0	43.0	19.5	21.0	34.9	34.0
1950	12.4	11.9			46.0	45.0	24.9	23.0	40.4	38.0
1951	13.3	13.0			49.8	47.0	26.8	27.0	42.6	43.0
1952	15.5	14.8			51.9	49.0	35.1	32.0	47.3	49.0
1953	16.8	16.0			52.7	52.0	37.5	37.0	52.6	55.0
1954	16.9	17.5	2.5	2.5	54.7	54.0	42.8	42.0	67.3	62.0
1955	18.8	18.5	4.1	4.1	56.0	57.0	47.7	46.5	76.1	68.5
1956	19.1	19.4	5.5	5.3	58.2	61.0	50.4	51.0	82.2	76.0
1957	20.5	19.9	6.2	6.2	63.4	64.0	54.7	55.0	87.7	83.0
1958	20.6	20.4	6.8	7.0	64.9	68.0	58.1	59.0	88.8	90.0
1959	20.5	20.5	7.7	7.7	67.3	70.0	62.0	61.0	93.5	98.0
1960	20.6	20.6	8.4	8.4	73.9	73.0	62.6	65.5	100.3	106.0
1961	21.3	20.4	9.1	9.0	77.6	75.0	64.8	68.0	109.9	113.0
1962	20.4	20.0	9.6	9.6	78.5	77.0	70.4	70.0	118.2	120.0
1963	18.5	19.4	10.2	10.1			72.4	71.5	128.3	126.0
1964	18.8	18.8	10.3	10.4			73.9	73.0	134.5	132.0

A. Dollar consumption adjusted by C.P.I.
B. Estimated secular trend.

EXHIBIT 56 (Continued)

Data Used in Estimating Product Life Cycles
(Millions of Dollars)

	Black and White TV — Adjusted by Black and White TV C.P.I.		Portable Mixers — Adjusted by Appliances C.P.I.		Automatic Washing Machines — Adjusted by Washing Machine C.P.I.		Electric Blankets — Adjusted by Appliances C.P.I.	
	A	B	A	B	A	B	A	B
1947					286	310	22.4	20.0
1948			0.3	0.4	260	320	23.5	21.0
1949			2.2	0.6	229	340	14.0	22.0
1950		1,460	2.2	1.5	413	360	27.3	24.0
1951	1,350	1,620	1.9	3.2	408	380	26.9	27.0
1952	1,550	1,720	7.3	6.0	429	410	29.8	30.0
1953	1,895	1,760	10.0	9.9	534	450	30.9	35.0
1954	1,697	1,760	16.9	14.8	620	490	34.0	40.0
1955	1,858	1,680	29.9	20.5	824	540	42.0	46.0
1956	1,489	1,600	48.5	30.0	909	590	57.9	53.0
1957	1,236	1,500	43.9	36.8	777	640	56.6	60.0
1958	1,007	1,430	37.1	40.9	791	700	62.1	69.0
1959	1,333	1,380	40.0	43.5	846	760	76.1	77.0
1960	1,242	1,340	44.4	45.4	727	800	77.5	83.0
1961	1,299	1,310	43.7	46.8	752	850	84.4	88.0
1962	1,316	1,290	46.2	47.8	853	890	93.5	92.0
1963	1,372	1,290	44.7	48.3	927	920	105.2	95.0
1964	1,465		50.8	48.9	991	950	93.5	97.0

A. Dollar consumption adjusted by C.P.I.
B. Estimated secular trend.

EXHIBIT 56 (Continued)

Data Used in Estimating Product Life Cycles
(Millions of Dollars)

	Replacement Tires	Footwear (exc. rubber)	Refrigerators Single Door	Refrigerators Double Door
	Physical Units	Physical Units	Physical Units	Physical Units
	B	B	B	B
1947	34.8	470.0		
1948	35.9	480.5		
1949	37.0	490.5		
1950	38.7	500.5		
1951	40.4	515.0		
1952	42.5	525.0	3250	325
1953	45.0	535.0	3300	375
1954	48.9	545.0	3300	425
1955	52.0	555.0	3250	500
1956	55.9	565.0	3075	650
1957	59.2	575.0	2800	850
1958	63.0	585.0	2450	1075
1959	66.5	590.5	2150	1350
1960	69.9	600.0	1850	1600
1961	73.2	605.0	1625	1900
1962	76.4	610.5	1550	2250
1963	80.0	615.5	1500	2550
1964	83.0	620.0	1500	2950

B. Estimated secular trend.

were developed for each product from percentage estimates of double and single door refrigerator unit shipments obtained from various annual statistical issues of *Merchandising Week*. For both replacement tires and footwear, data on unit volume of shipments were obtained from trade association sources. These data were used in the product life cycle analysis because they were the best available and did not entail price change calculations.

The preceding exhibits present data used in estimating the product life cycle for each of 24 products. The exhibits include:

Column A. Estimated trends in consumption for each product after adjustment for price changes. The Consumer Price Price Index (C.P.I.) used to make the adjustment is noted.

Column B. Estimated secular, or long-term trend after adjustment for cyclical variation.

The product life cycle estimates presented in Chapter III were taken as the value of year-to year changes (first derivative) in the secular trend of consumption in constant dollars. (Column B in each exhibit.)

Appendix C

The Economic Value of Consumer Preference for a Brand

THE COURTS, REGULATORY agencies and even business custom have long recognized the economic value of the trademark.

> If it is true that we live by symbols, it is no less true that we purchase goods by them. A trademark is a merchandising shortcut which induces a purchaser to select what he wants. The owner of a mark exploits this human propensity by making every effort to impregnate the atmosphere of the market with the drawing power of a congenial symbol. Whatever the means employed, the aim is the same—to convey through the mark, in the minds of potential customers, the desirability of the commodity upon which it appears. Once this is attained, the trademark owner has something of value.[1]

In more specific terms,

> ... reviewing a recent anti-merger case the Federal Trade Commission noted that the XYZ Company paid more than $30 million for the assets of the acquired company although they were valued at only $15 million. The FTC pointed out that the difference represented the value of the [latter's] trademark and goodwill.[2]

Unfortunately, this explicit recognition of the "economic value" of a trademark has not been consistently applied in all regulatory action of the Federal Trade Commission. In enforcing Sec. 2 of the Robinson–Patman Amendment to the Clayton Act, the Commission has denied the economic value of consumer preference for a brand several times. The cases involved the question of what constituted "like grade and quality" in price discrimination proceedings.

Section 2(a) of the Robinson–Patman Act reads in part:

> It shall be unlawful for any person engaged in commerce, in the course of such commerce, either directly or indirectly, to discriminate in price between different purchasers of commodities of *like grade and quality* ...[3] (Italics inserted.)

Here, the phase "like grade and quality" is a jurisdictional element which is necessary for the establishment of *any* Robinson–Patman Act violation.

Since the passage of the Act in 1936, the Commission has usually not considered the economic value of consumer preference for a brand in determining the grade or quality of products for the purposes of enforcing Sec. 2(a), but has considered trademark value to be important in enforcing other sections of the Act.

HISTORICAL BACKGROUND

The first important Federal Trade Commisssion case[4] which involved the issue of the economic value of consumer preference for a brand, centered on the marketing activities of The Goodyear Tire & Rubber Company (Goodyear) in its sale of distributors' brand tires to Sears, Roebuck and Co. (Sears).

In 1926, Sears began selling automobile tires under its own Allstate brand, and, by 1933 had become the largest tire distributor in the United States. Goodyear was the original supplier of the Allstate brand tires. On March 1, 1935, the Federal Trade Commission issued a complaint against Goodyear which stated that the

... respondent in the course and conduct of interstate commerce ... has, since May 1, 1926, discriminated in price, and is now discriminating in price, between the different purchasers of its said products, by giving and allowing said Sears, Roebuck & Co. a lower price than given or allowed other purchasers competitively engaged in said line of commerce ... Said discrimination in price has not been made, and is not now made, on account of differences in the grade, quality, or quantity sold, nor has said discrimination made only due allowance ... for difference in the cost of selling or transportation, nor has said discrimination in price ... been made ... in good faith to meet competition.[5]

Goodyear, in trying to meet these complaints, involved the cost justification defense.

According to evidence presented by Goodyear and subsequently analyzed and interpreted by the Federal Trade Commission, this defense was declared weak and finally rejected. The evidence indicated that:

the average gross discrimination [price difference] on these four sizes for the entire period of time ... was approximately 40%. On other sizes the gross discrimination over the entire period varied from 32% to 42%.[6]

Taking into consideration what it believed justifiable cost differences in serving a large chain customer, the Commission concluded that:

The net average sales discrimination remaining after deductions had been made from the dealer prices for discounts and allowances and transportation over the entire period varied from 29% to 40% on eight sizes of tires.[7]

With cost justification rejected and with the meeting of competition in good faith not an issue to either party, there remained the important question of "grade and quality."

Results of the hearings give an indication that the respondent did not voluntarily select, nor in fact use, the question of "quality" differences between "Goodyear" and "Allstate" tires as a key point of defense. Evidence of this is found in the respondent's admission that:

> for the purposes of this case, ... corresponding grades of Goodyear and Sears, Roebuck & Co.'s tires, such as the Goodyear "All Weather" brand and the "Companion" and Sears, Roebuck & Co.'s "Allstate" brand the "Pathfinder," respectively, may be considered as comparable in quality. [8]

However, Goodyear was not prepared to agree that "All Weather" and "Allstate" tires were the same product in the mind of the customer. This raised an implicit question as to the economic value of the market acceptance of the Goodyear brand as an attribute of the product.

The notion that strong market acceptance may significantly increase the value of a branded product was introduced as evidence by several of the dealer witnesses testifying on behalf of Goodyear. Among the several factors which these dealers "contended gave them the ability to sell Goodyear brand tires at higher prices than those received by Sears, Roebuck & Co.'s tires offering competition"[9] were:

1. Greater public acceptance or public preference for the Goodyear "All Weather" brand.
2. The Sears "Allstate" brand is as distinct from Goodyear brands as are the tires of other manufacturers.
3. The Goodyear national advertising program, which involved an annual investment of $4,500,000 or roughly $72,000,000 during the existence of such programs, "was pointed to as giving and maintaining respondent's public acceptance or public preference and its extensive goodwill."[10]

In answer to these statements, the Commission chose not to deal directly with the issue of market value in the brand name as an attribute of the product. Instead, the issue was avoided by evidence which indicated that Sears was "trading on the Goodyear brand name" by selling its "Allstate" brand tires as the products of the "world's foremost tire manufacturer." The Examiner apparently established that both the trade and a large portion of consumers were aware of the arrangements existing between the two firms.

Rather than give weight to the importance of this issue, in filing opinions and the cease and desist order which followed, the Commission chose to dwell upon the "lack of due allowance" for cost differences in the prices of Goodyear brand and Sears brand tires.

The subsequent appeal by Goodyear was based in part upon the Commission's interpretation of Sec. 2 of the new Robinson-Patman Amendment to the Clayton Act.[11]

...That section declares it to be unlawful to discriminate in price between purchasers of commodities where the effect of such discrimination may be to substantially lessen competition or tend to create a monopoly in any line of commerce, subject to the proviso: "That nothing herein contained shall prevent discrimination between purchasers of commodities on account of differences in grade, quality, or quantity of the commodity sold, or that makes only due allowance for difference in cost selling or transportation, or discrimination in price in the same or different communities made in good faith to meet competition." The petitioner contends that a discrimination in price is permitted if based upon the commodity sold, without respect to whether it makes only due allowance for difference in cost of selling or transportation.[12]

However, the order of the Federal Trade Commission was set aside on other grounds, and the specific issue of economic value in the market acceptance of a brand name was left unsettled in the courts.

Neither judicial inquiry nor legislative debate arising from the Robinson-Patman Amendment gave reasoned consideration to this issue.

At one point during the subcommittee hearings on Representative Patman's bill, the suggestion was made to change the first paragraph to read:

... unlawful ... to discriminate in price between different purchasers of commodities of like grade and quality *and brands* ... (Emphasis added to show change.)

Apparently, supporters of the bill feared that the courts would construe this to mean that the sale of commodities which differ only as to the label would be outside the reach of the statute. In the Congressional Record, one such supporter, Mr. H. B. Teegarden, then counsel to the United States Wholesale Grocers Association is quoted as follows:

... To amend the bill by inserting "and brands," after the words "commodities of like grade and quality," ... although it may seem harmless at first sight, is a specious suggestion that would destroy entirely the efficacy of the bill against large buyers... Under the Patman bill as it stands, manufacturers are still free to put up their products under private brands, but if they do so for one purchaser under his private brands, then they must be ready to do so on the same terms, relative to their competitive costs, for a competing purchaser under his private brand; and, unless that equity of treatment be required and assured, the discrimination at which the bill is aimed cannot be suppressed.[13]

The importance of administrative precedents[14] can be seen in the following statement by Federal Trade Commissioner, Paul Rand Dixon:

> The Commission in a number of prior proceedings has held that goods which are the same in all respects except labels are comparable goods for the purposes of Section 2, or goods of like grade and quality. In The Goodyear Tire & Rubber Company ... (1936), reversed on other grounds ... , a pre-Robinson-Patman Act proceeding, the Commission held, *in effect* [italics inserted] that private label tires and Goodyear's own brands of tires were comparable in grade and quality. Under the Clayton Act, as amended by the Robinson-Patman Act, the Commission in United States Rubber Co., et al., ... (1939) and United States Rubber Company ... (1950) prohibited discriminatory price differentials between sellers' brands and customers' private labels. In these cases the Commission *disregarded brand differences* [italics inserted] and found the products to be of like grade and quality. Similarly, in Page Dairy Co., ... (1953), different label markings were held to be without significance.[15]

As evidenced by the history of litigation traced in the preceding pages, the fundamental issue of the economic value of consumer preference for a brand name recognized within the meaning of the statute and administrative precedent was not dealt with explicitly. In effect, the precedent cited by the Commissioner developed independently from the issue over which he implied its jurisdiction.

Adjudication in the courts was of little help in providing a foundation of reasoned evaluation and precedent. The Federal Trade Commission's decisions simply were not challenged on the specific basis of their disregard for important brand differences.

Even one who does not support the basic intentions of Sec. 2 of the Robinson-Patman Act must agree with Representative Patman that:

> The mere fact that [a firm] may have placed [its] brand on one article and does not brand another of like grade and quality does not perceptibly change the *cost* [italics inserted] of either article.[16]

It is one thing to argue that differences in brand ownership do not cause "perceptible differences" in the production cost of articles of like grade and quality. It is quite another to argue that differences in the market acceptance of brand names on goods of like physical grade and quality cannot cause perceptible differences in free market value of either article. Such a statement would be unreasoned in the face of clear market evidence to the contrary.

For example, in assessing the value of a trademark as an asset, one cannot look to "cost" for fair value. A trademark, per se, costs very little. Its real value as an asset is determined wholly by its strength in a free market. Whatever value is embodied in the trademark, over and above the worth of tangible assets, is derived from the market in which the goods are sold under the mark. Few would argue that value so determined is not real.

Yet, for purposes of enforcement of Sec. 2(a) of the Robinson-Patman Act, the Federal Trade Commission has not considered the economic value of consumer preference for a brand name to be important in determining the grade and quality of products. The reasoning seems to be that applying different labels to physically similar products does not appreciably change product costs; therefore, the products carrying these different brands cannot be of different value, and must be considered of "like grade and quality."

On this issue, The Report of the Attorney General's National Committee to Study the Antitrust Laws concluded:

Actual and genuine physical differentiations between two different products adapted to the several buyers' uses, and not merely a decorative or fanciful feature, probably remove differential pricing of the two from the reach of the Robinson-Patman Act. To that extent, we believe, the [Federal Trade Commission] decisions take realistic account of the limitations which must qualify the scope of the statute.

Some Committee members nevertheless think that business actualities may often contradict the Federal Trade Commission's policy of ignoring brands and trade names in determining what are "goods of like grade and quality" under the Act. They emphasize that in some industries heavy national advertising and sales promotion have cultivated significant consumer preferences in a brand-conscious American public. Particularly on commodities for resale, they urge that resale value and mobility is an aspect of "grade and quality." For commodities containing precisely identical ingredients but packaged under a distinctive mark or label may not command equal consumer acceptance. Nationally advertised "premium" goods are "competitive" with unknown entities or "economy" brands only at a significant margin in price. In their opinion, a price discrimination law can consider heavily advertised and anonymous or private-brand merchandise on an equal legal footing only at a serious distortion of economic facts. Accordingly, they propose that demonstrable *economic* differences be evaluated under the statutory term "grade" as distinct from any purely physical consideration of "quality."

The majority of this Committee, however, recommends that the economic factors inherent in brand names and national advertising should not be considered in the jurisdictional inquiry under the statutory "like grade and quality" test. They do not dispute that heavy expenditures in advertisement and promotion of certain commodities have built up distinct consumer preferences that manifest themselves in real price margins as between branded and unbranded products the buying public is willing to pay. However, the Committee majority believes that abandonment of a physical test of grade and quality in favor of a marketing comparison of intrinsically identical goods might not only enmesh the administrators of the statute in complex economic investigations for every price discrimination charge, but also could encourage easy evasion of the statute through artificial variations in the packaging, advertising or design of the goods which the seller wishes to distribute at differential prices. For a determination that the goods are not of "like grade and quality" entirely exempts the transaction from all pricing restrictions of the Act. Moreover, a construction of the statutory concept of "like grade and quality" to exclude price differentials in a *sellers' simultaneous* [italics inserted] distribution of branded and unbranded goods would, in the opinion of the Committee majority, depart from the plain intent of the statute's draftsmen who, in 1936, sought to amend the Clayton Act to reach those exorbitant discriminations favoring private brand customers over the seller's regular distributors exemplified in the Goodyear Tire & Rubber case.

Rather, the Committee majority believes that tangible consumer preferences as between branded and unbranded commodities should receive due legal recognition in the more flexible "injury" and "cost justification" provision of the statute.[17]

Within varying degrees of consensus, the economic actualities of trademark value were recognized by the Attorney General's

Committee. However, a belief that the abandonment of a physical test of grade and quality in favor of an economic test would involve complexity in administration and easy evasion took precedent in the majority recommendation.

THE BORDEN CASE

Although the legal construction of "like grade and quality" is vital to the Robinson-Patman Act, approximately thirty years passed before the Supreme Court rendered an interpretation of the phrase. The case which served as the vehicle for this ruling was the Borden Company versus the Federal Trade Commission.[18] In this complaint, the Borden Company (Borden) was charged with price discrimination in the sale of "like grade and quality" evaporated milk under the Borden brand and under various private labels.[19] Borden responded to the charge by attempting to prove that there was no substantital lessening of competition and that the price differences were cost justified. In addition, the company argued that there were important differences in consumer prefernce between Borden brand milk and the distributors' brand milk it supplied that must be recognized at law. Borden did not:

> contend that all brand differences result in goods of unlike or different grade and quality ... Respondent argue [d] instead, that a distinction should be made between differing situations as follows:
> (a) the situation where the brand name is not shown to represent any significant added value being sold by the manufacturer, and
> (b) the situation where, as is asserted in the present case, the manufacturer's well-known brand name has a very substantial and commercially demonstrated significance.[20]

The decision of the Federal Trade Commission Hearing Examiner, Abner E. Lipscomb, was rendered on December 30, 1961. He found that evaporated milk under the Borden brand and the private labels are commodities of "like grade and quality" for purposes of the Act. However, the examiner held that no price discrimination in violation of the Act was established because it had not been shown that competition had been substantially lessened or that a reasonable probability existed of damage to competition in the future. The examiner also held that Borden had fully cost-justified the price differences shown. The complaint was subsequently dismissed.

Both parties appealed the decision to the full Commission. Counsel supporting the complaint challenged the finding of a lack of competitive injury and the validity of the cost-justification of the price differences. Borden mainly disagreed with the examiner's conclusion that the Borden brand and the private label evaporated milk should be considered commodities of "like grade and quality."

The full Commission reviewed the case and set aside the examiner's decision. A cease and desist order was entered against Borden on November 28, 1962.

The Commission based its decision on four salient points of law: [21]

1. The Borden brand and private label evaporated milk are of "like grade and quality." The Commission cited several past F.T.C. orders wherein it was held that goods which are the same in all respects except labels are goods of like grade and quality for purposes of Sec. 2 of the Robinson-Patman Act (i.e., Goodyear, Page Dairy). Then citing legislative hearings and the Attorney General's Report (1955), the Commission stated that it is obvious that no distinction was intended by Congress for different brands and that this is upheld by the majority of the Attorney General's Committee.
2. A price difference existed in the case, and, under the Act, a price discrimination is merely a price difference.
3. It is not necessary to show competitive injury, only a reasonable probability of it. Borden was a large, diversified manufacturer competing against smaller dairy processors for evaporated milk business. The smaller firms did, in fact, lose business to Borden as the latter increased its private label production. Several smaller firms had left the industry in recent years. The Commission held that competitive injury had been shown.
4. Borden's cost defense was based on average per case revenue and expense. The Commission deemed this cost study inadequate because of the use of "broad averaging" which leveled the extremes of both sales prices and costs and ignored specific situations which may have resulted in competitive injury.

Thus, the Commission rejected the "substantial and commercially demonstrated brand" differences in the interpretation of "like grade and quality."

Borden filed a petition in the Fifth Circuit Court of Appeals requesting that the cease and desist order of the Federal Trade Commission (November 28, 1962) be set aside.

In continuing the arguments set before the Federal Trade Commission, Borden did not contend that *all* brand differences were important and should receive full recognition under the law. The petitioner did

conten[d] that the grade and quality of products may vary either because of differences in "intrinsic superior quality" or because of "intense public demand" for one product as compared with another... Petitioner says that the higher price commanded by Borden brand at all levels of distribution is due to the "intense public demand" for the product rather than to any "intrinsic superior quality."[22]

There was no question of the fact that Borden brand milk and the distributors' brand milk produced by the company were exactly the same product chemically. By the same token, there was no question that placing distributor-owned brands on one portion and Borden labels on another portion of the output did not perceptibly change the cost of producing the different brands of milk. The primary issue revolved around the carefully demonstrated commerical value of the Borden brand.

Over a period of many years, final customers and intermediaries had willingly paid a premium for Borden milk, even with the clear choice of rejecting the brand in favor of a lower-priced milk sold under distributors' brands. Instead of taking this opportunity, both classes of customers continued to purchase the higher-priced Borden brands. Indeed, the distributors who purchased milk under their own labels continued to purchase the Borden brand milk in approximately the same quantities. Moreover, these distributors expressly agreed not to promote or sell their own brand milk by making reference to the supplier's "nationally advertised brand."

In examining the arguments advanced both by petitioner and respondent, the court precisely defined an issue that was held in ambiguity for three decades:

> Our initial determination must necessarily be whether or not the Commission applied the correct legal test in deciding that the commodities sold at different prices were of "like grade and quality." The facts on this element of the case are undisputed. The question is purely one of law, turning on the proper construction of the statutory phrase "of like grade and quality." If the products were not of like grade and quality, within the meaning of the [Robinson-Patman] Act, then their sale does not fall within the prohibition of Section 2(a). It is vigorously asserted by the Petitioner that Borden brand evaporated milk and the private label evaporated milk sold by Borden are not "commodities of like grade and quality."[23]

Thus, the court's initial point of law was "whether the demonstrated consumer preference for the Borden brand product over the private label product is to receive legal recognition in the "like grade and quality" determination.[24]

In evaluating the arguments presented, the court "did not find the administrative precedents urged upon [it] by the Commission applicable to this case."[25] The court recognized that these precedents were developed without explicit challenge of the "like grade and quality" requirement.

> In none of these cases was there any showing that the purchasers paying the higher prices had received brand name products which readily commanded a premium price in the market, which the purchasers paying the lower prices did not. The brand names were not shown to have any effect on the ultimate price the products could command.[26]

On December 4, 1964, the Appeals Court upheld the propositions advanced by Borden, and set aside the cease and desist order of the Federal Trade Commission. The opinion of the court implied that important brand differences based on market acceptance and consumer preference alone should remove the seller from the reach of the Robinson-Patman Act.

The Federal Trade Commission appealed the decision of the Court of Appeals to the Supreme Court. On March 23, 1966, the Supreme Court reversed the judgment of the Appeals Court on the question of "like grade and quality," and returned the case for further proceeding on the questions of competitive injury and cost defense.[27] The majority of the Supreme Court rejected the construction of "like grade and quality" which considers significant the commercial value of brand acceptance, and, in doing so, validated the position of the Federal Trade Commission in its previous decisions in this area.

AN INTERPRETATION

The consistent rationale behind the disregard for the economic value of consumer preference for a brand name in determining product grade and quality for purposes of Sec. 2(a) of the Robinson-Patman Act seems expediency of enforcement rather than sound economic reality.

The Attorney General's Committee Report, quoted in the Supreme Court's Borden decision, objected to the recognition of trademark value in the jurisdictional inquiry of a Robinson-Patman Act action mainly on two grounds:

1. That a change in the "like grade and quality" test to admit economic criteria would prove too complex to be practicably administered, and
2. That to make such a change would encourage easy evasion of the statute.

The "like grade and quality" requirement was not construed by the Committee as a defense of a price discrimination action but as an escape from the reach of the Act. In effect, however, it would have been a defense. The respondent has the burden of introducing evidence that products are not the same grade and quality, and, if this evidence is convincing, he has defended the price difference. In addition, it is difficult to believe that easy evasion would result from the addition of market tests in judging grade and quality. There is a long line of cases dealing with the market value of a trademark, and it is doubtful that the Commission or the courts would be easily fooled by "artificial variations in packaging, advertising or design" as the Attorney General's

Committee suggests. Regardless of their strength, these arguments have assumed considerable importance in justifying the physical-only construction of "like grade and quality." The Federal Trade Commission, in its opinion on the Borden case, said of the reasoning of the Attorney General's Committee Report:

> This we believe to be sound analysis. In our view, the discriminatory price trans-actions should first be subject to scrutiny under the statute; the *market factors* which may dictate that there will be different prices between seller's brand and private label can then be considered in connection with the provisions of Section 2.[28] (Italics inserted.)

The logic of this treatment of "market factors" breaks down when one examines the provisions of the Act. Continuing its opinion in Borden, the Commission said:

> For example, if cost savings are involved, these can be raised in connection with a cost defense. Thus economic factors may be considered, but the price relationship between different brands of intrinsically like goods remains subject to the terms of statute.[29]

The cost defense is based, of course, on a supply-side pricing force, and is only one of many price-determining market or econ-omic factors. There is no specific provision in the Act for one of the most important price-determining market factors—consumer demand. Thus, there is no legal justification for prices of similar products to be different simply because they are differentiated in the minds of the consumer and have different demand schedules, or preferences. The majority of the Supreme Court held:

> The Commission's view is that labels do not differentiate products for the purpose of determining grade or quality, even though one label may have more customer ap-peal and command a higher price in the marketplace from a substantial segment of the market. These views of the agency are entitled to respect, ... and represent a more reasonable construction of the statute than that offered by the Court of Appeals.[30]

In the past, the Commission has considered demand in price discrimination proceedings—i.e., it has recognized the commercial importance of consumer preference for a brand. These cases have involved the good faith meeting of compeittion, found in Sec. 2(b) of the Robinson-Patman Act. In the view of the Commission, "the issue under Sec. 2(b) of whether a seller's lower price is a good faith meeting of competition involves considerations dif-ferent from those presented by the jurisdictional question of "like grade and quality" under Sec. 2(a)."[31] The Supreme Court did not attempt to resolve the conflicting applications of the value of consumer preference for a brand by the Federal Trade Com-mission in enforcing various sections of the Robinson-Patman Act. The Court held, in effect, that the conflict was not salient to the major jurisdictional problem presented in the interpre-tation of "like grade and quality."

Appendix D

Estimates of Market Share
by Type of Brand
in Ten Major Industries

Packaged Foods

(1)

Type of Brand	No. of Product Lines	Share of Market (Dollar Sales Basis)*					
		1960	1961	1962	1963	1964	1965
Manufacturers' Advertised Brand	} 65	NA	70.6	71.3	73.2	72.4	74.9
All Other Brands		NA	29.4	28.7	27.8	27.6	27.1
		NA	100.0%	100.0%	100.0%	100.0%	100.0%
		Share of Market (Unit Sales Basis)*					
Distributors' Brand	21	11.4	12.1	13.1	13.6	13.8	NA

Source: Authors' calculations based on data from the A. C. Nielsen Company.

NA Not Available

*At the request of A. C. Nielsen Company, share of market data for the 65 specific product lines are not published in this report. Though the detailed data were used in the study itself, only summary measures could be presented here.

Household Supplies

(2)

Type of Brand	No. of Product Lines	Share of Market (Dollar Sales Basis)*					
		1960	1961	1962	1963	1964	1965
Manufacturers' Advertised Brand	16	NA	77.3	78.1	77.8	77.1	77.6
All Other Brands		NA	22.7	21.9	22.2	22.9	22.4
		NA	100.0%	100.0%	100.0%	100.0%	100.0%
			Share of Market (Unit Sales Basis)*				
Distributors' Brand	3	4.5	6.3	7.6	8.5	10.1	NA

Source: Authors' calculations based on data from the A. C. Nielsen Company

NA Not Available

*At the request of A. C. Nielsen Company, share of market data for the 16 specific product lines are not published in this report. Though the detailed data were used in the study itself, only summary measures could be presented here.

Toiletries

(3)

Type of Brand	No. of Product Lines	Share of Market*				(6 Mos.)
		1961	1962	1963	1964	1965
Manufacturers' Advertised Brand	9	66.4	68.4	69.3	70.9	70.9
All Other Brands		33.6	31.6	30.7	29.1	29.1
		100.0%	100.0%	100.0%	100.0%	100.0%

Source: Authors' calculations based on data from the A. C. Nielsen Company.

*It was agreed that share of market data for the 9 specific product lines would not be published in this report. As a result, only summary measures appear here though the detailed data were used in the study itself.

Proprietary Drugs and Other Health Aids

(4)

Type of Brand	No. of Product Lines	Share of Market*				(6 Mos.)
		1961	1962	1963	1964	1965
Manufacturers' Advertised Brand	12	78.4	78.4	78.6	79.3	79.2
All Other Brands		21.6	21.6	21.4	20.7	20.8
		100.0%	100.0%	100.0%	100.0%	100.0%

Source: Authors' calculations based on data from the A. C. Nielsen Company

*It was agreed that share of market data for the 12 specific product lines would not be published in this report. As a result, only summary measures appear here though the detailed data were used in the study itself.

Gasoline

(5)

Year	Manufacturers' Brand	Distributors' Brand
1954	90.3	9.7
1955	89.4	10.6
1956	88.6	11.4
1957	87.7	12.3
1958	86.7	13.3
1959	86.0	14.0
1960	85.2	14.8
1961	84.3	15.7
1962	83.0	17.0
———	———	———
1964	86.1	13.9

Source: Authors' estimates based on data from oil companies.

Footwear

(6)

Year	Manufacturers' Brands (Percent)	Distributors' Brands (Percent)	Total Millions of Pairs*
1955	52.0	48.0	585
1960	51.0	49.0	600
1964	49.0	51.0	613

*Non-rubber conventional footwear.

Source: Iver M. Olson, National Footwear Manufacturers' Association, Inc.

The data were based upon the unit output of the 70 largest shoe manufacturers in the United States. The 70 largest shoe manufacturers were determined on the basis of pairage production.

Replacement Tires

(7)

Year	Manufacturers' Brand	Distributors' Brand
1930	79.5	20.5
1931	78.6	21.4
1932	77.5	22.5
1933	78.2	21.8
1934	76.7	23.3
1935	74.4	25.6
1936	72.8	27.2
1937	71.2	28.8
1938	67.6	32.4
1939	66.2	33.8

Replacement Tires (Continued)

(7)

Year	Manufacturers' Brand	Distributors' Brand
1940	65.5	34.5
1941	65.1	34.9
1946	69.8	30.2
1947	67.8	32.2
1948	63.3	36.7
1949	61.4	38.6
1950	62.0	38.0
1951	70.5	29.5
1952	67.1	32.9
1953	65.2	34.8
1954	65.7	34.3
1955	65.5	34.5
1956	64.6	35.4
1957	67.5	32.5
1958	67.7	32.3
1959	68.7	31.3
1960	66.7	33.3
1961	64.1	35.9
1962	66.8	33.2
1963	65.1	34.9
1964	64.4	35.6

Source: Authors' estimates based on *Look* National Automobile and Tire Survey, tire company data, and figures prepared and published by Warren Leigh, (consultant to the tire industry).

Major Appliances

(8)

Indices of Market Share and
Unit Volume by Type of Brand

Electric Refrigerator

	1953-1954	1958-1959	1963-1964
Distributor Brands			
Share of Market	100	116	228
Number of Units	100	95	221
Manufacturer Brands			
Share of Market	100	99 NS	85 NS
Number of Units	100	82	83
All other Brands*			
Share of Market	100	80	79
Number of Units	100	66	77

Source: Starch Marketing Data Service. Market shares converted to index numbers to protect clients.

*In all years, all other brands accounted for less than 10 percent of the total.
NS-Change from previous period not significant at 0.95 confidence level.

Major Appliances

(8)

Automatic Washing Machine

	1953-1954	1958-1959	1963-1964
Distributor Brands			
Share of Market	100	126	170
Number of Units	100	154	254
Manufacturer Brands			
Share of Market	100	98^{NS}	86
Number of Units	100	120	126
All other Brands*			
Share of Market	100	47	33
Number of Units	100	57	49

Source: Starch Marketing Data Service. Market shares converted to index numbers to protect clients.
*In all years, all other brands accounted for less than 10 percent of the total.
NS-Change from previous period not significant at 0.95 confidence level.

Major Appliances

(8)

Clothes Dryers, Home Freezers
and Room Air Conditioners**

	1953-1954	1958-1959	1963-1964
Distributor Brands			
Share of Market	100	130	230
Number of Units	100	183	374
Manufacturer Brands			
Share of Market	100	105	88^{NS}
Number of Units	100	146	144
All other Brands*			
Share of Market	100	69	47
Number of Units	100	95	75

Source: Starch Marketing Data Service. Market shares converted to index numbers to protect clients.
* In all years, all other brands accounted for less than 25 percent of the total.
**The reason for this grouping is given in Appendix A.
NS-Change from previous period not significant at 0.95 confidence level.

Portable Appliances
Electric Housewares**

(9)

Indices of Market Share and
Unit Volume by Type of Brand

	1953-1954	1958-1959	1963-1964
Distributor Brands			
Share of Market	100	141	180
Number of Units	100	143	255
Manufacturer Brands			
Share of Market	100	94	92
Number of Units	100	97	133
All Other Brands*			
Share of Market	100	131	132
Number of Units	100	135	188

Source: Starch Marketing Data Service. Market shares converted to index numbers to protect clients.
  * In all years, all other brands accounted for less than 20 percent of the total
  **Includes stand and portable food mixers, electric toasters, and steam irons.
The reason for this grouping is given in Appendix 2.

Television Sets

(10)

Indices of Market Share and
Unit Volume by Type of Brand

	1953-1954	1958-1959	1963-1964
Distributor Brands			
Share of Market	100	268	278
Number of Units	100	214	280
Manufacturer Brands			
Share of Market	100	108	112
Number of Units	100	86	112
All other Brands*			
Share of Market	100	47	32
Number of Units	100	38	32

Source: Starch Marketing Data Service. Market shares converted to index numbers to protect clients.
  *In all years, all other brands accounted for less than 25 percent of the total.

Footnotes

CHAPTER 2. THE CONTEMPORARY
MARKETING STRUCTURE

1. United States Department of Commerce, Office of Business Economics, *Survey of Current Business*.

CHAPTER 3. ENVIRONMENTAL FORCES
AFFECTING BRAND POLICY

1. Willis K. Jordan, "Approaches to the Statistical Measurement of Capacity," presented at the annual meeting of the American Statistical Association, Cleveland, Ohio, September 4-7, 1963, p. 1.

   Other material which contributed to the measure of excess capacity used in this report are:

   L. R. Klein, and R. S. Preston, "Some New Results in Capacity Utilization," Discussion Paper No. 7, Economics Research Services Unit, University of Pennsylvania, February, 1965.

   Almarin Phillips, "An Appraisal of Measures of Capacity," *American Economic Review*, LIII, 2 (May, 1963), pp. 275-92.

   U.S., Congress, *Measures of Productive Capacity*, Report of Subcommittee on Economic Statistics, July 24, 1962.

   Almarin Phillips, "Notes on Measuring Capacity by Census Enumeration," *Measuring the Nation's Wealth*, report presented to the Subcommittee on Economic Statistics, 88th Cong., 2nd Sess., December, 1964, pp. 321-28.

2. Robert H. Cole, *et al.*, *Manufacturer and Distributor Brands* (Urbana, Ill.: Bureau of Economic and Business Research, University of Illinois, 1955), p. 10.
3. Neil H. Borden, *The Economic Effects of Advertising* (Homewood, Ill.: Richard D. Irwin, Inc., 1942), p. 599.
4. In Chapter II, page 13.
5. This is a standard definition of concentration in manufacturing or the "concentration ratio." Government statistics based on this approach are generally available. Additional information on the concept of economic concentration may be found in:

Willard F. Mueller, and Leon Garoian, *Changes in the Market Structure of Grocery Retailing* (Madison, Wisc.: The University of Wisconsin Press, 1961), pp. 18-47.

U.S., Federal Trade Commission, Staff Report, *Economic Inquiry into Food Marketing, Part I* January, 1960, pp. 236-49.

Concentration Patterns in Manufacturing, Studies in Business Economics Number Sixty-Five (New York: National Industrial Conference Board, Inc., 1959).

6. *Management & Advertising Problems in the Advertiser-Agency Relationship* (New York: Association of National Advertisers, Inc., 1965), p. 89.
7. J. O. Peckham, "Manufacturers' Advertised Brands: The Consumer's Choice," A presentation to the 57th Annual Meeting, Grocery Manufacturers of America, Inc., New York, N.Y., November 9, 1965, p. 12.
8. For other definitions of the "product life cycle" see:

   Arch Patton, "Top Management's Stake in the Product Life Cycle," *Management Review,* XLVIII, 6 (June, 1959), pp. 9-14 ff.

   E. Jerome McCarthy, *Basic Marketing: A Managerial Approach* Rev. ed.; Homewood, Ill.: Richard D. Irwin, Inc., 1964, pp. 332-36.

CHAPTER 5. DISTRIBUTORS' BRANDING POLICIES

1. "A New Report From the Brand Battlefront," *Grey Matter,* XXXIV, 3, (March, 1963), pp. 7-8.
2. *The Economics of Food Distribution,* McKinsey-General Foods Study (White Plains, N. Y.: General Foods Corporation, 1963).

APPENDIX A. RESEARCH METHODS

1. *Look Magazine National Gasoline Survey* (New York: Cowles Magazines and Broadcasting, Inc., 1961, 1962, & 1964).
2. *Look Magazine National Automobile and Tire Survey* (New York: Cowles Magazines and Broadcasting, Inc., 1949 to 1964).

APPENDIX B. TECHNICAL MATTERS

1. L. R. Klein and R. S. Preston, "Some New Results in Capacity Utilization," Discussion Paper No. 7, Economics Research Services Unit, University of Pennsylvania, February, 1965, p. 1.
2. U.S. Department of Commerce, Bureau of the Census, *Business Cycle Developments;* Series ESI No. 65-12 (December, 1965), p. 1.
3. *Ibid.,* inside back cover.
4. *Ibid.,* p. 2.
5. *The Conference Board's New Index of Help-wanted Advertising,* Technical Paper Number Sixteen (New York: National Industrial Conference Board, Inc., 1964), p. 15.
6. *Ibid.*
7. *Ibid.,* p. 17.

APPENDIX C. THE ECONOMIC VALUE OF
CONSUMER PREFERENCE FOR A BRAND

1. *Mishawaka Rubber & Woolen Mfg. Co. v. S.S. Kresge Co.,* 316 U.S. 203, 205 (1942).
2. *Trademarks -- Orientation for Advertising People* (New York: American Association of Advertising Agencies, 1964), pp. 2-3.
3. 15 U.S.C sec., 13(a).
4. *The Goodyear Tire & Rubber Co.,* 22 F.T.C. 232 (1936).
5. *Idem.,* p. 238.
6. *Idem.,* pp. 325-26.
7. *Idem.,* p. 326.
8. *Idem.,* p. 290.
9. *Idem.,* p. 311.
10. *Ibid.*
11. *Goodyear Tire & Rubber Co. v. F.T.C.,* 101 F. 2d. 620 (6th Cir. 1939).
12. *Idem.,* p. 621.
13. Letter from Mr. Teegarden, author of the bill, to Congressman Utterback, in Hearings before the Subcommittee of the House Committee on the Judiciary, 74th Congress, 2d Session, ser. 10, pt. 2, 469 (1936).
14. *Page Dairy Co.,* 50 F.T.C. 395 (1953): *Hartley & Parker, Inc., v. Florida Beverage Corp.,* 307 F. 2d. 916 (5th Cir. 1962).
15. Federal Trade Commission Complaints (CCH) 1961-1963, Para. 16191 (Transfer Binder).
16. Wright Patman, *Complete Guide to the Robinson-Patman Act* (Englewood Cliffs, N. J.: Prentice Hall, Inc., 1963), p. 23.
17. S. N. Barnes and S. C. Oppenheim (Co-chairmen), *The Attorney General's National Committee to Study the Antitrust Laws* (Washington, D. C.: United States Government Printing Office, 1955), pp. 158-159.
18. Federal Trade Commission Complaints (CCH) 1961-1963, Para. 15,633 (Transfer Binder).
19. Federal Trade Commission Complaints (CCH) 1957-1958, Para. 27,156 (Transfer Binder).
20. Federal Trade Commission Complaints (CCH) 1961-1963, Para. 16,191 (Transfer Binder).
21. Federal Trade Commission Docket No. 7129.
22. *Borden Co. v. F.T.C.,* 339 f. 2d. 135.
23. *Ibid.*
24. *Idem.,* p. 136.
25. *Idem.,* p. 137.
26. *Ibid.*
27. *Federal Trade Commission v. The Borden Company* 34 LW 4288 (1966).
28. Federal Trade Commission Complaints (CCH) 1961-1963, Para. 16,191 (Transfer Binder).
29. *Ibid.*
30. *Supra.,* note 49.
31. *Idem.,* p. 4290.

Bibliography

Agnew, Hugh E., Conner, Harold A., and Doremus, William L. *Outlines of Marketing.* 3rd ed.; New York: McGraw-Hill Book Co., Inc., 1950.

Alderson, Wroe. *Dynamic Marketing Behavior.* Homewood, Ill.: Richard D. Irwin, Inc., 1965.

————. *Marketing Behavior and Executive Action.* Homewood, Ill.: Richard D. Irwin, Inc., 1957.

Alexander, Ralph S., Surface, Frank M., and Alderson, Wroe. *Marketing.* 3rd ed.; New York: Ginn and Company, 1953.

"The American Trademark Index," *Thomas Register of American Manufacturers.* 55th ed.; IV, New York: Thomas Publishing Co., 1965.

Bain, Joe S. *Barriers to New Competition.* Cambridge, Mass.: Harvard University Press, 1962.

Banning, Douglas. *Techniques for Marketing New Products.* New York: McGraw-Hill Book Co., Inc., 1957.

Barnes, S. N., and Oppenheim, S. C., (Co-Chairmen). *The Attorney General's National Committee to Study the Antitrust Laws.* Washington, D. C.: United States Government Printing Office, 1955.

Baum, Daniel Jay. *The Robinson-Patman Act.* Syracuse, N. Y.: Syracuse University Press, 1964.

Beckman, Theodore N., and Davidson, William R. *Marketing.* 7th ed.; New York: The Ronald Press Company, 1962.

Borden, Neil H. *The Economic Effects of Advertising.* Homewood, Ill.: Richard D. Irwin, Inc., 1942.

Callmann, Rudolf. *The Law of Unfair Competition and Trade-Marks.* 2nd ed.; III, Chicago: Callaghan & Company, 1950.

Chamberlin, E. H. *The Theory of Monopolistic Competition.* 7th ed.; Cambridge, Mass.: Harvard University Press, 1958.

Clark, John Maurice. *Competition as a Dynamic Process.* Washington, D. C.: The Brookings Institution, 1961.

————. *Studies in the Economics of Overhead Costs.* Chicago: The University of Chicago Press, 1923.

Cole, Robert H., et al. *Manufacturer and Distributor Brands.* Urbana, Ill.: Bureau of Economic and Business Research, University of Illinois, 1955.

Committee on Marketing. *Principles of Marketing.* New York: Pitman Publishing Corporation, 1961.

Converse, Paul D., Huegy, Harvey W., and Mitchell, Robert V. *Elements of Marketing.* 7th ed.; Englewood Cliffs, N. J.: Prentice-Hall, Inc., 1965.

Corbaley, Gordon C. *Group Selling by 100,000 Retailers.* New York: American Institute of Food Distribution, Inc., 1936.

Cox, Reavis. *Distribution in a High-Level Economy.* Englewood Cliffs, N. J.: Prentice-Hall, Inc., 1965.

Dean, Joel. *Managerial Economics*. Englewood Cliffs, N. J.: Prentice-Hall, Inc., 1951.
Duddy, Edward A., and Revzan, David A. *Marketing: An Institutional Approach*. 2nd ed.; New York: McGraw-Hill Book Co., Inc., 1953.
Ferry, John W. *A History of the Department Store*. New York: The Macmillan Co., 1960.
The Food Industry Yearbook 1965-66. New York: Profit Press, 1965.
Galbraith, John Kenneth. *American Capitalism: The Concept of Countervailing Power*. Boston: Houghton Mifflin Company, 1956.
Grether, E. T. "External Product and Enterprise Differentiation and Consumer Behavior," *Marketing in Transition*. Alfred L. Seeyle (ed.), New York: Harper & Brothers, Publishers, 1958, pp. 180-96.
Hansen, Harry L. *A Study of Competition and Management in the Shoe Manufacturing Industry*. New York: National Shoe Manufacturers Association, Inc., 1959.
Hillery, Victor J. "Supermarkets Step Up Use of Private Labels," *Marketing in Transition*. Alfred L. Seeyle (ed.), New York: Harper & Brothers, Publishers, 1958, pp. 107-10.
Holtzclaw, Henry F. *The Principles of Marketing*. New York: Thomas Y. Crowell Company, 1935.
Hower, Ralph M. *The History of an Advertising Agency*. Rev. ed.; Cambridge, Mass.: Harvard University Press, 1949.
Knight, Frank H. *Risk, Uncertainty, and Profit*. Boston and New York: Houghton Mifflin Company, 1921.
Learned, Edmund P., and Ellsworth, Catherine C. *Gasoline Pricing in Ohio*. Boston: Division of Research, Graduate School of Business Administration, Harvard University, 1959.
Leather and Shoes Blue Book of the Shoe and Leather Industry. 33rd ed.; Chicago: The Rumpf Publishing Company, 1963.
Lebhar, Godfrey. *Chain Stores in America 1859-1962*. 3rd ed.; New York: Chain Store Publishing Corporation, 1963.
Leigh, Warren W. *Automotive Tire Sales by Distribution Channels*. Akron, Ohio: University of Akron, Bureau of Business Research, 1948. (Out of print).
Levitt, Theodore. *Innovation in Marketing*. New York: McGraw-Hill Book Co., Inc., 1962.
Markin, Rom J. *The Supermarket: An Analysis of Growth, Development, and Change*. Pullman, Wash.: Washington State University Press, 1963.
Matthews, John B. Jr., Buzzell, Robert D., Levitt, Theodore, and Frank, Ronald E. *Marketing: An Introductory Analysis*. New York: McGraw-Hill Book Co., Inc., 1964.
McCarthy, E. Jerome. *Basic Marketing: A Managerial Approach*. Rev. ed.; Homewood, Ill.: Richard D. Irwin, Inc., 1964.
McKittrick's Directory of Advertisers. New York: George McKitterick and Company, 1964 & 1965.
McNair, Malcolm P. "Significant Trends and Developments in the Postwar Period," in *Competitive Distribution in a Free High-Level Economy and Its Implications for the University*. Albert B. Smith (ed.), Pittsburgh: University of Pittsburgh Press, 1958, pp. 1-25.
McNair, Malcolm P., and Applebaum, William, and Salmon, Walter J. *Cases in Food Distribution*. Homewood, Ill.: Richard D. Irwin, Inc., 1964.
McNair, Malcolm P., and May, Eleanor G. *The American Department Store 1920-1960*. Boston: Division of Research, Graduate School of Business Administration, Harvard University, 1963.
Mueller, Willard F., and Garoian, Leon. *Changes in the Market Structure of Grocery Retailing*. Madison, Wisc.: The University of Wisconsin Press, 1961.
Nelson, Walter Henry. *The Great Discount Delusion*. New York: David McKay Company, Inc., 1965.
Oxenfeldt, Alfred R. "The Formulation of a Market Strategy," in *Managerial Marketing: Perspectives and Viewpoints*. William Lazer and Eugene J. Kelley (eds.), Rev. ed.; Homewood, Ill.: Richard D. Irwin, Inc., 1962, pp. 34-44.
————. *Marketing Practices in the TV Set Industry*. New York: Columbia University Press, 1964.
Palamountain, Joseph C. Jr. *The Politics of Distribution*. Cambridge, Mass.: Harvard University Press, 1955.
Patman, Wright. *Complete Guide to the Robinson-Patman Act*. Englewood Cliffs, N. J.: Prentice-Hall, Inc., 1963.

Phelps, D. Maynard, and Westing, J. Howard. *Marketing Management.* Rev. ed.;
Homewood, Ill.: Richard D. Irwin, Inc., 1960.
Phillips, Charles F. (ed.) *Marketing by Manufacturers.* Rev. ed.; Homewood, Ill.:
Richard D. Irwin, Inc., 1951.
Phillips, Charles F., and Duncan, Delbert J. *Marketing: Principles and Methods.*
5th ed.; Homewood, Ill.: Richard D. Irwin, Inc., 1964.
Pyle, John Freeman. *Marketing Principles.* Rev. ed.; New York: McGraw-Hill Book
Co., Inc., 1936.
Rowe, Frederick M. *Price Discrimination Under the Robinson-Patman Act.* Bos-
ton: Little, Brown and Company, 1962.
Schechter, Frank I. *The Historical Foundations of the Law Relating to Trade-Marks.*
New York: Columbia University Press, 1925.
Sevin, Chales H. *Marketing Productivity Analysis.* New York: McGraw-Hill Book
Co., Inc., 1965.
Stanton, William J. *Fundamentals of Marketing.* New York: McGraw-Hill Book Co.,
Inc., 1964.
Taylor, Weldon Jr., and Shaw, Roy T. *Marketing: An Integrated Analytical Approach.*
Cincinnati, Ohio: South-Western Publishing Company, 1961.
Trademark Management: A Guide for Businessmen. 3rd ed.; New York: The United
States Trademark Association, 1960.
Vaile, Roland S., Grether, E. T., and Cox, Reavis. *Marketing in the American Economy.*
New York: The Ronald Press Company, 1952.
Weiss, E. B. *Management and the Marketing Revolution.* New York: McGraw-Hill
Book Co., Inc., 1964.
————. *The Vanishing Salesman.* New York: McGraw-Hill Book Co., Inc., 1962.

MONOGRAPHS, NEWSPAPER ARTICLES, AND GOVERNMENT PUBLICATIONS

Active and Associate Membership Directory 1964-65. New York: Toiletry Mer-
chandisers Association, Inc., 1964.
"A Guide to Precision Marketing." *This Week Magazine 9th Biennial Grocery Study.*
New York: United Newspapers Magazine Corp., 1961, pp. 20-21, Book I.
18th Annual Consolidated Consumer Analysis. Milwaukee, Wisconsin: The Mil-
waukee Journal, 1963.
Annual Costs of Doing Business Survey. Chicago: National Appliance & Radio-TV
Dealers Association, 1963.
Annual Statement Studies. Philadelphia: Robert Morris Associates, 1965.
"Approved Appliances," *Directory.* Cleveland: American Gas Association, Inc., July,
1964.
Bart, Peter. "Advertising: A Campaign for Brand Names," *The New York Times,*
June 26, 1963, p. 59.
The Battle of the Shelf—Past, Present, and Its Extension into the 1960's. Chicago:
A. C. Nielsen Co., July, 1960.
"The Big Challenge in Food Marketing," *This Week Magazine 8th Biennial Grocery
Study.* New York: United Newspapers Magazine Corp., 1959, pp. 22-23.
Blundell, William E. "The Naming Game—Legal Problems Beset Firms in the Brand-
ing of Many New Products," *The Wall Street Journal,* May 7, 1964, p. 1.
"Borden Co. Wins Fight Against FTC Decision on Antitrust Charge," *The Wall Street
Journal*, December 7, 1964, p. 13.
"Borden Milk Loses Trust Plea in High Court," *The Philadelphia Inquirer,* March 24,
1966, p. 4.
Boyd, Harper W., Jr., and Frank, Ronald E. "The Importance of Private Labels in Food
Retailing," Working Paper No. 70, Graduate School of Business, Stanford University,
Undated.
Brand Loyalty as a Function of the Consumer's Expressed Needs. New York:
Advertising Research Foundation, Inc., Undated.
Carlson, Bjorn and Kusoffsky, Bertil. "Distributor Brands Versus Producer Brands,"
The Economic Research Institute at the Stockholm School of Economics, Stockholm,
Sweden, 1966.

The Case for Quality Stabilization. Washington, D. C.: Quality Brands Associates of America, Inc., Undated.

Colonial Study--A Report on Super Market Operations and Customer Habits. New York: Progressive Grocer, Undated.

Concentration Patterns in Manufacturing. Studies in Business Economics Number Sixty-Five. New York: National Industrial Conference Board, Inc., 1959.

The Conference Board's New Index of Help-wanted Advertising. Technical Paper No. 16, New York: National Industrial Conference Board, Inc., 1964.

Consumer Attitudes Toward Brand Names and Product Satisfaction--A Pilot Study for Good Housekeeping. New York: The Hearst Corporation, April, 1964.

"Contribution to Profit," This Week Magazine 10th Biennial Grocery Study. New York: United Newspapers Magazine Corp., 1963, pp. 34-35.

Crosby, William Ross. "National and Private Brands 1920 to Date." Unpublished Master's thesis, Graduate Division of the Wharton School, University of Pennsylvania, 1951.

Cupp, Paul J. "The Brand Facts of Life for the Food Retailers." Paper read before the American Association of Advertising Agencies' Central Region Annual Meeting in Chicago on October 17-18, 1962.

Dilworth, Robert S. "Discount Stores: New Sales Builders for Brand Name Manufacturers." Paper read before the Central Region Annual Meeting of American Association of Advertising Agencies, October 17-18, 1962.

Economic Concentration Measures: Uses and Abuses. Studies in Business Economics Number Fifty-Seven. New York: National Industrial Conference Board, Inc., 1957.

The Economics of Food Distribution. McKinsey-General Foods Study, General Foods Corporation. White Plains, N. Y., 1963.

Facts in Grocery Distribution--1963 Edition. New York: Progressive Grocer, 1963.

"Fedders Will Market Studebaker Appliances Under New 5-Year Pact," The Wall Street Journal, March 4, 1964, p. 7.

1964 Financial Analysis of Thirty-One Petroleum Companies. New York: The Chase Manhattan Bank, June, 1965.

"On Fleecing Consumers," The Wall Street Journal, June 10, 1964, p. 14.

"Food Chain Control Over Prices Rapped," The Evening Bulletin, April 8, 1964, p. 2.

Frank, Ronald E., and Boyd, Harper W. Jr. "Are Private-Brand-Prone Food Customers Really Different?," Working Paper No. 68, Graduate School of Business, Stanford University, August, 1965.

Grier, Dave, and Honomichl, Jack. "House Brands." A Study conducted for the Chicago Tribune Organization, September, 1958.

Grocery Business Annual Report--1964--31st Edition. New York: Progressive Grocer, 1964.

"High Court Curbs 2-Label Pricing," The New York Times, March 24, 1966, p. 31.

Jordan, Willis K. "Approaches to the Statistical Measurement of Capacity." Presented at the Annual Meeting of the American Statistical Association, Cleveland, Ohio, September 4-7, 1963.

Keith, Robert J. "Trademark Brands: Why We Have Them, and What They Mean to Consumers." Presented at the Annual Meeting of the Grocery Manufacturers of America, New York, November 14, 1961.

Klein, L. R. and Preston, R. S. "Some New Results in Capacity Utilization." Discussion Paper No. 7, Economics Research Services Unit, University of Pennsylvania, February, 1965.

Larsen, Spencer A. "Manufacturer Versus Distributor Control of Markets as Revealed in the 'Battle of the Brands'." Unpublished Ph.D. dissertation, Graduate School of Business Administration, New York University, 1933.

Law, Alfred. "Cuts in Liquor Prices by Macy's Trigger War With Big Distiller," The Wall Street Journal, February 5, 1965, p. 1.

Lewis, Edwin, Holloway Robert J., and Hancock, Robert S. "The Acceptance and Growth of Private Brands." University of Minnesota, Undated.

Look Magazine National Gasoline Survey. New York: Cowles Magazines and Broadcasting Inc., 1961, 1962 and 1964.

Look National Appliance Survey. Vol. I, Major Household Appliances; Vol. II, Portable Household Appliances. New York: Cowles Magazines, Inc., 1959 and 1963.

Look National Automobile and Tire Survey. Volumes 13 through 28. New York: Cowles Magazines, Inc., 1949 through 1964. (Volumes 13 through 24 out of print).

"Lower Court Ordered to Reconsider Attack by FTC on Supermarkets' 2-Price Systems," *The Wall Street Journal,* March 24, 1966, p. 2.

"Magnavox to Produce Private-Label TV Sets, Stereo Phonographs," *The Wall Street Journal,* January 8, 1964, p. 12.

Management & Advertising Problems in the Advertiser-Agency Relationship. New York: Association of National Advertisers, Inc., 1965.

McFarlane, Alexander N. "The Brand." Paper read to the Central Region Annual Meeting of the American Association of Advertising Agencies, October 17-18, 1962.

Mergers and Markets: A Guide to Economic Analysis of Case Law. Studies in Business Economics, No. 85. New York: National Industrial Conference Board, Inc., 1964.

————. *An Economic Analysis of the 1964 Supreme Court Merger Decisions.* Studies in Business Economics, No. 87. New York: National Industrial Conference Board, Inc., 1965.

Miller, Norman C. Jr. "Chain Tries New Tacks in Selling Groceries but Share of Market Drops," *The Wall Street Journal,* April 21, 1964, p. 1.

Moffitt, Donald. "Ads Under Fire," *The Wall Street Journal,* May 27, 1964, p. 1.

Mueller, Willard F. "Processor vs. Distributor Brands in Food Distribution." Remarks before the 35th Annual Meeting, National Council of Farm Cooperatives, Houston, Texas, January 13, 1964.

"National Brand or Private Label," An advertisement in *The New York Times,* November 12, 1963, p. 84.

National Petroleum News Fact Book Issue. New York: McGraw-Hill, Inc., May, 1964.

Nixon, H. K. "Advertising: A Functional Approach—Brand Preference." Unpublished monograph from the United States Trademark Association, Undated.

Otteson, Schuyler F. "Some Insights into Customers of Major Appliances and Their Dealers." A mimeographed address presented at the Convention of the National Appliance and Radio-TV Dealers Association, January 14, 1965.

Package Store Brand Switching and Impulse Buying. New York: Point-of-Purchase Advertising Institute, Inc., 1963.

Peckham, J. O. "Formula for Marketing New Brands of Toilet Goods." An address to Toilet Goods Association Dixville Notch, New Hampshire, June 27, 1964.

————. "Manufacturers' Advertised Brands: The Consumer's Choice." A presentation to the 57th Annual Meeting, Grocery Manufacturers of America, Inc., New York: November 9, 1965.

————. "Recipe for Marketing." A presentation to the 55th Annual Meeting of the Grocery Manufacturers of America, Inc., New York: November 12, 1963.

Phillips, Almarin. "Notes on Measuring Capacity by Census Enumeration," *Measuring the Nation's Wealth.* Report presented to the Subcommittee on Economic Statistics, 88th Cong., 2nd Sess., December, 1964, pp. 321-28.

"Private Brand Hats," *The Philadelphia Inquirer Magazine,* January 17, 1965, p. 24.

The Proprietary Association Directory. Washington, D. C.: The Proprietary Association, July, 1964.

"The Quality Revolution—New Hope for National Brands," An advertisement in *The New York Times,* March 7, 1962, p. 72.

Rabb, Norman S. "Private Brands—1957," Lecture delivered at Michigan State University, January 29, 1957.

RMA Recommended Minimum Standards for New Passenger Car Tires. New York: Rubber Manufacturers Association, Inc., 1964.

Rubber Industry Facts. New York: The Rubber Manufacturers Association, Inc., September, 1964.

Selecting and Evaluating Distributors. Studies in Business Policy, No. 116. New York: National Industrial Conference Board, Inc., 1965.

"The Shopper and the Supermarket," 6th duPont Consumer Buying Habits Study, Part I. E. I. duPont de Nemours and Company, Wilmington, Delaware, 1959.

Siegel, Noel S. "Brand Name Promotion of Synthetic Apparel Fibers and Fabrics—Channel Problems and Limitations." Unpublished Master's thesis, Graduate Division of the Wharton School, University of Pennsylvania, 1958.

Sloane, Leonard. "Daroff Accepts Clothiers' Stand," *The New York Times,* February 18, 1964, p. 49.

Stanton, Ted. "Battle of the Brands: Price Conscious Buyers Help Private Labels Expand Market Share," *The Wall Street Journal,* May 24, 1965, p. 1.

Stern, Louis William. "Some Aspects of the Changing Role of Marketing Management:
   The Evolution of Brand Management in Consumer Goods Industries." Unpublished
   Master's thesis, Graduate Division of the Wharton School, University of Pennsyl-
   vania, 1959.
A Study of Consumer Attitudes Towards Prescription Medicines, Non-prescription
   Medicines, Health Facilities—Good Housekeeping Panel Report. New York: The
   Hearst Corporation, 1964.
"A Study of the Magazine Market—Its Size, Quality, and Buying." The Magazine Ad-
   vertising Bureau of the Magazine Publishers Association, 1959.
Tire Guide—Who Makes It? and Where? Directory. Farmingdale, N. Y.: Tire Guide,
   1964 & 1965.
Trademarks—Orientation for Advertising People. New York: American Association of
   Advertising Agencies, 1964.
U.S. The Bureau of National Affairs, Inc. The United States Law Week, XXXIV (March
   22, 1966), pp. 4288-295.
U.S. Bureau of the Census. Concentration Ratios in Manufacturing Industry 1958 Part
   I. Report prepared for the Subcommittee of the Committee on the Judiciary, United
   States Senate, 1962.
U.S. Congress, House, Subcommittee 4 Select Committee on Small Business, Hearings,
   on H. Res. 13, The Impact Upon Small Business of Dual Distribution and Related
   Vertical Integration, Vol. 5. 88th Cong., 1st Sess., 1963.
U.S. Congress, Measures of Productive Capacity. Report of Subcommittee on Economic
   Statistics, July 24, 1962.
U.S. Congress, Senate, Subcommittee of the Committee on the Judiciary, Hearings,
   on S. Res. 262, Economic Concentration, Part 1. 88th Cong., 2nd Sess., 1964.
———. Hearings, on S. Res. 40, Economic Concentration, Part 2. 89th Cong., 1st
   Sess., 1965.
———. Hearings, on S. Res. 70, Economic Concentration, Part 3. 89th Cong., 1st
   Sess., 1965.
U.S. Department of Commerce. Basic Information Sources on Private-Label Manu-
   facturing of Cosmetics and Related Products. Business Service Bulletin, July,
   1954.
U.S. Department of Commerce, Bureau of the Census, Business Cycle Developments,
   Series ESI No. 65-12 (December, 1965).
U.S. Department of Commerce, Office of Business Economics, Survey of Current
   Business.
U.S. Executive Office of the President, Bureau of the Budget. Standard Industrial
   Classification Manual. 1957.
U.S. Federal Trade Commission, Chain Store Inquiry, Vol. III. 1933.
U.S. Federal Trade Commission Staff Report, Economic Inquiry into Food Marketing,
   Part I. January, 1960.
———. Economic Inquiry into Food Marketing, Part II. December, 1962.
———. Economic Inquiry into Food Marketing, Part III. June, 1965.
U.S. National Commission on Food Marketing, Food From Farmer to Consumer, June,
   1966.
U.S. National Commission on Food Marketing, Special Studies in Food Marketing. Tech-
   nical Study No. 10, June, 1966.
U.S. Small Business Administration, Small Business and the Federal Trade Commission.
   Small Marketers Aids No. 24, June, 1957.
Weiss, E. B. The Coming Battle with the Giant Retailers' Advertised Brands. New York:
   Doyle Dane Bernbach, Inc., 1959.
———. Meet the New Pre-sold National Brand: The Private Label. New York: Doyle
   Dane Bernbach, Inc., 1965.
———. Vertical Integration—The Coming Era of Scrambled Marketing. New York:
   Doyle Dane Bernbach, Inc., 1965.
"What About These New Consumers? Which Brand Will They Buy—National or Private
   Brand?," An advertisement in The New York Times, March 2, 1964, p. 28.
"Which Half of the Market Needs National Brands?," An advertisement in The New
   York Times, May 16, 1962, p. 84.

JOURNALS AND PERIODICALS

"Accomplishment Shapes an Image," Printers' Ink, CCLXXXI, 11 (December 14, 1962),
   pp. 52-56.

Agnew, Hugh E. "Fair Trade and the Consumer," *Journal of Marketing*, II, 4 (April, 1938), pp. 301-02.

"The Alarming Marketplace Truth on Advertised Brands vs. Private Labels," *Liquor Store*, LVIII, 6 (June, 1963), pp. 26-27.

Allen, Audrey, "Drug-Ad Formula: Big Dollars in TV," *Printers' Ink*, CCLXXXVIII, 3 (July 17, 1964), p. 27.

Anderson, Richard. "Private Label for New Ideas," *Drug and Cosmetic Industry*, LXXXVIII, 2 (February, 1961), p. 159.

Applebaum, William, and Carson, David. "Supermarkets Face the Future," *Harvard Business Review*, XXXV, 2 (March-April, 1957), pp. 123-35.

"Are Brand Names Important in Selling Piece Goods?," *Department Store Economist*, XXV, 12 (December, 1962), pp. 50-52.

"Are Brands Losing Out to Private Labels?," *Boot and Shoe Recorder*, CLIX, 7 (March 1, 1961), pp. 56-57.

"Are Gas Price Wars at an End?," *Business Week*, Number 1865 (May 29, 1965), pp. 134-36.

"The Arrival and Survival of a National Brand: The Story of the Arrow Shirt Company," *Department Store Economist*, XXV, 12 (December, 1962), p. 34.

"Baby Foods: An Ever-New Market," *Printers' Ink*, CCLXXXVII, 13/CCLXXXVIII, 1 (June 26/July 3, 1964), pp. 55-56.

Banks, Seymour. "The Relationships Between Preference and Purchase of Brands," *Journal of Marketing*, XV, 2 (October, 1950), pp. 145-57.

Begin, Jean. "Farmers', Sacramento, Hails Own-Label Dual-Grade Beef," *Supermarket News*, XII, 31 (July 29, 1963), p. 35.

Bernsohn, Al. "The Manufacturer: As Seen by the Retailer," *Home Appliance Builder*, XXXI, 5 (May, 1966), p. 30.

Bier, Nancy. "Who Can Control Brand-Switching:," *Printers' Ink*, CCLXXXVI, 5 (February 7, 1964), pp. 25-28.

"Big Price Test: Can Marketers Weather a Year of Chaos?," *National Petroleum News*, LIV, 1 (January, 1962), pp. 93-102.

Blickstein, Steve. "Gas: Where Did Brand Loyalty Go?," *Printers' Ink*, CCLXXXV, 1 (October 4, 1963), p. 25.

Bonwich, William T. "Will Private Brands in Nonfoods Invade the Supermarket Industry?," *Journal of Retailing*, XXXIX, 2 (Summer, 1962), pp. 29-33.

Borden, Neil H. "The Concept of the Marketing Mix," *Journal of Advertising Research*, IV, 2 (June, 1964), pp. 2-7.

"Bouquets to Weiss! Series on Scrambled Marketing," *Advertising Age*, XXXVI, 3 (January 18, 1965), p. 91.

"Brand Control Study," *Discount Store News*, III, 3 (February 10, 1964), p. 2.

"Brand Leaders Outline Steps to Meet Private-Label Challenge," *Food Engineering*, XXXI, 10 (October, 1959), p. 52.

"Brand Loyalties: How Wide-Ranging?," *Printers' Ink*, CCLXXXI, 4 (October 26, 1962), pp. 60-61.

"Brand-Name Battle: Grocer's Profits vs. New Consumer Foods," *Time*, LXXIII, 24 (June 15, 1959), p. 88.

"The Brand Name Dilemma," *Advertising Age*, XXXVII, 14 (April 4, 1966), p. 18.

"Brand Names Foundation Plans Enlarged Drive," *Advertising Age*, XXXIV, 27 (July 1, 1963), p. 56.

"Branded Goods," *Forbes*, XCV, 1 (January 1, 1965), p. 53.

"Brands Across the Table," *Department Store Economist*, XXVI, 12 (December, 1963), pp. 40-43.

"Brands Are Waning, French Tells Container Corporation Meeting; No Shift from Brands: Cleaves," *Advertising Age*, XXXII, 41 (October 9, 1961), p. 72.

Brown, George H. "Brand Images Among Low Priced Cars," *American Marketing Association Proceedings*, Winter, 1959, pp. 61-65.

Brown, Robert H. "Gas & Oil: Beleaguered but Fighting," *Printers' Ink*, CCLXXXVIII, 5 (July 31, 1964), pp. 21-24.

"Bumps on the Shelf," *Dun's Review and Modern Industry*, LXXX, 5 (November, 1962), p. 65.

"Can Wines Achieve Brand Identity?," *Printers' Ink*, CCLXXXVI, 2 (January 17, 1964), p. 14.

"Cashes in on Own Label," *Food Engineering*, XXXI, 11 (November, 1959), p. 45.

Christopaulos, G. "Dark Horse in Tomorrow's Marketing," *Management Review*, XLIX, 1 (January, 1960), p. 4.

Christy, Marian. "Supreme Markets: 'Big Job' with Controlled Labels," *Supermarket News*, XII, 13 (April 1, 1963), p. 50.

Clement, Dick. "Philadelphia Units Stress Private Label," *Supermarket News*, XII, 13 (April 1, 1963), p. 49.

————. "Private Brand Price Cut—Too Little is Just Right," *Women's Wear Daily*, CVIII, 78 (April 20, 1964), p. 10.

————. "Small Saving Sells Private Label; Big Variance Hurts, Borden Finds," *Supermarket News*, XIII, 15 (April 13, 1964), p. 4.

Cole, Robert. "The Battle of the Brands in Canned Goods," *American Marketing Association Proceedings*, 1954, pp. 153-59.

"Company Name or Brand Name? The Problems of Corporate Endorsement," *Management Review*, LI, 12 (December, 1962), pp. 34-37.

"Competitive Strategy for the Independent Store," *Stores*, XLV, 4 (April, 1963), p. 18.

"Compulsory Differentials Get Blasts," *National Petroleum News*, LVII, 9 (September, 1965), p. 77.

Conn, Anthony G. "The Grocer's Stake in New Product Introduction," *American Marketing Association Proceedings*, Summer, 1957, pp. 228-29.

"Consumer Confidence in Private Labels Poses Ad Challenge," *Printers' Ink*, CCLXXIV, 13 (March 31, 1961), p. 5.

"Consumer Shopping Habits: Are They Predictable?," *Printers' Ink*, CCLXXXI, 9 (November 30, 1962), pp. 48-50.

"Corporate Identity Programs Get New Look," *Printers' Ink*, CCLXXXI, 9 (November 30, 1962), p. 5.

"Crossroads for Private Labels and/or Brand Names," *Spirits*, XXX, 8 (August-September, 1963), pp. 21-24.

Cunningham, Ross M. "Brand Loyalty—What, Where, How Much?," *Harvard Business Review*, XXXIV, 1 (January-February, 1956), pp. 116-28.

————. "Customer Loyalty to Store and Brand," *Harvard Business Review*, XXXVIV, 6 (November-December, 1961), pp. 127-37.

"CU Report Hits Reliability of Brands as Aids to Consumer: Calls Ad Claims Hard to Check," *Advertising Age*, XXXIV, 39 (September 23, 1963), pp. 36-37.

Dakins, J. Gordon. "National Brands, Private Brands: The Current Debate," *Stores*, XLV, 2 (February, 1963), pp. 5-6.

Davidson, William R. "The Shake-out in Appliance Retailing," *Home Appliance Builder*, XXX, 3 (March, 1965), pp. 21-29.

Detman, Art Jr. "Comparative Pricing: New Threat to Brand Names," *Sales Management*, XCV, 10 (November 5, 1965), pp. 30-31.

————. "Survival of the Fittest," *Sales Management*, XCVI, 11 (June 1, 1966), p. 43.

Diamond, Sidney A. "Private Brands and the Federal Trade Commission," *Advertising Age*, XXXVI, 3 (January 18, 1965), p. 85.

Diamond, Sidney A. "Private Brands—The Borden Case is Not Over Yet," *Advertising Age*, XXXVII, 16 (April 18, 1966), p. 80.

"Diaper Field Needed Change; Kendall Vied with Discounts, Private Labels," *Advertising Age*, XXXV, 6 (February 10, 1964), p. 12.

"Discounters Jack Up Sales of Auto Accessories and Services," *Discount Store News*, III, 2 (January 27, 1964), p. 111.

"Discredit 'Malignant' Private Label Items: Bronfman Advises," *Advertising Age*, XXXV, 12 (March 23, 1964), p. 112.

Dixon, P. R. "Private Label May be Device for Price Discrimination Offenses," *Advertising Age*, XXXII, 51 (December 18, 1961), p. 10.

"Do' Private Labels Violate the R-P Law?," *American Druggist*, CXLV, 1 (January 8, 1962), p. 23.

Dodd, Allen R. Jr. "Appliances: Focusing on Function," *Printers' Ink*, CCLXXXVIII, 8 (August 21, 1964), p. 27.

————. "Cigarettes: The Splintered Market," *Printers' Ink*, CCLXXXIV, 10 (September 6, 1963), p. 21.

"Does the Label 'Change' the Taste?," *Printers' Ink*, CCLXXXVIII, 2 (January 12, 1962), pp. 55-57.

"Don't Devote Inordinate Attention to Private Brands, Hanes Warns NRMA," *Advertising Age*, XXXIII, 3 (January 15, 1962), p. 68.

"'Don't Tread on Me'—Anymore," *National Petroleum News*, L, 5 (May, 1958), p. 82.

Dragonetti, Joseph J. "Private Label Detergents," *Soap and Chemical Specialties*, XXXV, 10 (October, 1959), p. 51.

Drucker, Peter. "Find Your Company's Hidden Strength," *Nation's Business*, LII, 3 (March, 1964), pp. 80–84.
"Drug Prices Again—But a New Approach," *Business Week*, Number 1822 (August 1, 1964), p. 30.
Dubbs, Ed. "The Private-Label Duel in Housewares: Where Does the Retailer Stand?," *Merchandising Week*, XCVII, 21 (May 24, 1965), pp. 23–25.
DuBois, Peter C. "Competition in Tissue," *Barron's*, XLI, 42 (October 16, 1961), p. 5.
"Dynamic Role of National Brands," *Boot and Shoe Recorder*, CLXIII, 7 (March 1, 1963), pp. 45–76.
"The East's Newest Private-Brander," *National Petroleum News*, LIII, 3 (March, 1961), pp. 23–24.
"Emerson Sees Private Label Growing," *Television Digest*, IV, 5 (February 3, 1963), p. 8.
Emond, Mark. "How Private Brands are Burgeoning in the Interior West," *National Petroleum News*, LV, 10 (October, 1963), p. 24.
———. "Split-Pumps, Subsidies: The Anatomy of a Chronic Price-War 'Gas' Market," *National Petroleum News*, LV, 2 (February, 1963), p. 23.
Evans, Franklin B. "Psychological and Objective Factors in the Prediction of Brand Choice," *Journal of Business*, XXXII, 4 (October, 1959), pp. 340–69.
"Exclude Brand's Value in Private Pricing: FTC," *Advertising Age*, XXXIII, 51 (December 17, 1962), p. 1.
Farley, John V. "'Brand Loyalty' and the Economics of Information," *Journal of Business*, XXXVII, 4 (October, 1964), pp. 370–79.
Fassler, Sally. "Private Labels No 'Brand' Bar, Bottinick, Daitch Buyer, Says," *Supermarket News*, XII, 13 (April 1, 1963), p. 51.
"Fight Private Label 'Marauders,' Bronfman Asks," *Advertising Age*, XXXIII, 46 (November 12, 1962), p. 3.
"Financing Product Growth," *Printers' Ink*, CCXC, 5 (February 26, 1965), p. 28.
Finn, Richard. "What's in a Brand Name?," *American Legion Magazine*, LXXIV, 6 (June, 1963), pp. 22–24.
Ford, Kenneth. "Autos: Will the Boom Continue?," *Printers' Ink*, CCLXXXIV, 6 (August 9, 1963), p. 21.
———. "Liquor: Beset by Changing Tastes," *Printers' Ink*, CCLXXXIV, 2 (July 12, 1963), p. 19–29.
———. "What's Missing in Beer Marketing?," *Printers' Ink*, CCLXXXV, 9 (November 29, 1963), p. 25.
Freer, Robert E. "Fair Trade in Operation," *Journal of Marketing*, II, 4 (April, 1938), pp. 303–08.
Frisselle, Parker. "Creating a Company Brand to Protect a Market," *American Marketing Association Proceedings*, Summer, 1960, pp. 517–22.
"FTC Asked to End Wholesale Price Advantage of Branded Gasolines," *Advertising Age*, XXXV, 12 (March 23, 1964), p. 110.
"FTC Asks Review by Supreme Court on Borden Case," *Advertising Age*, XXXVI, 5 (February 1, 1965), p. 8.
"FTC's New Stance," *National Petroleum News*, LVII, 5 (May, 1965), pp. 65–67.
"FTC Questionnaires Show Unbranded Gasoline Sales," *National Petroleum News*, LVII, 11 (November, 1965), p. 78.
Gardner, Burleigh B. "Qualitative Research and Brand Image," *American Marketing Association Proceedings*, Winter, 1959, pp. 55–60.
Garson Arnie. "Brands—Private Label 'Battle' Hit for 'Outdated' Thinking" *Supermarket News*, XII, 31 (July 29, 1963), p. 4.
"Gaseteria's Dream: A Franchised Trademark for Private Branders," *National Petroleum News*, XLIX, 11 (November, 1957), pp. 123–26.
"Gem's QS View: 'Aim Is Resale Price Maintenance'," *Discount Store News*, III, 3 (February 10, 1964), p. 9.
"The Giants Plan to Get Still Bigger," *Business Week*, Number 1814 (June 6, 1964), p. 100.
"Greater Own Label and Brands Stress Twin A&P Policies," *Supermarket News*, XII, 24 (June 10, 1963), p. 1.
Greenberg, Manning. "Fair Trading in L.A., N.Y. Attributed to Desperation," *Home Furnishings Daily*, XXXV, 71 (April 11, 1963), p. 42.
Grether, Ewald T. "Trade Marks and Differential Gain," *The Ronald Forum*, (May, 1928), pp. 67–74.
Groenveld, Leonard. "A New Theory of Consumer Buying Intent," *Journal of Marketing*, XXVIII, 3 (July, 1964), pp. 23–28.
Gross, Walter. "Strategies Used by Major Department Stores to Compete with Low Margin Retailers," *Journal of Retailing*, XL 2 (Summer, 1964), pp. 11–18.

Hall, William P. "Franchising—New Scope for an Old Technique," *Harvard Business Review*, XLII, 1 (January-February, 1964), pp. 60-72.

Hancock, Robert S. "Factors Motivating Consumer Choice of Private Brands," *American Marketing Association Proceedings*, Winter, 1959, pp. 66-74.

Hanenberg, Paul. "Private Label Trend Growing in Sportswear," *Women's Wear Daily*, CVI, 90 (May 8, 1963), p. 42.

Harrison, Roy. "Will You Bring Me Up to Date on That Borden Case?," *The Food Institute: Weekly Digest*, LXXII, 41 (April 16, 1966), p. 1.

Harting, Philip H., and Fisher, James L. "Brand Switching and Mathematical Programming in Market Expansion," *Management Science*, XI 10 (August, 1965), pp. 231-43.

"He's Half Wildcatter, Half Big Businessman," *Business Week*, Number 1837 (November 14, 1964), pp. 103-04.

Hoffman, Manny. "Major Retailing Chains Taking Steps to Strengthen Private Label Programs," *Home Furnishings Daily*, XXXVII, 24 (February 4, 1965), p. 1.

———. "See Retail Fate a Wrestle with Angel of Private Label," *Home Furnishings Daily*, XXXVII, 23 (February 3, 1965), p. 1

"How Do 'Private-Brand Spreads' Affect Competition?," *National Petroleum News*, LII, 4 (April, 1960), pp. 162-65.

"How Do Private-Branders Buy?," *National Petroleum News*, LV, 5 (May, 1963), pp. 67-68.

"How Heavily Product Is Advertised Doesn't Affect Retailer; Markup Does," *Advertising Age*, XXX 18 (May 4, 1959), p. 32.

"How to Expand a Market by Using Private Brands," *Printers' Ink*, CCXC, 13 (June 25, 1965), p. 29.

"How to Save $200 a Year at a Supermarket," *Consumer Reports*, XXVI, 2 (February, 1961), pp. 64-67.

Howell, Ken. "Major Coast Chains Push Private Label Health Aids," *Supermarket News*, XII, 13 (April 1, 1963), p. 50.

———. "Own-Label Buildup Seen as Big Chains Enter L.A.," *Supermarket News*, XII, 31 (July 29, 1963), p. 4.

Hughes, Lawrence M., and Nicholas, George P. "Private vs. National Brands," *Sales Management*, LXXXI, 1 (July 4, 1958), pp. 81-104.

Hughes, Lawrence M. "The 'Secret' Hand in Private Brands," *Sales Management*, LXXXV, 8 (September 16, 1960), p. 35.

"The Impact of Brands," *Hardware Retailer*, 5 (May, 1962), pp. 71-97.

"Impulse Sparks 22% of Purchases," *American Druggist*, CXLVII, 7 (April 1, 1963), p. 59.

"Interurbia—Brand Battle Salient," *Food Engineering*, XXXI, 9 (September, 1959), pp. 46-47.

Jacobson, A. L. "Private Brands: Has the Cream Been Skimmed?," *Food Business*, XI, 1 (January, 1963), pp. 29-30.

———. "Profit in Private Labels? Where," *Printers' Ink*, CCLXXVIII, 8 (February 23, 1962), p. 66.

Judelle, Beatrice. "National Brands and Private Brands in the Fashion Departments," *Stores*, XLIV, 9 (September, 1962), p. 28.

"Justice Department on QS: 'Consumer High Price Act'," *Discount Store News*, III, 3 (February 10, 1964), p. 9.

Kelly, Patrick J. "Cereals: Blowing Hot and Cold," *Printers' Ink*, CCLXXXIX, 7 (November 13, 1964), pp. 29-31.

———. "Cereals: Snap, Crackle, Boom," *Printers' Ink*, CCLXXXVIII, 7 (August 14, 1964), pp. 25-28.

Kiefer, Frank X. "Building Business with National Brands," *Department Store Economist*, XXVI, 12 (December, 1963), pp. 38-39.

———. "A World Without Brand Names," *Department Store Economist*, XXXV, 12 (December, 1962), pp. 26-27.

King, Roy. "Private Labels Often Harder to Sell Than Established National Brands," *Advertising Age*, XXXIII, 28 (July 9, 1962), p. 84.

Klapper, Marvin. "Red Hot Brand Needed to Make Mark in Man-Mades," *Women's Wear Daily*, CVI, 90 (May 8, 1963), p. 58.

Knapp, J. Gordon. "What's Wrong (and Right) with Today's Trademarks?," *Industrial Marketing*, XLVIII, 8 (July, 1963), pp. 101-04.

Kuss, R. L. "Running Hard to Stand Still—The Private Brand Marketer," *The Oil Daily*, No. 3,346 (November 10, 1964), p. 19.

Levitt, Theodore. "Branding on Trial," *Harvard Business Review*, XLIV, 2 (March/April, 1966), pp. 20-22.

Lifshey, Earl. "If You Ask Me," *Home Furnishings Daily*, XXXV, 136 (July 15, 1963), p. 58.

————. "Whose Brand Will Be at the Point of Sale,"*Home Furnishings Daily*, XXXVII, 160 (August 18, 1965), p. 31.

"A Link with Retail Realities," *Modern Packaging*, XXXVII, 3 (November, 1963), pp. 152-54.

Lippincott, J. Gordon, and Margulies, Walter P. "Missing Person in the Battle of Brands," *Food Engineering*, XXXIII, 7 (July, 1961), pp. 40-41.

"Liquor Labels Get BNF Attention," *The Key Report*, (February 24, 1964), p. 2.

Lockley, Lawrence C. "Avoidance of Direct Competition at the Retail Level," *American Marketing Association Proceedings*, Winter, 1960, pp. 143-51.

"Loss Leader, 'Bait' Bills May Delay QS,"*Discount Store News*, III, 5 (March 9, 1964), p. 11.

"Lower Price for Private Brands?," *Printers' Ink*, CCLXXXI, 12 (December 21, 1962), p. 90.

"Lucerne Brand Push by Safeway," *Supermarket News*, XII, 10 (March 11, 1963), p. 44.

"Mail-Order Giants Multiply Outlets for Private Labels," *Printers' Ink*, CCLXXXV, 5 (November 1, 1963), p. 8.

Manchester, Allen W. "Packaging Catalyst for a Produce Come-Back,"*Food Business*, XL, 6 (June, 1963), pp. 16-18.

"Market Skirmishes with Private Labels of Growing Concern," *Home Furnishings Daily*, XXXV, 71 (April 11, 1963), p. 42.

"Marketing Briefs," *Business Week*, Number 1753 (April 6, 1963), p. 52.

"Marketing Develops into Alliance for Profit," *Grey Matter*, XXXVI, 6 (June, 1965), 4 pp.

Marquardt, Raymond, Makens, James, and Larzelere, Henry. "Measuring the Utility Added by Branding and Grading," *Journal of Marketing Research*, II, 1 (February, 1965), pp. 45-50.

Marsh, W. W. "Tire Dealers Are Emerging as Important Growing Part of Automotive Transportation," *NTDRA Dealer News*, XXVIII, 4 (January 25, 1965), pp. 12-13.

"Masters Only Wants Big Pre-Sold Brands," *Editor and Publisher*, XCIV, 8 (February 25, 1961), p. 28.

Maxwell, John C. Jr. "Soft Drinks: Market on the Move," *Printers' Ink*, CCLXXXVII, 11 (June 12, 1964), p. 27.

————. "Soup: An Industry in Ferment," *Printers' Ink*, CCLXXXVII, 5 (May 1, 1964), p. 45.

McCammon, Bert C. Jr. "The Emergence and Growth of Contractually Integrated Channels in the American Economy, *American Marketing Association Proceedings*, Fall, 1965, pp. 496-515.

McKitterick, J. B. "What is the Marketing Management Concept?," *American Marketing Association Proceedings*, Winter, 1957, pp. 71-82.

McLaughlin, Ed. "Own Labels in Philadelphia Counter Operation Rises," *Supermarket News*, VII, 21 (May 26, 1958), p. 16.

McNair, M. P. "Fair Trade Legislation and the Retailer," *Journal of Marketing*, II, 4 (April, 1948), pp. 295-300.

McNamara, H. V. "The Shifting Pattern of Consumer Goods Distribution," *American Marketing Association Proceedings*, Summer, 1960, pp. 529-38.

McVey, Phillip. "Are Channels of Distribution What the Textbooks Say?," *Journal of Marketing*, XXIV, 1 (January, 1960), pp. 61-65.

"Meadville Corp. Enters D.C. Market," *National Petroleum News*, LVI, 1 (January, 1964), p. 72.

Mendelson, Nathaniel. "Are Your Vendors Serving Two Masters?," *Department Store Economist*, XXVI, 12 (December, 1963), p. 114.

"Mom Feels Quality Not Ad Cost, Makes Brand Item Costlier," *Advertising Age*, XXV, 49 (December 7, 1964), p. 30.

"Mom Will Pay More for Advertised Brand But Not Too Much More, Food Brokers Told," *Advertising Age*, XXXIII, 51 (December 17, 1962), p. 6.

"More Growth for Private-Label Foods," *Printers' Ink*, CCLXXXVI, 11 (March 20, 1964), p. 5.

"More New Price Thinking on the Way? It's a Must, Say Two Independents," *National Petroleum News*, LIII, 5 (May, 1961), pp. 72-74.

"More on Private Brands," *Printers' Ink*, CCLXXXIV, 6 (August 16, 1963), p. 3.

Morris, Betty. "Distribution Edge Seen for Private-Label Giants," *Home Furnishings Daily*, XXXVII, 36 (February 23, 1965), p. 1.

Morse, Leon. "The Battle of the Brands," *Dun's Review and Modern Industry*, LXXXIII, 5 (May, 1964), p. 53.

Mosley, G. E. "Ads Not Enough; Retailer Must Be Sold," *Advertising Age*, XXX, 15 (April 13, 1959), p. 50.

Moulson, T. J. "Danger Signals: How to Spot Erosion in Brand Loyalty," *Printers' Ink*, CCXC, 6 (March 12, 1965), p. 55.
Mueller, R. W. "New Attitudes Toward Private Brands," *Progressive Grocer*, XLII, 1 (January, 1963), p. 6.
Mullen, Wadsworth H. "Some Aspects of Chain Store Development," *Harvard Business Review*, III, 1 (October, 1924), pp. 69-80.
Munn, Henry L. "Brand Perception As Related to Age, Income, and Education," *Journal of Marketing*, XXIV, 3 (January, 1960), pp. 29-34.
――――. "Should Retailers Reduce Number of Brands Stocked?," *Journal of Retailing*, XXXVIII, 4 (Winter, 1962-1963), p. 1.
"National Ads Won't Keep Price-Squeezed Grocer from Going to Private Labels: Rabb," *Advertising Age*, XXXII, 11 (March 13, 1961), p. 61.
"National Brands Ahead in Vague Cleveland Brand Picture," *Supermarket News*, VII, 21 (May 26, 1958), p. 18.
"National Brands & Private Labels," *Boot and Shoe Recorder*, CLXII, 9 (October 1, 1962), p. 103.
"Negroes More 'Brand Conscious' Than Whites, Bauer Says," *Advertising Age*, XXXV, 12 (March 23, 1964), p. 73.
"New Crowd Minds Store for the Tea Company," *Business Week*, Number 1815 (June 13, 1964), p. 88.
"New Look in Private Labels," *Food Engineering*, LXIX, 6 (June, 1959), p. 69.
"New Plan Devised to Spur National-Brand Acceptance," *Printers' Ink*, CCLXV, 7 (November 14, 1958), pp. 81-82.
"New Products Outlook," *Printers' Ink*, CCLXXXVII, 8 (May 22, 1964), p. 24.
"A New Report From the Brand Battlefront," *Grey Matter*, XXXIV, 3 (March, 1963), 16 pp.
"A New Report from the Brand Battlefront," *Grey Matter*, XII, 4 (July, 1966).
"New Study Details Scramble for Share of Gasoline," *The Oil and Gas Journal*, LXIII, 6 (February 8, 1965), pp. 50-51.
"New U.S. Drug Rules," *Modern Packaging*, XXXVI, 4 (December, 1962), p. 201.
"A New Wrinkle on Private Labels," *Sales Management*, LXXXVI, 11 (May 19, 1961), pp. 85-86.
"Newness Losing Consumer Appeal, Capitman Finds," *Advertising Age*, XXXIV, 46 (November 11, 1963), p. 3.
O'Farrell, Larrie. "Detergents: Suds Down, Sales Up," *Printers' Ink*, CCLXXXVIII, 2 (July 10, 1964), p. 29.
――――. "How Detergents Fight for Difference," *Printers' Ink*, CCLXXXIV, 4 (July 26, 1963), pp. 20-26.
――――. "Pet Foods: Lucrative Wary Industry," *Printers' Ink*, CCLXXXV, 11 (December 13, 1963), p. 27.
"One Brand Name in Place of Four," *Business Week*, Number 1739 (December 29, 1962), p. 40.
"One Name to Girdle the Globe," *Business Week*, Number 1822 (August 1, 1964), pp. 74-75.
Orth, Penelope. "Coffee: Relying More on Advertising," *Printers' Ink*, CCLXXXVII, 2 (April 10, 1964), p. 27.
――――. "Cosmetics: The Brand is Everything," *Printers' Ink*, CCLXXXV, 5 (November 1, 1963), p. 27.
Oak, Richard. "Drugs: The Big Shift to Proprietaries," *Printers' Ink*, CCLXXXIV, 12 (September 20, 1963), p. 37.
"Penna. Solons Get Anti-QSB Pleas," *Discount Store News*, III, 9 (May 4, 1964), p. 7.
"Packaging Notes," *Printers' Ink*, CCLXXXV, 9 (November 29, 1963), p. 21.
Patton, Arch. "Top Management's Stake in the Product Life Cycle," *Management Review*, XLVIII, 6 (June, 1959), p. 9.
Perkins, Al. "See Brand-Name Impact Growing," *Home Furnishings Daily*, XXXV, 71 (April 11, 1963), p. 46.
"Person to Person: Retailers Speak Out About Brands," *Department Store Economist*, XXVI, 12 (December, 1963), pp. 50-58.
Phelen, Patrick. "Honor Consumer, Operators Told," *Supermarket News*, XII, 10 (March 11, 1963), p. 32.
Phillips, Almarin. "An Appraisal of Measures of Capacity," *American Economic Review*, LIII, 2 (May, 1963), pp. 275-92.
"A Place for the Private Label," *Business Week* Number 1434 (February 23, 1957), p. 57.
"Power Play at Retail Level Tightens Vise on Manufacturers," *Food Engineering*, XXXI, 8 (August, 1959), pp. 42-45.
"Prestige Packaging Sparks Private-Label Push," *Food Engineering*, XXXI, 1 (January, 1959), pp. 62-63.

"Private Brand Gains Are Slowing, A. A. Finds," *Advertising Age*, XXX, 28 (July 13, 1959), p. 1.

"Private-Brand Lubricants Gets Bigger," *National Petroleum News*, LVI, 11 (November, 1964), p. 68.

"Private Brand Stress Seen Hurting Stores," *Daily News Record*, No. 6, Whole No. 21251 (January 9, 1962), p. 1.

"Private Brander: He's Confident," *National Petroleum News*, L, 2 (February, 1958), p. 137.

"The Private Brander No One Really Knows," *National Petroleum News*, L, 3 (March, 1958), pp. 95-99.

"Private Branders from the Midwest Move into East Coast Markets," *National Petroleum News*, LIII, 9 (September, 1961), p. 19.

"Private Brands Are Spreading," *Super Market Merchandising*, XXVIII, 6 (June, 1963), p. 7.

"Private Brands Cut into Sales of Tire Giants," *Advertising Age*, XXXIII, 27 (July 2, 1962), p. 63.

"Private Brands Dominate Big Food Chain Sales: FTC," *Advertising Age*, XXXII, 7 (February 13, 1961), p. 8.

"Private Brands: The Inside Story," *Changing Times*, XIX, 11 (November, 1965), pp. 25-29.

"Private Brands Salvage Retailer Caught by Margin Pinch, High Operating Costs: Rabb," *Advertising Age*, XXX, 33 (August 17, 1959), p. 68.

"Private Brands Sell Better, Net More for Retailers, Food Commission Finds," *Advertising Age*, XXXVII, 27 (July 4, 1966), p. 4.

"Private Brands to Suffer," *Progressive Grocer*, XLII, 6 (June, 1963), p. 35.

"Private Label Health, Beauty Aids Fail in Supers: 'McCall's' Panelists," *Advertising Age*, XXX, 44 (November 2, 1959), p. 3.

"Private Label Hose Kick in with Bigger Share of Booty," *Women's Wear Daily*, CXI, 6 (July 9, 1965), p. 1.

"Private Label Ice Cream," *Super Market Merchandising*, XXIV, 11 (November, 1959) p. 87.

"Private Label Identification High," *Super Market Merchandising*, XXVIII, 5 (May, 1963), p. 41.

"Private Label Impact Light in Chicago Except at Jewel," *Supermarket News*, XII, 13 (April 1, 1963), p. 49.

"Private Label: New Round in the Retail Revolution," *Drug and Cosmetic Industry*, XCII, 3 (March, 1963), p. 285.

"Private Label Penetration," *Sales Management*, CIII, 3 (August 7, 1964), p. 16.

"Private-Label Selling," *Drug and Cosmetic Industry*, LXXXIII, 2 (August, 1958), p. 180-81.

"Private Label Threat Due to Brand Makers Weak Merchandising: Motorola's Herkes," *Advertising Age*, XXXVI, 32 (August 9, 1965), p. 8.

"Private-Label Topic Constantly Recurred at GMA Convention," *Food Field Reporter*, XXVI, 24 (November 24, 1958), p. 1.

"Private Labels Growing in Europe," *Printers' Ink*, CCXCI, 1 (July 9, 1965), p. 3.

"Private Labels Held Asset, But Brands Indispensable for Arousing Interest," *Supermarket News*, XIII, 16 (April 20, 1964), p. 22

"Private Labels Pervade N.Y. Area Markets But Maker Brands Dominate, Study Shows," *Advertising Age*, XXXV, 31 (August 3, 1964), pp. 18-19.

"Private Labels Pose Bigger Problem Than Ever," *Printers' Ink*, CCLXXX, 13 (September 28, 1962), p. 5.

"Private Labels 'Submerging' National Brands, GMA Told," *Food Field Reporter*, XXVI, 24 (November 24, 1958), p. 6.

"Private Labels vs. National Brands: Another Round," *Printers' Ink*, CCLXXXI, 8 (November 23, 1962), p. 5.

"Private Labels Win Greater Consumer Recognition," *Printers' Ink*, CCLXXXII, 9 (March 1, 1963), p. 5.

"Private vs. National Brands," *Sponsor*, XVI, 46 (November 12, 1962), p. 33.

"Pro Ten Private Label Deals Granted," *Supermarket News*, XII, 9 (March 4, 1963), p. 33.

"Probe P. B., Justice Advises Senators; Big Stores Not Discounters Should be Studied," *Advertising Age*, XXIX, 26 (June 30, 1958), p. 52.

"Produce Changes on Way for A&P," *Supermarket News*, XII, 27 (July 1, 1963), p. 1.

"Program for a Two Billion Dollar Market," *Modern Packaging*, XXXVI, 12 (August, 1963), pp. 89-94.

"Publix Rides the National Brand-Wagon," *Super Market Merchandising*, XXII, 10 (October, 1957), p. 68.

"QSB 'Constructive,'" Eliz. Arden V.P. Says," *Discount Store News*, III, 4 (February 24, 1964), p. 13.

"QSB Foes Have Cut Chances of Passage," *Discount Store News*, II, 26 (December 30, 1963), p. 9.

"QS Won't Work in Oil Industry," *Discount Store News*, II, 26 (December 30, 1963), p. 9.

"A Quick History of Oil Marketing," *National Petroleum News*, LI, 2 (February, 1959), pp. 95–110.

Read, Harry S. "What's in Store for the Private Brand Marketer?," *National Petroleum News*, LI, 2 (February, 1959), p. 130–31.

Reed, Raymond S. "Rambling with Ray," *Home Furnishings Daily*, XXXV, 130 (July 5, 1963), p. 2.

"Retailer Brands Gaining," *Supermarket News*, XII, 10 (March 11, 1963), p. 42.

"Retailing Shifts to Affect Advertisers," *Printers' Ink*, CCLXXXII, 7 (February 15, 1963), p. 3.

Reynolds, William H. "Brand Images and the Consumer," *Management Review*, LII, 5 (May, 1965), pp. 49–52.

"The Rise of the Cheapies," *Time*, LXXXIII, 15 (April 10, 1964), p. 97.

Robbins, W. David. "A Marketing Appraisal of the Robinson-Patman Act," *Journal of Marketing*, XXIV 1 (July, 1959), pp. 15–21.

Rossi, Bill. "The Growing Influence of Brands," *Boot and Shoe Recorder*, CLXVIII, 3 (July 1, 1965), p. 23.

———. "National Brands: Demand is Command," *Boot and Shoe Recorder*, CLXIII, 7 (March 1, 1963), p. 11.

"Safeway's Labels Prosper Despite Cuts, Consolidation," *Supermarket News*, VII, 6 (February 10, 1958), p. 1.

"Sage Anticipates Trends," *Soap and Chemical Specialties*, XXXIX, 10 (October, 1963), p. 111.

Sanchagrin, Ted. "Battle of the Brands: Soft Drinks," *Printers' Ink*, CCXC, 8 (April 9, 1965), p. 21.

———. "Frozen Foods: Can Brands Survive?," *Printers' Ink*, CCLXXXV, 3 (October 18, 1963), p. 29.

Sanderson, William. "Brands: National, Private, and Invisible," *Stores*, XLV, 4 (April, 1963), pp. 16–17.

Schroeder, Richard C. "Major Brand vs. Private Brand: Are They Really That Different?," *National Petroleum News*, LI, 2 (February, 1959), p. 144–46.

"Sears Makes It Look Easy," *Fortune*, LXIX, 5 (May, 1964), p. 120.

Shapiro, Max. "Private Label Role Cited in Small Specialty Store," *Women's Wear Daily*, CVI, 78 (April 22, 1963), p. 2.

"Shopper Resistance to Substitute Found," *Food Field Reporter*, XXVI, 24 (November 24, 1958), p. 22.

"Shop-Rite Label Paints," *Progressive Grocer*, XLII, 4 (April, 1963), p. 10.

Silberman, Charles E. "The Department Stores Are Waking Up," *Fortune*, LXVI, 1 (July, 1962), p. 143.

———. "The Discounters Choose Their Weapons," *Fortune*, LXV, 5 (May, 1962), p. 118.

Sinclair, Frank. "Esbeco Asks U.S. to Watch Attacks on Private Labels," *Advertising Age*, XXXIV, 26 (June 24, 1963), p. 32–33.

"Small Refiners Ask Government Help to End Price Wars," *The Oil and Gas Journal*, LXII, 11 (March 16, 1964), pp. 68–69.

"Small Towners Loyal to Brands, 'Grit' Reports," *Advertising Age*, XXXII, 50 (December 11, 1961), p. 60.

Smith, M. Blake. "Private Label Sales Hit 30%," *Supermarket News*, VII, 21 (May 26, 1958), p. 18.

Snyder, James D. "Neither Whitewash Nor Witchhunt," *Sales Management*, XCVI, 11 (June 1, 1966), pp. 25–27.

"The Soap Wars: A Strategic Analysis," *Fortune*, LXVII, 6 (June, 1963), pp. 122–25.

"Store Brass Echo Refrain for Better Vendor Harmony," *Women's Wear Daily*, CXI, 5 (July 8, 1965), p. 1.

"Study Shows 5 of 6 Brand Switches Made on Impulse, Popai Meeting Told," *Advertising Age*, XXXIV, 12 (March 18, 1963), p. 3.

"Surgical Stockings Stride into Fashion," *Business Week*, Number 1817 (June 27, 1964), p. 96.

"Sweeping Revision of Food Marketing Urged," *Advertising Age*, XXXVII, 10 (March 7, 1966), p. 1.

"Swing to Private Brand Tires in the Making?," *National Petroleum News*, LVI, 3 (March, 1963), p. 158.

Taft, J. Richard. "For Appliances: True Growth at Last," *Printers' Ink*, CCLXXXIV, 7 (August 23, 1963), p. 21.

Taylor, Thayer C. "Regulators Eye Private Labels," *Food Engineering*, XXXIV, 2 (February, 1962), pp. 55-56.

————. "Will Chains Do More Manufacturing?," *Food Engineering*, XXXII, 10 (October, 1960), pp. 103-04.

Teegarden, Tom J. "Don't Be Bluffed into Brand Name Buying," *Purchasing*, LIII, 9 (October 22, 1962), pp. 94-95.

"Teens Show Little Loyalty to Brands," *Drug Trade News*, XXXIX, 6 (March 16, 1964), p. 24.

"Tells Quickie Stockholders Name Brands Spell Profits," *Home Furnishings Daily*, XXXV, 143 (July 24, 1963), p. 14.

"Tire Buyers Confronted with Bewildering Jungle of Terms," *The Car*, LXIV, 11 (November, 1964), p. 1.

"Tire Makers Drive Deeper into Discountland," *Discount Store News*, III, 2 (January 27, 1964), p. 1.

"The Tissue-Paper War," *Forbes*, XCV, 2 (January 15, 1965), pp. 21-23.

Toles, George E. "Buffalo Chains Selling 35-50% Private Labels," *Supermarket News*, VII, 21 (May 26, 1958), p. 26.

"'True' Product Profit," *The Key Report*, (February 10, 1964), p. 1.

Tucker, W. T. "The Development of Brand Loyalty," *Journal of Marketing Research*, I, 3 (August, 1964), pp. 32-35.

Tyler, William D. "The Image, The Brand, and The Consumer," *Journal of Marketing*, XXII, 2, (October, 1957), pp. 162-65.

"Uncle Sam: Consumers' Champion," *Business Week*, Number 1909 (April 2, 1966), p. 76.

"United Fruit Breaks from the Bunch," *Sales Management*, XC, 13 (June 21, 1963), p. 55.

"U.S. Likes Familiar Brands in New Environs, Forum Told," *Food Field Reporter*, XXVI, 24 (November 24, 1958), p. 8.

"Users of Brand Read Its Ad More Faithfully Than Non-Users Do: Starch," *Advertising Age*, XXXIV, 44 (October 28, 1963), p. 3.

"USWGA Puts Private Label Plan in Effect," *Supermarket News*, XII, 22 (May 27, 1963), p. 4.

"VA View: QS Would Hurt the Weakest the Most," *Discount Store News*, III, 3 (February 10, 1964), p. 9.

"The Values of the Brand Concept as Applied to Liquor Marketing," *Liquor Store*, LVIII, 6 (June, 1963), pp. 21-27.

Vautin, Peter. "Day of the Private Label," *Drug and Cosmetic Industry*, XCV, 1 (July, 1964), pp. 27-28.

————. "The New Face of Cosmetic Retailing," *Drug and Cosmetic Industry*, XCIII, 5 (November, 1963), p. 618.

————. "The Private Label Challenge," *Drug and Cosmetic Industry*, XCI, 1 (July, 1962), p. 29.

————. "Private Label: A New Round in the Retail Revolution," *Drug and Cosmetic Industry*, XCII, 3 (March, 1963), p. 285.

"A Victory That Turned Sour," *Business Week*, Number 1816 (June 20, 1964), p. 114.

"Volume Footwear and the Mass Market," *Boot and Shoe Recorder*, CLXII, 12 (November 15, 1962). (Reprint)

"Von's Central Deli Preparation Makes the Most of Automation," *Progressive Grocer*, XLII, 2 (February, 1963), p. 73.

Wedding Nugent. "Contemporary Brand Policies," *American Marketing Association Proceedings*, 1954, pp. 143-51.

Weiner, Jack B. "Myth of the National Market," *Dun's Review and Modern Industry*, LXXXIII, 5 (May, 1964), p. 40.

Weinstein, Steve. "Private Brands Gain in New York," *Supermarket News*, VII, 21 (May 26, 1958), p. 20.

Weiss, E. B. "Advertising Trends Among Retail Giants," *Printers' Ink*, CCXXXIII, 9 (December 1, 1950), p. 38.

————. "Are Discount Outlets Utterly Dependent on Pre-Sold Brands?," *Advertising Age*, XXXIII, 8 (February 5, 1962), p. 78.

————. "Are You Financing Retailer Competition for Your Brand?," *Printers' Ink*, CCXXXIII, 11 (December 15, 1950), p. 35.

————. "The Coming Age of National Retail Brands," *Advertising Age*, XXVII, 27 (July 2, 1956), p. 60.

————. "Coming Era of International Store-Controlled Brands," *Advertising Age*, XXXI, 19 (May 9, 1960), p. 98.

————. "Competitive Status of Controlled Brands in Foods," *Printers' Ink*, CCXXXIII, 5 (November 3, 1950), p. 46.

————. "The Controlled Brand in the Drug Industry," *Printers' Ink*, CCXXXIII, 6 November 10, 1950), p. 45.

————. "The Controlled Brand in Soft and Hard Goods," *Printers' Ink*, CCXXXIII, 7 (November 17, 1950), p. 44.

————. "The Day of the Known Brand Is Here: Make the Most of It," *Printers' Ink*, CCXXXIII, 12 (December 22, 1950), p. 33.

————. "Distributors' Advertised Brand vs. Manufacturers' Advertised Brand," *Printers' Ink*, CCXXXIII, 3 (October 20, 1950), p. 32.

————. "Five New Trends for Marketing Men to Ponder," *Advertising Age*, XXXV, 2 (January 13, 1964), p. 96.

————. "How Controlled Labels are Pushing Retailer into Manufacturing," *Advertising Age*, XXXV, 46 (November 16, 1964), p. 127.

————. "Retailers Are 'Trading Up' Price and Quality of Private Labels," *Advertising Age*, XXXVII, 26 (June 27, 1966), p. 62.

————. "30 Road Blocks for the Controlled Label," *Advertising Age*, XXXVII 43 (October 24, 1966), p. 88.

————. "To Make or Not to Make Private Labels?," *Printers' Ink*, CCXXXIII, 10 (December 8, 1950), p. 36.

————. "Managers of 2,000 Chain Super-Stores Seen Emerging as Individual Super-Forces in Marketing," *Advertising Age*, XXXII, 2 (January 9, 1961), p. 83.

————. "The Manufacturer's Billion Dollar Private Label Ad Budget," *Advertising Age*, XXXVI, 28 (July 12, 1965), p. 92.

————. "Meet Our Newest Mass Retailer—the 100 Department Store Chains," *Advertising Age*, XXXVI, 23 (June 7, 1965), p. 124.

————. "The New Battle of the Brands," Printers' Ink, CCXXXIII, 2 (October 13, 1950), p. 27.

————. "The Sophisticated Shopper and Over-Priced Status Brands," *Advertising Age*, XXXVI, 3 (January 18, 1965), p. 86.

————. "Sophisticated Shoppers and Over-Priced Brands," *Advertising Age*, XXXII, 40 (October 2, 1961), p. 84.

————. "Sticks and Stones Won't Kill Off Private Labels," *Advertising Age*, XXX, 28 (July 13, 1959), p. 68.

————. "Store-Controlled Brands Will Be Stronger in 1960," *Printers' Ink*, CCXXXIII, 8 (November 24, 1950), p. 36.

————. "Study Successful 'Unadvertised' Brands," *Advertising Age*, XXXV, 42 (October 19, 1964), p. 112.

————. "Time: The Shoppers Number One Problem," *Advertising Age*, XXXV, 4 (January 27, 1964), p. 68.

————. "Weiss vs. Nielsen," Advertising Age, XXXVII, 4 (January 24, 1966), p. 82.

————. "What's the Future for Retailers' Own Brands?," *Advertising Age*, XXXV, 17 (April 27, 1964), p. 84.

————. "When Is a Brand Not a Brand," *Advertising Age*, XXXI, 48 (November 28, 1960), p. 74.

————. "When Is a Label a Private Label?," *Advertising Age*, XXXVI, 4 (January 25, 1965), p. 105–06.

————. "Why Do Large Retailers Push Their Own Brands?," *Printers' Ink*, CCXXXIII, 4 (October 27, 1950), p. 34.

————. "Will Retailer-Controlled Brands Seek Broader Distribution?," *Advertising Age*, XXVIII, 38 (September 23, 1957), p. 106.

Weitz, Joseph. "A Study of Trade Name Confusion," *Journal of Marketing*, XXV, 2 (October, 1960), pp. 54-56.

Welles, Sara. "On National Brands," *Printers' Ink*, CCLXXVIV, 13 (June 29, 1962), p. 57.

Wesson, Sheldon. "Brand Name Magic: Induced, Not Inherent," *Home Furnishings Daily*, XXXVIII, 73 (April 13, 1966), p. 43.

————. "Brand Switching Poison and Antidotes Described," *Home Furnishings Daily*, XXXVIII, 74 (April 14, 1966), p. 32.

————. "National Brands vs. Market Focus," *Home Furnishings Daily*, XXXVIII, 72 (April 12, 1966), p. 31.

"What's Behind Shell's '1¢ Policy'," *National Petroleum News*, LIV, 8 (August, 1962), p. 82.

"What's in the Future for Private Brands?," *Electrical Merchandising Week*, XCIV, 22 (May 28, 1962), p. 9.

"What Goes into an Incentive Plan?," *Printers' Ink*, CCLXXXVII, 3 (April 17, 1964), p. 29.

"What's Macy's Up to Now?," *Printers' Ink*, CCXC, 4 (February 12, 1965), p. 9.

→"What's in a Name? Everything!," *Printers' Ink*, CCLXXXIV, 4 (July 26, 1963), p. 3.
"What's in a Name? Macy's Shows 'Em," *Electrical Merchandising Week*, XCIII, 35 (August 28, 1961), p. 6.
"What Trademark Types Tell Consumers About a Company," *Business Week*, Number 1627 (November 5, 1960), p. 104.
"What Will FTC Probe of Private Labels Mean to Advertisers?," *Printers' Ink*, CCLXXVII, 12 (December 22, 1961), pp. 13–14.
"When Do 'Cents-off' Offers Work?," *Printers' Ink*, CCLXXXVI, 7 (February 21, 1964), p. 45.
→"When Not to Trade on a Brand Name," *Sales Management*, XCI, 2 (July 19, 1963), p. 75.
"Which Way: Brand Names in Today's Retailing Revolution?," *Department Store Economist*, XXV, 12 (December, 1962), p. 30.
"Whirlpool Corporation: From Little Benton Harbor, Michigan, Elisha Gray II Runs a Peculiar Kind of Company-Part Sears Roebuck Supplier, Part Independent Merchandiser," *Forbes*, XCI, 3 (February 1, 1963), pp. 18–22.
"Wholesaling—Super Value Attraction," *Investors' Reader*, XLIV, 11 (June 2, 1965), p. 17.
"Whose Label?," *The Economist*, CXCVIII, 6133, (March 11, 1961), pp. 983–85.
"Why Alcoa Changed Its Trademark," *Printers' Ink*, CCLXXXII, 9 (March 1, 1963), pp. 52–54.
"Why Babbitt is Proud to Sell for Private Labeling," *Sales Management*, LXXXV, 13 (November 18, 1960), p. 35.
"Why Is Bata Bringing Out Its Own Brand?," *Printers' Ink*, CCLXXXVI, 5 (February 7, 1964), pp. 12–13.
"Why Brand Name Owners Turn Gray," *Sales Management*, XCI, 1 (July 5, 1963), p. 11.
"Why Farmer's Share Is Shrinking," *Business Week*, Number 1863 (May 15, 1963), p. 174.
"Why Liquor-Brand Promotion Grows," *Printers' Ink*, CCLXXXVI, 4 (January 31, 1964), pp. 35–37.
"Will FTC Find Price Discrimination in Private Labels?," *Printers' Ink*, CCLXXXV, 7 (November 15, 1963), p. 11.
"Will Inflation Create More Private Brands?," *Tide*, XXXII, 16 (October, 1958), pp. 34–36.
"Will Private Cigarette Labels Become Threat to Major Brands?," *Printers' Ink*, CCLXXVII, 4 (October 27, 1961), p. 18.
"Will Strictures Mount?," *Printers' Ink*, CCLXXXVI, 1 (January 10, 1964), p. 68–70.
Williams, Art. "Private Label Viewpoint," *Spirits*, XXX, 8 (August-September, 1963), pp. 24–25.
Williams, Ronald. "'Premature' Private Labeling Hit at Frozen Packers Meet," *Supermarket News*, XII 11 (March 18, 1963), p. 50.
Winans, Derek. "Insurance Ads: Reappraisal Coming?," *Printers' Ink*, CCLXXXV, (November 15, 1963), p. 27.
Winkler, Jack. "Private-Branders Grow in Britain," *National Petroleum News*, LIV, 9 (September, 1962), pp. 15–20.
Winters, Alvin M. "Private Label Lines: More the Merrier," *Home Furnishings Daily*, XXXV, 163 (August 21, 1963), p. 1.
Wolfe, Charles E. "Private Labels in St. Louis, Strongest Ratiowise in Sales," *Supermarket News*, VII, 21 (May 26, 1958), p. 24.
"Women 18-35: What Do They Buy?," *Printers' Ink*, CCLXXVI, 2 (January 17, 1964), p. 36.
"Women Flunk Identity Test," *Business Week*, Number 1753 (April 6, 1963), pp. 50–52.
Wood, Wallis E. "Marketing Through Retailers: What Management Foresees," *Merchandising Week*, XCVIII, 11 (March 14, 1966), p. 28.
——. "The Private-Brand Invasion," *Merchandising Week*, XCVII, 20 (May 17, 1965), pp. 15–21.
"Working Together. . .How Brand Name Manufacturers and Retailers Can Help One Another," *Department Store Economist*, XXV, 12 (December, 1962), p. 28.
Wortman, Victor. "Cereals: Competition Stiffens as Sales Continue to Rise," *Printers' Ink*, CCXC, 10 (May 14, 1965), p. 67.
→"You Can't Stay Cozy Forever," *Printers' Ink*, CCLXXXIII, 6 (May 10, 1963), p. 3.
"You and the Private Label—A Look into the Future," *Electrical Merchandising Week*, XCIII, 37 (September 11, 1961), p. 3.
"Zayre Chief on QS: 'Reward to Least Efficient'," *Discount Store News*, III, 3 (February 10, 1964), p. 9.
Ziemba, John V. "Private Labels Climb into Key Marketing Positions," *Food Engineering*, XXX, 7 (July, 1958), pp. 52–54.
Zimmerman, Richard G. "National Advertisers Must Block Private Brands in Supermarkets or Get Hurt," *Advertising Age*, XXX, 33 (August 17, 1959), p. 67.

Index